KIERAN READ

KIERAN
READ
STRAIGHT 8

THE AUTOBIOGRAPHY

HEADLINE

First published in 2019
by HEADLINE PUBLISHING GROUP

1

Cataloguing in Publication Data is available from the British Library

Photography courtesy of the author and Getty Images

Hardback ISBN 978 1 4722 6809 9
Trade paperback ISBN 978 1 4722 6811 2

Typeset in Adobe Jenson Pro
Printed and bound in Great Britain by Clays Ltd, Elcograf S.p.A.

HEADLINE PUBLISHING GROUP
An Hachette UK Company
Carmelite House
50 Victoria Embankment
London EC4Y 0DZ

www.headline.co.uk
www.hachette.co.uk

For Bridget, Elle, Eden & Reuben

CONTENTS

CONTENTS

WRITER'S NOTE

He's a complex man, Kieran Read. He's at once everything you expect him to be and nothing like you imagined. Yes, he is an All Blacks captain, which is of course an honour and a privilege, not to mention a massive responsibility and a heavy burden, but he is also just a humble Kiwi lad who fell in love with sport and forged a remarkable rugby career from a childhood dream.

I have known Kieran for many years, though of course I now know him a lot better than I used to. Throughout the writing of this book he was always open, thoughtful, honest and emotionally revealing. He was a kid in a hurry, as his earliest recollections of sibling rivalry well show, and because of that he has remained impatient for success and hardwired to constantly prove his worth to himself and to others. In the following pages I am sure you will gain an insight into that intense personal drive.

Professional athletes all share a blazing ambition to succeed, and Kieran is no different. As a player, his record speaks for itself. In his 127 tests for New Zealand, Kieran started and finished in more than 100. That statistic alone illustrates his enormous value to the team and his equally enormous physical capability. Furthermore, only two players — Richie McCaw and Keven Mealamu — boast more test caps and more test victories. The 2019 Rugby World Cup was Kieran's opportunity to surpass Sean Fitzpatrick on the list of captain's appearances in All Blacks tests too. As the saying goes, you are judged by the company you keep.

It would be easy to assume that everything has come to Kieran as a matter of course, as if all he has achieved was somehow preordained. The real story is not so simple. In fact, if anything this is a record of the immense physical and mental challenges he has faced and overcome on the way to becoming one of the game's modern-day giants. He has done it all with his family by his side, even when the rough and rutted road was his to walk alone, and that connection reveals much of his humility, character and vulnerability.

Ultimately, Kieran's place in the order of all things All Blacks will be for others to judge, but what is not up for debate is the fact this is the story of a good man with a big heart and a bottomless well of determination and resilience who never lost sight of the Kiwi kid within.

As always, many thanks go to publishers Warren Adler and Kevin Chapman who continue to amaze me with their faith. To Kieran, Bridget and the entire Read family, thank you for your support and for trusting me with your story. All the love goes to my own family, who make everything possible.

Scotty Stevenson
November 2019

1

IN THE END . . .

The tears stopped on Monday, but the hurt refused to leave. I doubt there is a hole deep enough to bury it. There will be days to come this week, and next, and then the month after that, and maybe in a couple of years, when I will trip over some jagged, rusting edge of it and open afresh a wound that refuses to fully heal. That's the way defeat works, especially when all I had thought about for four years was victory.

The tears stopped on Monday and frustration filled the void. We sat slumped in the All Blacks team room, in a forest of Tokyo high rises, where two days after the semi-final of the 2019 Rugby World Cup we reviewed the game. Okay, let's be honest here: we reviewed the loss. In every frame, a missed opportunity; in every clip an alternate reality: a technicolour tragedy rendered in slow motion serving first to magnify regret and then to strengthen resolve. We watched in disbelief to begin with, a room of shaking heads and downcast faces.

And then we snapped out of it.

'Are you happy, Daddy?' That was all my little boy Reuben had wanted to know the day before, which was the day after: my 34th birthday, my toughest night as All Blacks captain. He had looked up at me, his tight curls of hair as blond as pine shavings tumbled around his cheeky face, and I had smiled then and thought I was.

11

Right in that moment, I was. Pain comes in waves, though, and Monday had been tough again. The review had made it tougher still — the honesty, the clarity, the sheer ease with which we could see things then that on Saturday had been so uncharacteristically hidden from view. We had to draw a line under it, then and there. We were lucky to have one more chance that week to show what we could do. We had one more chance to play for our country.

My body was wrecked after the England test. I had run further in the game than in all but a handful of test matches before. The usual aches and pains taunted me, taking turns with all-new areas of interest and inflammation to protest against a full range of movement. Movement, however, was what was required. We needed to move forward, to accept that what might have been will never compete with what was. On Monday night we drew a line in the sand. Yes, a semi-final loss was a long way from what we had wanted, but there was no do-over. We had been beaten, fairly and squarely, and now we had one more game left. It would be my last.

The laughs started on Tuesday. I had invited the boys of New Zealand operatic trio SOL3 MIO to the hotel and they spent the evening singing for us and bringing the house down with their jokes. It was a classic night, one that was very much needed by all of us. In those few hours together, I think we began to remember what was important: being around the people you cared about and appreciating everything that went with being a part of this famous team. On Wednesday that notion was reinforced when all the families came for dinner with us. The same people who four days earlier had been there to console us were back to their encouraging best. Across those two evenings, we rediscovered our emotional centre. We knew then that we had to enjoy the few days we had left. By the final Thursday training run, we were thinking only of what was in front of us: we had a test match to play, against Wales.

There was something else, too. The messages of support we received during the week were overwhelming. I had been so disappointed for everyone after the semi-final, for the team and for myself, yes, but also for the many thousands of fans who wanted us to deliver them another title. I had carried that weight with me over those first few days, but with each new email, or text, or phone call, the burden was eased. There had also been an incredible gift: the Minister for Sport and Recreation, the Hon. Grant Robertson, presented Steve Hansen and me with taiaha on behalf of the government as we prepared to say goodbye to the team we both loved. It was a humbling gesture, and a taonga that will hold pride of place in my home.

On Friday, 1 November, I gave my final pre-match talk. The guys will tell you I almost lost it, and they're probably right. It was hard not to be emotional in that moment, but the tears had been used up. 'Do it for yourself, do it for your mates, and do it for the people closest to you — those you really care about.' I think in all honesty I was talking to myself more than anyone. A few moments later, I led the team out onto Tokyo Stadium, smiling, just as I had at the coin toss alongside Alun Wyn Jones, the great Welsh captain. He had smiled back. 'Well, mate, what the hell are we doing here?' I asked him, ruefully and rhetorically. It was his 143rd test match that night, making him the northern hemisphere's most capped international. A man of great integrity and immense talent, Alun Wyn had been a sensational rival over many years. To stand there next to a captain of his class was an honour, and that moment brought fresh perspective. Yes, we were playing a day earlier than both of us had hoped, but how lucky we were to lead our teams in a test match. 'You said it, not me,' came his cheeky response.

When the team was named early in the week and TJ Perenara had been given a rest, I knew I would be leading the haka. Only once before had that honour fallen to me and I felt an enormous sense of pride that I would get to act as kaea in my last appearance in black. We chose 'Ka Mate', only because it was still us. It felt right for the night for how we wanted to represent ourselves and the jersey and all who had come before. I had come to truly appreciate the significance of the haka, especially in the last few years. It was more than tradition for me — it had become a portal to a new world of learning, and that had made me a better person.

The Welsh lined up on halfway and accepted the challenge. We knew what we wanted to do and what we needed to do, and we also knew that they were as motivated as us. Yes, we were saying goodbye to our coach, but so were they. We knew they would give it everything they had. Unfortunately for them, their all would not be enough. Over the next 80 minutes, everything that didn't work the week before suddenly clicked into place. The sight of Joe Moody sprinting 30 metres to score the first try was one to savour. Beauden Barrett did Beauden Barrett things to score the second. Ben Smith — surely one of the classiest players in history — chimed in with a double that only he could have manufactured. My mate Ryan Crotty got served up a Sonny Bill special. Richie Mo'unga finished the job.

The smile stayed on my face for the entire game and when Wayne Barnes blew the final whistle, I felt an enormous rush of pride. Six days earlier I hadn't been able to look my teammates in the eye, but now I took everything in. It all felt hyper-real, the green of the grass, the glare of the lights, the noise from the crowd, the satisfaction on the faces of my mates who had done this with me one last time. One last time.

Through the chaos I found Bridget and the kids and one by one they joined me on the field where they ran around laughing and having the time of their lives. Everywhere I looked there were children giggling and playing, some dressed in black and others dressed in red. We stood there waiting for the presentation, chatting away with each other and with the men we had defeated. It felt like we were all back on the club field having played for the love of it alone. Maybe that was what we had just done that night. Played for the love of the game, and for each other. Could I think of a better way to finish? Sure, a little gold cup would have been a nice addition, but in those minutes after the match, my cup was full.

One last press conference. One last shower. One last beer in the sheds with the men I admire. What a pleasure it had been to captain them. We left the stadium and boarded the bus for the drive back to the team hotel, each of us feeling the satisfaction of victory. For some of us — Ryan Crotty, Ben Smith, Sonny Bill Williams, Matt Todd and me — it would be our last. We knew that before the game. We had each been given the chance to go out on our terms. I looked around the bus, a beer in hand, smiling still, and hoped that others would have the opportunity to be a part of this team for as long as I had been.

I felt time slipping away. I think a part of me wanted to hold on to these final hours forever, even though I had made my peace with letting go. I sat in the vast lobby of the Conrad Hotel and gathered my thoughts. Upstairs, hundreds of family and friends had gathered to celebrate the end of the tournament and the end of this All Blacks team's time together. We would always be bonded by the brotherhood forged in the furnace of international rugby, but this team's era would soon be over. That was always the way it was with the All Blacks: the desire to succeed remained the only thing that never changed. The cast was a revolving one. My time on stage had come to an end, all the lines written and performed.

I took a long sip on a can of cold Japanese beer. The body was beginning to ache again, but that would pass. It always did. Enjoy this, I told myself. Get yourself up those stairs and hold your wife, and hang out with your mum and dad, and your brother. Treasure the drinks and the laughs with them, and with all the other families. They are yours, too. They are the people who make us what we are, and who support us through it all. They're the ones who feel the pain like we do and feel the same pride. And, hell, be proud. You've done all right, mate. You gave it your best, and that has to be all you can ask. You had a dream and you chased it, and you chased it with everything you could muster.

It had all been amazing, really. I had been given the chance to represent my country in 127 test matches. I had won my first, and I had won my last, and I'd won 105 in between. I had gone the distance in 106 of those tests and led the side in 52. That was the simple accounting of it all, but numbers alone don't do justice to the story . . .

2

A DRIVE

It always feels like rush hour when you're standing next to a motorway, watching the processional convoy of economic progress droning its way north to south or south to north, filling six lanes of blacktop with the constant throb of agitated engines and restless souls. Even on Saturday mornings, when the city offices were closed for the weekend and the winter mists had pegged themselves to the Bombay Hills and hung across Auckland's southern green belt, the cars and trucks sped by, the constancy of their sound punctuated only by the sharp, angry blast of a horn or the descending bass scale of an engine brake.

I used to stand and watch them all go by on those Saturday mornings when I was just a wee lad, and now I stand and I watch again as an adult, as the dusk descends on a Wednesday night in January, and the minutes, and hours, and days and weeks and months tick by to the 2019 Rugby World Cup in Japan and the headlights start to outshine the summer sun draining away through the haze in the west. It will all come to an end, soon, this rugby story. I don't want to think about endings. Instead I think back through the years and ponder the faces that once peered from their windows and shared with us Southside boys a split second of our game in progress on the Drury playing fields, beside the southern motorway. We were a small part of their journey then, a snapshot of Kiwi kids' life on the furrowed outer arc of Auckland's radiating suburbs, a brief distraction from their road trip. From where? To where? These are essentially the only questions that roads ever answer: where did you start? And where do you want to go?

This is where I started. On the muddy fields beside Auckland's arterial connection with the south. It was all rugby back then, but nowadays the goalposts have largely given way to goals with nets and these same fields foster football more than they do footy. I stand in the potholed and puddling car park watching the cars whizz by and wondering where the time went. It feels like forever ago that I once rushed from Dad's car out to my mates all huddled on the sideline and ready for kick-off. It feels like only yesterday. I think about that short distance I have travelled and the many miles my body has clocked along the way, and with that thought in my head I get in a friend's car and pull out of that car park headed for a drive down everyone's favourite road: memory lane.

Papakura is just north of the Drury sportsgrounds along Great South Road, or the next exit off the motorway if you're travelling that way. It was once a roadside stop that became a town that became a city that morphed into a district before it was swallowed whole by Auckland's grand Supercity scheme. Papakura grew along the edge of that Great South Road, Sir George Grey's ambitious nineteenth-century military-minded public work scheme to connect Auckland with the thought of war and to allow passage for troops and supplies to the real action in the Waikato. War never did crest the Bombay Hills and Papakura was left to find other ways to define itself. It always felt to me like it was happy in its own vibe, a place that was quite content to be itself despite its obvious connection to greater Auckland. I liked that about the place. I like it still. Even now I think it retains a certain level of autonomy despite the fact it is being rapidly ingested by the Supercity's insatiable urban sprawl.

Terry and Marilyn Read called Papakura home and won the food bill booby prize when they got lumped with three boys. Gareth came first, followed by me a couple of years later, and Mark four years after that. Being younger than Gareth and me, Mark was on his own tour through childhood and adolescence, but Gareth and I were constantly engaged in the kind of fraternal benchmarking that invariably ended in arguments, property damage or tears. On many occasions it ended in all three. Gareth revelled in his role of tormentor-in-chief, running the spectrum from simmering older sibling to short-fused psychopath. In turn, I threw myself into my one key brotherly function: to move him from the former end of that spectrum to the latter in the quickest possible time. It was the easiest job of my life.

We lived on a classic suburban cul-de-sac called Kavanagh Place close to Great South Road, its 20 homes an eclectic mix of three decades of architectural experimentation which lent the entire street a quintessentially Kiwi pick-and-mix sentimentality. It was one of those streets that was always perfumed by flowering shrubs or freshly clipped grass or the evaporating oils of scruffy conifers on late summer afternoons, as if it was an advertisement for 1980s potpourri. If it looked and smelled as Kiwi as they came, then it certainly sounded that way too. The 'Kavanagh Crew', comprised of every mildly adventurous kid on the street with a sporting bone in his or her body, and a fully functional larynx, made sure of that.

The dead-end street gets a bad rap if you ask me. Kavanagh Place on weekday afternoons and long weekend days was the ultimate all-weather playing surface. It didn't matter what the game was — roller hockey, skateboard races, original compositions fashioned from the basic rules of AFL, touch rugby, cricket, tennis, football — if it could be played for points and for ultimate victory then we were into it. One house had a front garden filled with pumice stones, which we used to chalk out the field of play boundaries on the asphalt for whatever game had been agreed upon. No one had ever bothered building a fence so balls kicked or hit into backyards were always easily retrievable. We made as much noise as we needed to and never got told off. Traffic was never a problem. Looking back, it never struck any of us as strange that our parents would tell us to 'go play on the road'.

If none of the neighbours were available, there was always a healthy appetite for a Read brothers' duel. Games between Gareth and me could last all weekend or stretch through the holiday weeks. Neither of us ever wanted to lose, but I think I was that much more obsessed with winning. It was never just a game for me when it came to a one-on-one with Gareth. It was a proving ground, a study in self-worth. I had to beat him. There was a simple reason for this, one that does not require deep psychological evaluation: I knew I couldn't win the fight so I had to win the game. Problem was, if things got tight or there was a dispute over the rules, there inevitably would be a fight. And, just as inevitably, I would get beaten up. I couldn't count now the times I took the short march to the house licking my wounds and wiping away the tears after yet another hiding at the hands of my brother. What I do know is there were always a few tears left for my Mum's benefit. And don't start judging me. All younger brothers know this: if you're going to take a beating, at least make sure you get some form of revenge through parental sympathy.

This was the way things went with us for years. We would start a game, do our utmost to outlast each other, argue over a rule and finally come to blows. I swear some of the neighbours probably had stopwatches on us and could pick the exact moment when the intense competitiveness would boil over into open violence. It didn't matter. What mattered was that I would never say no to a challenge. If Gareth spent an hour occupying the cricketing crease, I would not rest until I could do the same. If he could kick a spiral punt over the tall tree on the last bend of the street, I would practise until I could too. If he started running faster, I would train until I could keep up. In fact, I would train until I could outrun him. Come to think of it, that was probably more about survival than any competitive drive.

When we weren't engaged in a sporting pretext for bloodshed, my circadian rhythm revolved around finding new and improved ways to provoke Gareth's outrage. I recall on one occasion I arrived home from school early and lined up an arsenal of water balloons on the balcony that overlooked our driveway, hiding from view until I heard him clomping up the concrete. Before he could take evasive action, I launched my elevated assault, soaking him to the bone and sending him into a death spiral of anger. I knew I could outrun him and, after a chase that lasted much of the next hour, he must have finally cottoned on to this notion too. In lieu of belting me he punched a hole through the wall of the house. Things truly peaked some weeks later when, after another protracted and adrenaline-filled pursuit, he cornered me in the rumpus room, collared me, and proceeded to throw me head-first through a window. Remarkably, I came away from the incident without a scratch.

In spite of his many fratricidal attempts on my life, Gareth largely tolerated my existence. He was stuck with me, really, because everything he did, I wanted to do too. There is little doubt that my drive was shaped in large part by my need to compete with him, and because I was always competing with him, I was also competing with his friends. As such, I never felt any fear when it came to playing sports with or against older, bigger kids. In fact, I couldn't wait to get among the action and to prove I was worthy of their company and their respect. I think back now to that time and realise how blessed I was to have that attitude then and to have parents who never once tried to dissuade me from mixing it with the older boys, even though they were likely certain there would be a few tears along the way.

Sport was everything to me. I would much rather be outside running about or kicking a ball than sitting inside on the gaming console. As it was, Gareth had dominion over our PlayStation anyway and, on the rare occasions I showed interest in playing, took great pleasure in making me wait so long for a turn that I would lose my will and head off to find one of the Kavanagh Crew to do something else with instead. I like to imagine that he had my best interests at heart, that he was teaching me a valuable lesson about the dangers of a sedentary lifestyle, but he was probably just being an asshole. Either way, it got me outside where I could enjoy the number one privilege of so many New Zealand kids: the freedom to roam.

Kavanagh Place was in the Opaheke suburb of Papakura, if you could call it a suburb at all. In fairness, it was first listed as an independent suburb in 1989 and its newfound status lasted all but a few months before the classification was revoked and Opaheke was once again considered simply a part of the Papakura district. To be perfectly frank, no one who lived there ever cared about that and nor would anyone still living there really care for its one remaining geopolitical distinction, that being it is the southernmost tip of the Auckland metropolitan area. To us kids it was simply a rabbit warren of walkway short cuts between avenues, dead-end streets and quiet cul-de-sac roads, all of which combined to form a masterpiece of topographical confusion that ensured no first-time visitor would ever find the right house before circumnavigating the entire area at least 17 times.

Papakura was a strangely tough location to navigate by car. Its arterial roads merged around the town cemetery before magically multiplying and splitting off into what felt like every imaginable direction: out to Red Hill and the Hunua Ranges in the east, Clevedon in the north-east, East Tamaki in the north, Drury in the south ... and all of this was further complicated by the railway that ran through the middle of the town. Like all places bisected by train lines, there was always a right and a wrong side of the tracks, but as kids we were never truly cognisant of the subtle class distinction, and because of that we grew up seeing ethnic and cultural diversity as the norm, rather than the exception. In this respect, Opaheke School was a perfect representation of the population, and a quintessentially Kiwi primary. The only problem was my mum sometimes worked as a relief teacher there, and when she did I would suffer through my irrational juvenile embarrassment by finding somewhere to hide.

I was blessed to have attended a school like that, really. To be able to walk from home and back with my mates, creating myriad kinds of mischief along the way. There was no uniform, and shoes were an optional extra. While Nirvana was busy releasing *Nevermind*, I was wandering the streets of Papakura in hand-sewn clothes carrying my packed lunch and wondering why all the other kids got bags of chips while we, without so much as a grain of gratitude, always had to make do with a slice of home baking and a ham sandwich. Many was the interval during which I pined for a packet of salt and vinegar chips or even a bag of Rashuns. I should have known that Mum had my best interests at heart; she and Dad always did, and that was a good thing as I seem to recall spending much of my childhood in tears. Maybe I was just that kind of kid, a bit of a sensitive soul who needed to find an outlet for the excess emotion. That outlet was destined to be sport.

I drive past the school now and the memories flood back, of escapades on the fields on summer afternoons filled with the noise of boisterous kids whose dreams and aspirations escaped with them from the classroom and ran with them on the sun-dried grass. Just down the road the old golf course is fenced off and closed for good awaiting some ambitious future development, its fairways now rough and its rough now a tangle of weeds and trees: the dereliction of time. I turn corners and swing through roundabouts and head past the cemetery and over the railway tracks, passing Massey Park where on sports afternoons they would let the Rosehill College kids out one side and the Papakura High School kids out the other lest surplus scores still needed settling. I turn onto the main street with its eclectic mix of takeaway bars with names like 'Grumpy's' and 'Lucky Day', and dollar shops and chain stores, bars and gaming rooms. The 'Mainly Men' hair salon is still there at the southern end of the strip, dispensing fades and fads. The Edmund Hillary Library is a few doors down dispensing fact and fiction.

In the descending darkness the cars stream past under the pale glow of the halogen streetlights, people are leaving work or coming home, suburban life is lit in kitchen windows and lounges illuminated by television news. I follow the traffic out of the town centre and along Great South Road, retracing my route back past the Drury playing fields and then turning west through the Karaka countryside towards the edge of the Manukau Harbour and to Mum and Dad. I know these roads, the blind corners and the narrow straights. I know the distances between the landmarks, even in the half light. I could tell you about those 3-kilometre runs between the rutted entrance to the family land and the third wooden power pole on Ellett Road. Home calls. Always. In the wall oven there will be a shoulder of lamb cooking and Mum's special roast vegetables will need to be turned. Dad will have a beer in his hand and his backside in a recliner. In the garage will be three decades of three boys and their games and the things they have left behind. On the walls inside, the story of us. I can't wait to get there now, back to home and to a delicious dinner and to the easy company of my parents. Things are only going to get more manic, more pressurised, in the coming weeks. It is less than nine months until I am expected to lead my national side to a Rugby World Cup victory. I need this one night to remind myself of how that came to be. I need this one moment to remember that at the end of it all, I am just another Kiwi kid. I needed this drive to remind myself of where I am from — and how far I still have to go.

3
BRUISER'S GIFT

My back is not right. My hamstring hurts, and my left leg feels like it's made of lead. It's now the end of January and I can't sit in the same spot for long before I have to reposition myself. I am having a glass of red wine after gate-crashing a mate's family dinner and devouring most of their roast chicken, much to the delight of his kids who I don't think have ever had an All Black arrive at their dining table after a day of fitness and strength testing. It's been more than a year since I first developed my herniated disc and the nerve issues that went with it, and still the ache has not yet fully subsided. I'm still cursing that gorgeous December day a few weeks back when I threw my back out throwing a goddamn frisbee, but we'll come to that later. What I do know now is that I am starting to wonder if I need to re-evaluate just where I am physically. I am starting to wonder whether I am going to make it through this year at all.

Only 24 hours before I had been in much brighter spirits, gathering for the first of the year's 'foundation days' with the rest of the boys in Auckland. I caught myself smiling during short moments of reflection, thinking that there were not going to be too many days left at the Heritage Hotel, our 'home away from home' during the All Blacks season. I felt like I knew every inch of the place, every creak of the old wooden floors, every angle of the city surrounding us, the short cuts in the service elevators, the way old black-and-white photos on hallway walls always look hopeful. It was great to see the guys arrive and to acknowledge, maybe with a sudden onset of sentimentality, how much I enjoyed being a part of this remarkable club.

There is a special, contagious kind of energy created by the group on that first day of any new All Blacks season. It is a nervous energy, born of the fact we all know we are about to be placed under the microscope of the strength and conditioning staff, but I loved the feeling of being plugged in to it, as if every part of me was instantly recharged purely by proximity. I needed that hit because the morning brought with it a good old-fashioned beep test and the afternoon comprised a hefty weights session and a full body scan. There is nowhere to hide on days like this, and it was encouraging to note that no one had shirked their fitness work over the short summer break.

When I am training or active my back doesn't seem to give me much bother, and already over the last month I have been able to load up in ways I was never able to during last season. When I am at rest, though, or when I have time just to sit and think about it, it is a constant irritation, and it is starting to wreak havoc on my mental state. I know my time in New Zealand and with the Crusaders and the All Blacks is coming to a close. I know

now that I have a finite period to get through. Knowing that gives me some comfort at least. I haven't told the doctors or physiotherapists too much about the ongoing problem. I have just told them that I can still get out there and do what I have to do.

My disc is obviously completely buggered, a misshapen abomination, really. I have to accept that. But what I can't accept is that it might prevent me from achieving what I want to achieve, to win a third Rugby World Cup. I know I must not think that way; we have been taught time and again to not allow that kind of negativity to pollute our minds. Acknowledge the problem, sure, but then believe in overcoming it. That is how we have long been conditioned to think, but even so there have been too many days lately during which I am struggling to see the finish line. I just want to get rid of this doubt. I just want to remember what it was like to play without pain and with confidence; what it was like not to feel a jolt down my spine every time I tie my bootlaces . . .

I still remember the first pair of rugby boots I ever owned. They were given to me by my grandfather, Arthur Lionel 'Bruiser' Read, and I cherished them. Every week I would come home from Thursday practice and head straight to the big laundry tub where I would scrub off every last bit of mud caked on them and leave them that night in front of the fire to dry. The next night I would sit in front of that same fireplace and nugget them up until they looked like new. Those boots were the tools of my trade and my dad had told me I should always take care of the tools of my trade. I would follow that routine right up until I started professional rugby, only stopping because we never trained or played in the mud.

Bruiser died when I was still in intermediate school and so never had the chance to see just how far that first pair of boots would take me. Mary, his wife and my nana, still watches every single game from the edge of her seat in her home on the edge of Stratford, and she will chat about rugby with anybody she bumps into. My maternal grandma Magdalene Harper, who lost her husband — my grandpa Norman — several years after Bruiser's passing, was still driving herself from Timaru to Christchurch for Crusaders home games well into her eighties. These wonderful women have followed me every step of the way and their support and love has been a constant source of comfort for me throughout my career, but it was Bruiser's gift that marks the starting point of this rugby story. Bruiser's gift, and my tears.

I cried until they let me play. That's at least how my parents remember it. Gareth was six and I was four and the only way to stop me bawling was to let me be a part of the same rugby team he was in. Even at that early age I just wanted to be out there testing myself against the older boys and doing the same things my big brother got to do. My parents wanted peace, and I wanted to play, and so the solution seemed pretty obvious to all involved: I got to play. I loved it immediately and could hardly wait for those winter Saturday mornings when I would pack my freshly shined boots in my bag and jump in Dad's car for the short drive to the game.

Winter was for rugby and summer was for cricket, and the story was the same for both. If Gareth was playing cricket, I wanted to be in the team too. So it went for my parents — and for my brother — for my entire childhood, and when there was no cricket or rugby, there was athletics instead. Mum and Dad were the ultimate backers of our sporting pursuits and Dad, especially, was right into it. A surveyor by trade and a quiet, diligent man who has never wasted a word in his life, Dad's language was sport, and he loved analysing it. Mum and Dad both played sport for the love of it, and they watched it with a wonderful passion. They imbued all three of us boys with that same passion but never once put any pressure on us to perform or to win. They instilled in us the joy of getting out there and giving it your absolute best every single time.

I must have been doing that, because by the time I had reached the final year of primary school I was invited to my first Counties trial. It was for the Goldfields team, an under-45-kilogram side and most of the other kids there were at least a couple of years older than me. Dad obviously didn't have a lot of faith in me making the team because on the way there he told me that if I was selected he would buy me an authentic All Blacks replica jersey, in those days made by Canterbury out of a material that could hold at least ten litres of water before it started to drip. It was a rare misstep from the old man. He should have known that nothing motivates a kid like the thought of an All Blacks jersey and, much to his surprise and cost, I made the team. I think I wore that jersey until it fell off me in pieces.

That Goldfields team was my first experience of representative rugby and I loved every second of it. I was pretty much a mute for the entire tournament — given the age difference between me and most of the boys there was some disconnect between what I was thinking about and their nascent pubescent preoccupations — but I enjoyed the challenge of taking on teams we all knew were better than us and matching up against the older kids. Was I a fearless kid? No. But sport had a transformative effect on me.

Once I was out there, on the field or on the pitch, I didn't care how big, how fast or how old the opposition was. I backed my instincts and tore into it.

I started to make representative teams on a regular basis after that, but I became somewhat of a club nomad. When I started at intermediate school we moved out of Papakura to a lifestyle block in Te Hihi, on the scruffy southern edge of the Manukau Harbour. The Drury club could no longer muster enough players so I went to play for Karaka instead, which was only a few kilometres down the road from the new family home and where I spent my summers playing cricket. It was a small side and after a handful of grading games we were dumped in the lowest grade. Two games into the season my coach asked me to play fullback and to take it a bit easy as I was hurting other kids. It was anathema to me, the concept of holding back on a footy field. I was out there to win and the only way to win was to play as hard as I could. I absolutely hated it.

My dad could see that I was going to have a tough time keeping up the charade and so I joined the Papakura club instead. The team was comprised mainly of Polynesian boys with a couple of Palagi ring-ins, of which I was one, and I think it is safe to say that year was when rugby got serious for me. We played in a decent grade and came up against some massive kids. I was an outsider in the team, but all that mattered to me was the rugby, which wasn't exactly complicated. The only move that seemed to matter was the classic 'on the burst', and I ended up being the kid who put his hand up to take down whoever the opposition threw at us. I delighted in being the one who was prepared to put his body on the line. There was no better feeling than sizing up the biggest kid on the field and sending him into reverse.

I loved those few years playing at Papakura, my seasons defined by club and representative commitments, the damp, dark winter mornings giving way to bright summer afternoons, the boots swapped for the bat, the boy becoming a teenager. When rugby and cricket weren't dominating my thinking, I would be at Massey Park competing in athletics against my friend and future rugby rival Onosai Auva'a. I loved athletics and was more nervous before a meet than I was before any rugby or cricket match, but with two sports already taking up most of my time my father eventually offered me a choice: I could have a new pair of spikes or a new cricket bat — but I couldn't have both. I chose the bat.

I couldn't blame my dad for wanting me to cut back on my sporting commitments. He and Mum had enough on their plates ferrying me to all the various rugby and cricket trainings and games, and my demands didn't end there. On winter weekend afternoons there was only one place I wanted to be: on the bank at Pukekohe watching the Steelers play. Man, I loved watching that team — Jonah and Joeli in full flight, a tough-as-teak pack with the likes of Jim Coe and Errol Brain and Glen Marsh scrapping in the mud, an intoxicating style of rugby that we all wanted to emulate. Gareth and I would make massive homemade signs and hold them up for the television cameras, and later we would drive home talking excitedly about the moves we had seen. For two magical years — 1996 and 1997 — the Steelers went all the way to the final but came up short on both occasions. I harboured an irrational hatred for Canterbury for many years after Jim Coe broke his ankle in the 1997 final at Lancaster Park. Funny how things work out . . .

Funnier still how they don't. My parents received a call from Saint Kentigern College after my third-form year at Rosehill in

Papakura, and I was offered a scholarship to play cricket for the school. It was not a full scholarship, but it did cover half the fees, and my parents thought it would be a good idea to try it out. I was hardly convinced. I was a homeboy, attached to my friends, and happy within my own school community where I knew the lay of the land and felt like I belonged. Mum and Dad urged me to give it a go, insisting that if I didn't like it I could always come back home and re-enrol at Rosehill. I'm glad we had come to that arrangement because I was barely a handful of weeks into my time at St Kent's when I made up my mind that it was not for me.

I was certainly aware of the opportunity I had been given and of the privilege I found myself surrounded with, but it was like being in a completely different world, one that I would never fully understand. I was a simple lad from a small, diverse community. This was a big city school with a vanilla complexion and it simply wasn't my flavour. The only close friend I made in my first few months there was an Australian lad who didn't play sport at all, which was mildly ironic considering I was there on a sporting scholarship. Sure, it was a place that possibly could have opened doors for me in terms of a potential sporting career, but it did not suit my personality and because of that it would never have got the best out of me.

Exacerbating the situation was the not insignificant issue of being on the bus for hours each day. I would catch the first of several buses at seven in the morning and would not, on nights when I had training, arrive back home until after seven in the evening. I would much rather have been kicking a footy around with mates or fighting with Gareth over a game of backyard cricket. At least my love of sport remained undimmed. I was still able to extend myself by playing in teams comprised mainly of seventh-form students. They were at a very different stage of their school lives, of course. When they were jumping into their cars and talking about that night's party, I was shuffling my feet waiting for my dad to pick me up!

I did wonder whether I had made up my mind too early about the St Kent's experience, but the passing weeks did nothing to assuage my unease. My parents encouraged me to see out the one year and, having agreed to that, I just knuckled down and got on with it. I still played a bit of senior cricket for Karaka when school commitments allowed and was selected for Counties age-group sides for both cricket and rugby that year. I was drawn to return home, back to people I could relate to and a place I understood. I completed my promised one year and returned to Rosehill and to senior school with a newfound enthusiasm for familiarity.

It probably seems too crazy to have foregone the opportunity to attend one of the big Auckland sporting schools, especially given the clamour today to get kids into that kind of institution, but I never once regretted my decision to return to Rosehill. Unlike St Kent's, it was certainly not what you would call a famous sporting school. Former Maori All Black and New Zealand Sevens player Kristian Ormsby was about the one recognisable rugby name we had produced. It was a big school — close to two thousand students — but in my fifth-form year we had enough rugby players to field precisely one team: a First XV. We had to search high and low to put that team together too.

It didn't matter to us that we were the underdogs every Saturday. Truth be known, we really enjoyed it. Moreover, we saw it as an opportunity to develop an identity for the team around the school, something that had not been done before. We were given ties and pullovers as our official team dress uniform and we wore them on Fridays, complete with our black pants and white shirts, in an attempt to create a bit of hype for the following day's fixture and to let the other students know that we were proud to represent them. Gareth was the team's captain and it was fantastic to play alongside him. We also played for the same club cricket team and that shared experience had helped to equalise our combative relationship.

It was wonderful to play footy with Gareth. He was a lock and a determined bastard. He was skinny as a rake — we both were — but it was great to be a part of his sporting world. From the moment we were named in that First XV side together there was something stronger than a fraternal bond between us. We were teammates, brothers in a very different sense. I was someone for him to protect and to watch out for and he was someone for me to respect and follow. I think he saw that I wasn't a bad player, actually, and figured I may be of some use after all. I was the youngest in the team, but I was comfortable with my brother as captain to assume some of the leadership. By virtue of being the only representative player in the squad, I felt that it was important to demonstrate what I could do on and off the field. If someone had deemed me worthy of playing for the province, the least I could do was attempt to be the very best for my school.

I considered representing my school to be an absolute privilege and my first taste of First XV rugby came against our arch-rivals Papakura High School on my old athletics stomping ground, Massey Park. While we lost the game, we felt like we were competitive, which was something at least. We were battlers really, but we trained hard on Tuesdays and Thursdays and dug in on Saturday. After my year away, everything about playing for Rosehill felt special. It was as if I was exactly where I needed to be. I rediscovered how much I loved playing the game. We were connected as a team, on the same wavelength, from the same place. The Saturday nights were always a lot of fun, too, especially after a rare victory.

Those were rare indeed over Wesley College, which was by far the most dominant school side in Counties-Manukau and one that was feared and revered all over the country for its traditions and history of success. A trip to Wesley was not for the faint-hearted. I absolutely loved it, but for boys who were 60 kilograms dripping wet, facing up against 110-kilogram wingers on a Saturday afternoon was not their idea of fun. Wesley was the kind of team that could score four or five tries against you in the space of as many minutes and be laughing the entire time. I remember on those occasions having to look around the deflated faces huddled under our own goalposts and deliver a pep talk that absolutely no one was buying.

There was one reason above all others that I loved fronting up to play Wesley College: it was the alma mater of Jonah Lomu. If I had one rugby hero growing up it was undoubtedly him. I mean, I was never going to be like him — there were some rather insurmountable differences between us — but I just loved watching him play. The things he could do in the game were so remarkable, so superior to anyone else of his time that I was in awe of him. His legend only grew for me the more we all got to understand how hard he had worked to overcome such a debilitating condition. He changed the game forever, electrified the rugby world, and he did it while battling health issues that would eventually lead to his premature death. Jonah was the man, and he made me want to knuckle down and be as tough and as good as I could be.

That first year, playing under my brother in the Rosehill First

XV, certainly whetted the appetite for more and when the next season rolled around I was blessed to have a mentor who had enormous belief in what I could achieve and who did everything he could to help me get there. His name was James Fraser, a young, compact energetic teacher with a permanently positive disposition and a genuine love for the school and its students. James could see that a couple of afternoon training runs a week were never going to be enough to develop my full potential and volunteered to meet me at school at 7 am twice a week to hold a tackle bag or run me through extra drills. It was an incredible gesture from him, really, to make that commitment to my development. Knowing that someone else was prepared to do that for me flicked a switch. His advice was timeless: I could get anywhere I wanted to if I was prepared to work for it.

James also helped me with my nutrition and every day a bottle of flavoured milk and a chicken roll would be waiting for me at the school tuck shop to supplement the lunch that I had packed at home. I don't know how he made that happen — he claimed that it was all part of the budget for the elite sports programme, something he had helped create alongside another teacher and great confidant, Merrick Rennell. As part of the programme James organised a number of guest speakers, one of whom was Olympic boardsailing legend Barbara Kendall. When she had finished her presentation, she asked each of us to write down what our sporting goal was. Mine was to be a great All Black. When she read what I had written down she looked at me with a smile and said, 'Just being an All Black would be amazing, wouldn't it?' I said, 'Yeah, but being a great one would be better.'

That year, James organised a trip for our First XV to a schools rugby festival on the Gold Coast. We had a great bunch of guys in the team and had worked hard to raise the money to make the trip happen. I didn't want to miss out, and as a result took myself out of contention for the Counties Schools side that year. I didn't regret that decision at all, but James still thought I was worthy of representative footy and when we returned he invited the Counties B coach to come watch a game. He must have talked me up because he was probably more gutted than I was when the coach took one look at me and told James that he thought I should stick to cricket.

So much for the future great All Black.

4
MAKING A CHOICE

A few weeks after the All Blacks opening training camp in late January 2019, I was sitting in the office of surgeon Rowan Schouten. The plan was to cut into my back and to scrape more of the disc away, followed by six weeks of rest and then perhaps a three-month recovery overall. I could get back in June if I tried, but if I saw any action in Super Rugby I would be doing well. The public had no idea, of course. Nothing to see here.

I had agonised over this decision and it was not a popular one. The surgeon's advice ran counter to everything my team medics wanted, and I knew that I would be cutting things fine in terms of the All Blacks' faith in me, but I just couldn't see any other option. Yes, I was training and ticking all the boxes on pre-season but there was no way around it — the problem was not going away. If I didn't have this done now, how great was the risk that I would need it later in the year? It was mathematics really — take the short-term hit for the long-term payout or close my eyes and roll the dice. I just couldn't live with that kind of gamble.

On the plus side, I would be heading into this surgery

in a much better physical state than the last time and that boded well for a faster recovery. Even so, March, April, May, June . . . My life had become a grand countback on the wall calendar, every day a calculated risk.

I had been in reasonable spirits at the start of the year. I had been incredibly open with Razor about what I felt I needed to get through for the Crusaders. We had agreed that I would miss the first four games of the season and he was comfortable that by the time I came back into the environment I would be good to go. That had been one non-negotiable with Razor since he had taken on the Crusaders job: there was no way we were to come marching back into Rugby Park underdone after our time off. He trusted the squad to get the job done in our absence and they in turn expected us to respect them by making sure we were working as hard as they were, even away from the team.

The hamstring issue that had come back with a vengeance in January was not preventing me from training, but I did pay a visit to John Roche, the Crusaders physiotherapist, just to let him know what was going on. The January All Blacks camp went by without too much of a hitch and I was trying to pretend that any ongoing discomfort was just the result of standard training fatigue. Over the next couple of weeks, though, it kept getting worse. Day by day the tightness would be more pronounced, the twinges of pain more frequent. The fact that it wasn't stopping me completely was a good thing, but when I was at rest the pain and heaviness in my leg were constant companions. I like to think I am strong mentally, at least in terms of handling the toll the game takes on the body, but this was driving me insane. Everyone was telling me it was going to turn around, it was going to get better, but it never did. It was with me every single second of the day.

Denial works. At least for a while. And then it doesn't. As the training began to get tougher, there were more and more things that I couldn't do at the level expected and required. I needed to front it with the medical staff and I put it like this: if there were five games left in the year and this was my cross to bear, then, sure, give me whatever painkillers I need and roll me on out there. But it's the first week of the Super Rugby season and there is no way I am going to be on a regime of serious medication until November. I had to be honest, I just could not see myself able to handle that course of action.

The medical staff knew I was struggling, but there was nothing showing in any of the neuro-testing they were doing with me. Because of that, the wait and see approach was deemed to be best. I was prescribed amitriptyline, a drug more commonly used to treat depression, to alleviate some of the pain. Another drug, pregabalin, came next. I was still battling symptoms rather than causes and it was becoming clear that we were reaching a point of no return on what the next solution might be.

I was booked in to see Rowan on the Thursday before the Crusaders' first game against the Blues, and on the following Monday I was admitted for full imaging. The news wasn't good. The bulge in the back was back. I trained Tuesday in the foulest mood imaginable, a mood made worse by the fact I now had a surgeon telling me one thing and two team doctors — Tony Page at the All Blacks and Crusaders doctor Martin Swan — telling me something else. I knew that they all had my best interests at heart and were doing their utmost for me, but it left me in a quandary. I knew Rowan would recommend another surgery when I met him the next day. Tony and Martin urged me to consider a non-surgical option. I didn't think there was one. If I was going to go under the knife it had to be now, not later.

Maybe I should have stuck to cricket . . .

Cricket consumed more of my school life than rugby ever did. Even in winter I was attending cricket training camps, and every spare Sunday was devoted to games or net practices or anything else that involved me swinging a bat. I believed then that if I was destined for a career as a sportsman it was going to be as a cricketer. From under-14 level right through high school I captained Counties representative teams and was also privileged to captain Northern Districts teams on occasion too. I loved the game and relished the technical aspects of a captain's job in the field, the constant search for a result, the endless tinkering with field placements, the impulses and inklings and gut feelings of a gambling man. I felt respected already as a cricketer and as such devoted much more of my time to it than I did to rugby.

Throughout my senior school years my father would drive me to the Karaka Cricket Club at 7.30 on frosty winter mornings and there waiting would be Alan Whimp, one of the great stalwarts of Counties Cricket, who had driven from Weymouth just to throw balls to me in the nets and to offer a sage word or two after every shot. His dedication was astounding and the investment he put into kids in cricket throughout the region can never be adequately repaid. All he cared about was that I was doing something to further my game every day. What a wonderful man.

As it was with rugby, I was playing in a team with much older lads, cutting my teeth as a 14-year-old in the reserve two grade side for the Karaka club, alongside my brother Gareth. The team was comprised of boys Gareth's age and much older and the opposition sides always featured a few gnarly veterans, but I was never worried about facing adults as a kid. Actually, I recall the year being a particularly fruitful one. I shared some good stands as an opener, including one memorable innings during which my opening partner Phillip Wood and I both scored 170-odd runs. All up I scored three centuries in that first senior season and had an absolute ball along the way. We had a big boom box on the sideline and played our own walkout tunes. I used to stroll out to 'Intergalactic' by the Beastie Boys, just in case you were wondering.

I never considered the idea of turning out for an age-group club team. I just figured if I was going to play, I may as well push myself. It was all I knew how to do. No one did me any favours out in the middle either, and there must have been some older guys who really hated being smashed to all parts by a 14-year-old. I was elevated to the Karaka premier side the next year, after I had turned 15. At the time, internationals like Daryl Tuffey, Ian Butler and Brent Arnel were throwing absolute heaters around the club competition in Counties and here I was, a 15-year-old kid, opening the batting. My highest score for the club was 190, enough to get me on the honours board at least. I was devastated to miss out on a double ton. I had been absolutely middling it and then tried a cute clip through the onside and holed out to midwicket off a leading edge. I'm not sure whether I got clapped off or copped a verbal spray, but it was certainly a day to remember.

I became well versed in taking abuse. When you are facing up as a batsman there is a great constant stream of adrenaline because you know an entire fielding team is out there coming for you, and the bowler is hell-bent on taking your wicket. There is nothing you can do about that fact so you just have to lock it in, embrace it and go for it, even while you're being verbally savaged. As a youngster, I didn't exactly have a reservoir of retorts. I can still recall one game playing for Counties against Northland as a 15-year-old and being emotionally tormented by the Marshall twins and Northern Districts stalwart Joey Yovich. I remember my innings so well because I scrounged a handful of runs, played a dire shot to be dismissed and then was absolutely roasted as I walked back to the pavilion. One thing was certain, even if I wasn't building scores, I was building a strong vocabulary.

When it came to watching New Zealand play I was a massive Roger Twose fan. I really admired how the doughty Englishman went about his work. He was nuggety and determined and just found a way to eke out an innings. I had a lot of respect for that and for his performance at the 1999 Cricket World Cup. From a batting point of view, Stephen Fleming was a great source of inspiration as well. It was not exactly a vintage era for New Zealand cricket, and I mean that with the utmost respect, but I loved following the game and had been to Eden Park on many occasions where I had watched the Black Caps take a towelling until Chris Harris came along and found some newfangled way to save the day. That was my favourite thing about 'Harry', how he embodied the idea that one person could change the direction and the outcome of a game.

Cricket and rugby continued to be the two interwoven extramural threads of my high school existence. I played for Counties and Northern Districts cricket sides all the way through high school, making the New Zealand tournament team at under-17 level in my sixth- and seventh-form years. Also, in my seventh-form year I was selected for the Counties Schools rugby team coached by one of my childhood idols, Jim Coe, and that selection would prove to be pivotal for my sporting career. From that point on, rugby, rather than cricket, would come to dominate my sporting life.

I knew most of the boys in the side because I had played with them for the last three or four years of representative rugby, but I wasn't overly close to them and I was so serious about being there and doing well that they probably wondered whether I had anything approximating a sense of humour. A few of the lads obviously thought it would be funny to head out on the booze the night after we had played our first game, but the next day was no laughing matter. Being a man of old-school standards, Jim gathered us on the field in the morning and, without raising his voice, said, 'Right, we know some of you guys have been on the piss. So, today, you're all running.' We ran shuttles one after another in the mud until we could not move. Needless to say, the rest of the tournament passed without further nocturnal drama and, playing openside, I was selected for the Northern Regions A team for the national tournament.

This was the first rugby rep team I had made outside of Counties. To be honest, before my name was called out I had no idea the team even existed. I probably had less of an idea of what I was doing there in the first place, but a few of the Wesley boys had also been picked in the team and we spent some time training together ahead of the national tournament in Rotorua. I organised to get a lift to the tournament in their team van, but when I turned up to the school with my dad at the pre-arranged time, there was no sign of anyone. I didn't have a number for any of the guys or even a contact for the team, at this stage. We waited there in the car park for what felt like an eternity before making some enquiries at the school dormitories. It turns out they had completely forgotten me and had already headed off!

'All right, mate, let's get in the car,' Dad said calmly, sensing I was about to lose it. 'We best be getting to Rotorua.' Dad was not prepared for a six-hour round trip that day but he never once complained, which was so typical of him. On the bright side, we caught up to the Wesley boys on the long straights north of Matamata, and Dad pulled out and drove alongside them tooting his horn and waving them over. Dad saved himself a few hours of driving, and I spent the next couple with a very apologetic vanload of boys and not much to offer the conversation.

I was absolutely out of my league. I knew it as soon as I arrived at the camp in Rotorua. Who was I to be a part of this? A skinny kid from Rosehill who a year before had been told to stick to cricket. I was now surrounded by the best schoolboy rugby talent north of the Bombays, all of whom seemed to be totally at ease with their place there, their easy-going confidence in stark relief to my awkward, shuffling shyness. I was wracked with self-doubt, convinced there had been a clerical error or that I was at most there to make up the numbers. I set myself to default mode, barely said a word to anyone, and kept my head down. Everything about that camp was just on a different level to what I was accustomed to. I mean, what kind of rugby team had meetings about trainings, before training?

I was surprised to be picked at openside for the opening game of the tournament, but given the opportunity, I made my tackles and made certain I was a nuisance at the breakdown. Being out there was an escape from those lingering pangs of insecurity. As long as I was doing, I didn't need to think, but no sooner had the game finished than the coaching staff told me the selectors wanted to see how I went as a lock. I was none too pleased, but I was hardly in a position to argue. If that's where they needed me to play, I would suck it up and do my best. I played lock in the final, in torrential rain, and scored a try from a towering high kick that I chased and caught over the top of the opposition fullback. It was a great moment, and my smile shone through the downpour and the darkness of that stormy afternoon.

After the match we sat spent but satisfied in the steamy concrete block changing sheds. The boys were talking excitedly about the naming of the New Zealand Secondary Schools team at the post-tournament function, which was about to take place upstairs. It finally dawned on me that 'the selectors' who wanted to see me play at lock were the *New Zealand* selectors. No, I thought, as my stomach suddenly turned and my jaw clenched, don't get ahead of yourself, mate. I mean, a few weeks earlier I had been surprised to learn that there was such a thing as a Northern Regions schools team and now I was contemplating selection for the national side? Come on. I busied myself getting dressed and squared away, all the while trying to dampen any expectations.

Anxiety filled the vast room upstairs at the stadium. Every kid was a hopeful, a starter's chance. Even those who knew in their heart of hearts that they were not going to hear their name read out that afternoon were still harbouring a little ship of hope. Crazy thing, hope. It's contagious. I started to hope too, despite my best efforts to keep a lid on the emotion that was suddenly threatening to swallow me whole. You can watch the way hope ripples through the room, the way every foot in the place shuffles with it, the way facial muscles tense up under its influence, how conversations become clipped and whispered and heads turn in every direction. We were called to attention and a serious man with a gravelly voice began reading names. Mine was one of them.

The New Zealand Secondary Schools team assembled in September that year at the Police College in Porirua for a pre-tour match against the Samoan schools side. Jamie 'Whoppa' Mackintosh, a hulking unit of a kid from Southland who had already played under-19 rugby for New Zealand, was the captain, and it seemed to me as if I was the only one who barely knew a soul there. Tevita Mailau, who was a Wesley boy and a Counties teammate, was about the one truly familiar face. In my eyes, everyone else shared a connection — real or imagined — potentially because almost all of them had played for more well-known rugby schools.

My eyes were as wide as saucers that week, and my mind devoured all that was thrown at it. The week was a procession of planning sessions, preview work, fitness testing, strength training and endless drills on windswept fields. By the time game day arrived I was living and breathing attack structures and set moves and running lines and had begun to emerge from my shell around the rest of the team. I lined up that day in a pack featuring six players who would all go on to professional careers, including Jeremy Thrush, Michael Paterson, Hika Elliot and Faifili Levave. I was stoked to get to the game to find Mum and Dad, along with a whole bunch of my mates, had taken the long drive down from Papakura to watch me play. Among them was a beautiful girl I had fallen for the year before while sitting around a bonfire at a friend's party. Her name was Bridget, and she was destined to become my most ardent supporter, and my wife.

Also, there was my younger brother Mark who would become a fixture on the sideline for me, whether it was cricket or rugby. His dedication to supporting me was unreal, and I cherished his presence at games. It didn't matter how far my career went, I knew Mark would find a way to be there to support me. I was blessed to have a little brother like him.

We put a big score on Samoa that day in Wellington and were soon en route to Australia for a three-match tour in Queensland. It was an old-fashioned trip with billeted stays in Noosa and Southport and a couple of good victories against Queensland Schools and Australia A. Many laughs were shared as uncertain introductions became fast friendships. I came off the bench for our final match against Australia Schools at Ballymore with simple instructions to make my tackles and that's exactly what I did. When the whistle blew for fulltime, we had scraped by with a two-point win. At that point I wasn't sure if we were supposed to celebrate or simply shake hands and move on. I had never been in a team that had defeated another country before; this was all new territory for me. I settled for a smile and ticked off another great experience.

Things moved fast once I returned home. I still had the school year to finish but, being a diligent student, I never fretted about schoolwork. I was no standout student, but I could hold my own in most subjects and I never mucked around in class. In short, I got on with my work so I could get back to doing the fun stuff. I was head prefect at the school and with that came a responsibility to give my best in all facets of school life. Perhaps because I liked to be involved with lots of different things at school, my friends reflected an incredible diversity of interests. Many of them didn't have the slightest interest in rugby or cricket, and that was just fine with me. I enjoyed being able to completely shut off from sport when I was in their company but, as it turned out, the selection in that Counties Schools side had put me on a fast track to a sporting career. I just wasn't yet fully aware of it.

I was straight back into cricket when I returned from Brisbane, and before the year was done, I had also signed a contract with the Counties-Manukau rugby academy. Counties was in the second division of the national championship then and I began training twice a week at Pukekohe under the watch of Phil Healey, who would go on to a strength and conditioning career with the Chiefs and the Blues. I was now immersed in a world of beep tests, skin folds and weights, all of which told me I was fast, skinny and weak. It was great to have a foot in the door, though, or maybe just a toe, and a couple of months later I was invited to the New Zealand under-19 trials which were taking place at the same time as the representative cricket window. For the first time in my life I had to make a genuinely tough call between rugby and cricket. I don't know which way I would have gone had I not had the New Zealand Secondary Schools experience. Fact is, though, I had. And wearing a black jersey for the first time had ignited something within me. I made the call to make myself unavailable for rep cricket and headed to Palmerston North to give rugby a decent crack.

We took a bus to Palmerston North, all the Auckland and Counties boys with our aspirations packed in gear bags with our spare underwear and our minds on the challenge that awaited. No sooner had we arrived than we were straight into a 3-kilometre run test followed by a full gym session. I still felt awkwardly shy around the other players, and I couldn't pinpoint exactly why. All the easy-going confidence I had around my school and mates seemed to abandon me as soon as I was thrust into this kind of environment. I still didn't have much of a clue about what to expect and what was expected of me, but I soon got some idea of the latter when I was told that I had to drop at least 30 seconds off my 3K time if I wanted to be in the frame. I had run 12 minutes and 15 seconds. This was going to hurt.

I had the chance to play both blindside and openside flanker during the camp, but I busted my thumb up a bit in the trial match, which could best be blamed on fate. When I got home, I received a call from Northern Districts cricket — they had an injury and wanted me to come down as cover at the national tournament. With my thumb the way it was, I couldn't hold a bat. Life has many pathways. Who knows where that one may have led if I had been in a position to walk down it? Instead, all summer long I ran a 3-kilometre route that we had marked out down the narrow country road leading to Mum and Dad's. The Counties academy programme was on hiatus over the holiday break so in January I decided to take up a place with Counties cricket on an invitational tour to Australia. Brent Arnel was our coach and understanding that I needed to keep fit for rugby, he made a point of training with me. Even if I had been out in the field all day I would still make sure I never missed a day of running or weights on that trip.

I returned to the final New Zealand under-19 trial in February and ran 11 minutes and 50 seconds. I think it was likely the fittest I had ever been and ever would be. I was still as skinny as a rake and clueless when it came to the gym work, but I did enough to make the team for the world championship that year in Durban. My good mate Onosai Auva'a had made it, too, and Whoppa was again my captain. It was a great crew of lads, coached by Aussie McLean and Russell Hilton-Jones with great men like Leicester Rutledge and Greg Shipton, Mark Plummer and Steve 'Doc' Kara on the management team. With backs like Aaron Bancroft, Richie Kahui and James Somerset, we adopted a free-flowing, high-paced game which perfectly suited how I wanted to play. We were jumping out of our skin to rip into it, but the first game would knock the stuffing out of us in the most tragic fashion.

We played Ireland first up at that tournament and during the match one of their lads, John McCall, collapsed on the field. We didn't think too much of it at the time, figuring he had been knocked out in a tackle and would soon recover after he was taken from the field. We were shocked to be told after the match that John had, in fact, died. He was just 18 years old, with dreams of becoming an architect. We were all in shock, and heaven knows how his own team were feeling at that moment, let alone his family. This was not supposed to happen. This was the most fun you would ever have playing the game, not a time to die. The next day we visited the Irish team at the hotel, presented them with our jerseys and sung waiata for them. Naturally they were heading home, and it was a deeply moving experience to be there that day and to pay our respects in that way.

Afterwards we sat together and talked about what we were all experiencing. There was no doubt that we were reeling from what had happened. None of us had ever been in a situation like it, and in those moments and the hours that followed, rugby was the least important thing on our minds. It would stay with me forever, that day, and even as the tournament progressed it was never far from my thoughts. In the end, we won the tournament, defeating South Africa in the semi-final and France in the final.

For the first time in my life I could call myself a 'world champion'. It was the first time I truly acknowledged that I just might be all right at this rugby business.

Aussie McLean wandered up to me after the final to congratulate me. 'You'll be playing for Canterbury soon,' he told me. I shrugged my shoulders and let the comment pass. He was a Canterbury man through and through and I was certain it was just a tongue-in-cheek comment, an oft-used throwaway line. Playing for Canterbury? Whatever, mate.

5

ON THE MOVE

It's now just a few days before I have to make a decision on surgery, with my 2019 Rugby World Cup chances as much under the knife as my back. I meet with Bert Enoka and Ceri Evans that afternoon as part of the All Blacks leadership programme. It's a crucial meeting because it will set the tone for the World Cup season. I'm in no mood for it, but I know I have to be on my game. Ceri is great in those meetings as he knows how to push all the right buttons to bring the excitement out of you, and Bert plays a vital role in making sure we can then sustain that head space throughout the year. As a psychological double act they make a formidable pairing. Of course, I was in no mental state for that kind of meeting, and they knew it within seconds, offering to reconvene another time. I didn't want that. I told them exactly where everything was at physically and dialled into what needed to be done mentally.

The key question in that session was a simple one: how was I going to be the world's best player in my position? The answer too was very simple. I based my ability as a number eight on defensive dominance, ball-carrying ability and being the best in the air, whether that is at lineout time or from kick-off. But simplicity can be a trap. We often have no trouble articulating what we want to do, but we fall down when it comes to describing how we are going to do it. That was where Ceri came into his own. His real skill lay in helping us all gain an insight into how we could become what we wanted to become. He took the outline and showed us how to colour it in.

I was so glad I had decided to push on with the meeting because by the time we had finished I felt as if much of the weight had been lifted. Yes, my back issue was a source of frustration and maybe it was even worse than that, but I still had the mental capacity to begin forming the foundations upon which my aspiration would stand. I left Bert and Ceri with a genuine sense of calmness and perspective, and my mood was further elevated later that evening when Martin Swan rang to tell me that he didn't think surgery was going to be required. I fell into bed that night, almost forgetting my hamstring was still hurting, and managed to fall asleep picturing high kick receipts and hard running lines.

I went back to Rowan the next day hoping that he shared Martin's optimism. What he shared with me, instead, were the percentages. I was among the 10 per cent of discectomy patients to suffer a recurrence and if I opted for no surgical intervention, I would have a 50 per cent chance that it would heal itself within six to eight weeks. Then again, I could have another surgery with an 80 per cent success rate, but if it did succeed, I would be back to 100 per cent fitness. If you have had any trouble following that brief detour through the scenario now presented to me, perhaps you can spare a thought for how hard my brain was working to process everything.

I trusted Rowan completely, and getting the scan done was the best decision I could have made. At least then I had facts in lieu of easy answers. I left his consultation room with all the permutations swirling in my mind. What was my priority for the year? It was to be in the best shape possible when the Rugby World Cup began in September. What was my best chance of that? Deep down I knew it was to have the surgery. Rowan's rationale was simple: the window of opportunity was closing fast. Could I afford to leave it to hope and chance for another two or three weeks? The recovery time was not going to change and the longer I left it the finer I would be cutting things at the other end of the season. Yes, surgery would mean missing most of the Super Rugby season — my last for the Crusaders — which was a sacrifice I didn't want to make. Then again, if it meant my World Cup dream was still very much alive . . .

The conflict was brutal. The Crusaders medical staff were still advising caution, especially as I was presenting well enough at training and getting through the majority of the work, but the conversation with Rowan had crystallised my thinking. I arrived at training on Thursday convinced I would not be able to get through the heavy contact afternoon session, thereby clearing any lingering doubts that surgery was the go-to play. Of course, it had to be the case that I felt really good and got through it with very few issues. It was a relentlessly brutal session too, with everyone absolutely throwing themselves into the collision and the breakdown drills. Confusion reigned once more. Martin Swan and his team devised a new painkiller plan for the coming week and we agreed to get through the first two days of the following week and make a final call on the Wednesday.

The following day I ran into Steve Hansen at the airport. Bridget and I were travelling to Auckland for a wedding that weekend and I had woken to find all the familiar symptoms had returned. Steve knew everything that had been going on — naturally the medical teams had been in constant contact — and we had a candid discussion about what was best for me and for the All Blacks. He reassured me that he would support whatever decision I made which gave me some peace of mind at least. On the way to the departure gate he chatted away to Bridget and once we were seated on the plane, I asked her what he had said. She smiled, knowingly, and without looking at me, said, 'His words were "tell him to get the surgery".'

That night I ran repetitions on the gravel road that snakes its way up a long steady incline to Mum and Dad's house, just as I had done as a kid. The sun was slowly sinking into the Tasman, casting the last of its late summer light across Waiau Pa, the waters of the Manukau Harbour awash in tints of orange and pink. I had all the facts now; I knew what was wrong and how it could be fixed. I had the support of the All Blacks coach and of my family. I knew the Crusaders would be disappointed but behind me all the same. I took deep breaths and I ran again and again, alone on the road with my thoughts as the lights came on in the family home above me and a waning full moon lay in wait below the horizon. It felt like yesterday that I lived here, like a lifetime ago that I left . . .

I moved to Hamilton after I finished school. It seemed as good a place as any to start something, and so I enrolled at Wintec to study for a degree in Sport and Exercise Science. Bridget enrolled at Waikato University and found a flat with some friends while I stayed in the halls and made some new ones. 'You'll be playing for Canterbury soon,' Aussie had said, but if there was any truth to that, I was yet to find any supporting evidence. I was still contracted to the Counties academy and they had allowed me to play my club rugby for University in Hamilton. I played my first game for the B team at the start of that season and four days later played an academy game for Counties against Waikato. Ten minutes in I managed to fully rupture my medial ligament and tear my ACL. I called Bridget to come get me from the hospital — she did, even though she had a university assignment to hand in that day — and I spent an uncomfortable night at her flat before heading to Auckland the next day for scans.

The news was not good: 2004 was done as far as rugby was concerned and the medial ligament rehabilitation would take at least three months before they could even contemplate operating on the ACL. It was a deflating time, especially as I had harboured high hopes of playing for Counties that season. It may have been a long shot, but my confidence had climbed after the world championship success in South Africa and now I was laid up until at least the middle of the 2005 season. Apparently, that was no problem for Canterbury who, just as Aussie had said they would, came calling.

I was definitely conflicted. On the one hand I was still such a Counties kid and still fiercely parochial about my province. Canterbury? This was the team that broke Jim Coe's ankle! Could I really see myself playing in red and black if there were no white stripes as well? It was a little childish of me. Professional rugby's development had already well and truly obliterated the old provincial lines, and Canterbury went to enormous trouble to fly me to Christchurch and show me around their operation and facilities. It was my first meeting with Rob Penney, the former hard-man number eight who was running the academy programme in the Garden City. It was fair to say I liked him immediately.

Counties knew that an offer had come in and the staff there did their best to generate some interest in me at the Chiefs and the Blues, hoping to keep me closer to home. There was none forthcoming but reverberating in my brain were the conversations I'd had with Rob and Aussie about how the Canterbury academy could improve my game. There shouldn't have been any real cause for equivocation — Canterbury was the province looking to make an investment in me and from the limited time I had spent there I could tell it was an organisation that looked after its investments. Ultimately, what young man doesn't long to feel valued and wanted? I have no doubt Rob and Aussie had perfected their sales pitch, and they had delivered it perfectly. After a long conversation with Bridget, we decided to give it a crack together. If it didn't work out, what had we lost?

The rest of the year was a lesson in self-motivation as I recovered from surgery and set my sights on a return to play in 2005. I pushed myself to train as hard and as often as I could manage and also completed my diploma. Bridget and I got to spend plenty of time together and our relationship bloomed as a result.

She arranged for her degree to be transferred to the University of Canterbury, and I made plans to attack further study once there through the academy's scholarship programme. I was rapt that she had agreed to take the punt with me, and, for me, to have the person I loved beside me on the start of a new adventure made everything seem right. After taking a Christmas break with family back in Auckland, we packed our meagre belongings into my 1990 red Toyota Corolla station wagon, bundled in a bunch of compact discs, and began the great trek south.

It was the beginning of February when we drove into our new city. Hagley Park had browned off in the summer sun and a dry wind cut across the playing fields and ruffled the tall pines lining Harper Avenue. We wound our way through the suburban streets of St Albans and Merivale and finally, after two days of driving, arrived at our academy flat — a compact weatherboard bungalow with a front garden of scruffy shrubs, directly opposite Rugby Park. The house came complete with three bachelors: Culum Retallick, Jonathan Poff and Isaac Ross. None of them knew how to cook anything other than chicken nibbles, but they were good men and I enjoyed their company. I'm not sure Bridget had envisaged this scenario when she had agreed to come to Christchurch, but after buying the necessary furniture and a few home comforts we settled in just fine.

There was a lot to get accustomed to. I had never been flatting before so everything was a novelty to me, as were the city's idiosyncrasies. Our first visit to New Brighton beach on a 30-degree summer's day was a salutary lesson in the difference between North and South Island ocean temperatures. We were going to need to acclimatise, that was for sure. The locals didn't seem to mind, which gave us some hope that in time we would get used to it. As summer turned to autumn, we also realised we may have moved into the coldest house in Christchurch. If this was autumn we thought, huddled under every blanket we could find, we'd hate to be here in winter.

Of course, these and the many other things about Christchurch (the one-way system) that we had to get our heads around were minor distractions. I was there for rugby and as such Academy Manager Rob Penney was already proving to be an outstanding guide and influence. He was genuinely one of the most helpful men you could hope to find, and he knew the lay of the land so well down there that you could ask him anything and he would have an answer. One of the top priorities was to find a club that wanted me, and a few called up to gauge my interest. Rob told me that I should be playing number eight so if I joined the Varsity club, I would find that position available. I missed the start of the season, but once I had the all-clear on the knee I was good to go.

Our home ground was at Ilam, in the middle of the sprawling university campus, and the club had a solid reputation for performing well off the field. I was not the only Canterbury hopeful who had found a home at the club. Andy Ellis and Ti'i Paulo were already knocking on the door of provincial selection and Steve Brett was a familiar face from representative rugby. We were coached by Victor Simpson who had played for Canterbury and the All Blacks in the 1980s. There was an apocryphal tale that he had once been knocked out by his own coach, Alex Wyllie, but none of us ever brought it up. Victor was a hard case, though, and hated spiral passes. He instituted a team-wide ban on them and we all had to learn to flick it from the hip. I thought it was absolutely hilarious, though I'm not sure Andy thought it was doing his game much good.

It didn't take long for me to realise that a special kind of welcome is reserved in senior club rugby for new kids on the block. The first time I donned the famous maroon and gold jumper I was given some fairly frank advice from the opposition pack on the importance of serving my time at that level before getting too far ahead of myself. Sometimes the advice came in verbal form and at other times more physical methods of instruction were enlisted. I remember giant lock Kevin O'Neill absolutely squaring me up and punching me straight in the face in one game, for no fathomable reason at all. I figured I must have been doing something right if everyone wanted to beat me up. Apart from a couple of black eyes and the odd bleeding nose, I managed to get through that first season on the field — and off it. It was a very social year.

The weeks took on an easy rhythm that revolved around rugby. We trained with the academy at Rugby Park on Monday and Wednesday, starting with a 6 am gym session and finishing with running in the afternoons. On Tuesday and Thursday nights we threw hip passes for Vic at the Ilam Fields. The remaining time was dedicated to study, and on Saturdays I received my weekly lessons in the finer points of senior club rugby. The academy shared facilities with the Crusaders and Canterbury teams, but we were very much a separate operation. Even so, you could walk through the gym and see the big dogs doing their thing. I found myself undertaking a silent roll call most days. 'Wow, there's Reuben Thorne!' Or, 'Holy shit, that's Dan Carter!' I never talked to them; I was far too shy. Worse, I never wanted to lift anything in front of them because I was using such small weights.

Trainer Luke Thornley wasted no time in getting me onto a bulk-up weights programme, introducing me to the wonderful world of 10 sets of 10 repetitions for every exercise. It was fundamental muscular hypertrophy training — increasing muscle tissue size through metabolic fatigue and progressive overload. I needed to put at least 10 kilograms on my frame, which was easier said than done. I had always been a bit of a beanpole and gym work had never been a forte. Not wanting to disappoint anyone, I set about making the necessary changes to my physique and hoovered as many protein shakes as I could lay my hands on.

The academy sessions were hard work but great fun. It was ultra-competitive because all our testing was done as a group and everyone there wanted to win at everything. It was an epic environment to be in, energising and encouraging. Importantly, I had a plan. Rob had sat me down when I arrived and outlined the year ahead. I was up for his idea of playing number eight. I knew the position was perfect for utilising my skills as a player and would also allow me the chance to roll up my sleeves and do the dirty work, which is what I relished in the game. I had New Zealand Colts trials later in the year too, and I knew I had two years — this one and the next — to make that team. I had a growing aspiration now to go as far as I could with rugby. I hadn't gone as far as to circle dates and create personal deadlines — I still had so much to learn and all I wanted to do was take full advantage of every opportunity I got — but it was becoming clearer by the day that this was going to be more than a game to me. It was going to be my profession.

Those first few months in Christchurch were a complete vindication of my decision to join the academy. We had access to an incredible bank of detailed information and we all felt like we were growing as players with every session. It was akin to being on a learning fast track; all we had to do in return was listen, watch, learn and work hard. I had no problem with any of that.

Rob mixed up the programme to ensure we had a range of voices at different stages of the season and he was also happy to take one-on-one sessions to offer specialist help. I sought his counsel as often as I dared and was never once turned away. He knew inherently how to get the best out of me, and I was fortunate enough to be selected for the New Zealand Colts that year.

The world championship was held in Argentina — specifically Mendoza — and we were all excited about touring somewhere new. Rudi Wulf may have been a little too excited as he jumped into the pool at the team hotel in Auckland during our final training camp and broke his neck. It was not the kind of start the team was after, but things could have been a lot worse for Rudi. Fortunately, he would eventually make a full recovery, after which he would be selected for the All Blacks and enjoy a lengthy professional career in New Zealand and France.

There were some talented loose forwards in the Colts team that year, including Liam Messam, who started in every game of the tournament, the relentless worker Serge Lilo, and Peter Nixon and Mikaele Tuu'u, who were also in the Canterbury set-up. Peter was preferred as the first-choice number eight, and apart from one start in a merciless shellacking of the Canadians, I was limited to sub minutes from the bench. The year before I probably would have been happy with that, but the expectations I had for myself had increased exponentially during my time in Christchurch. I wasn't content to be backup; I wanted to be playing, not least because Mum, Dad and Grandma had made the trip to watch us play.

The team had a great balance of humour and talent. Andy Ellis and I had already built a solid friendship through the academy and the University club and we were constantly at each other on tour.

While we got on well, we had very different attitudes towards the game. In later years many a young player new to the Canterbury environment could attest to wondering if we liked each other at all. Andy would push the rules past what I considered to be their breaking point. I would call him up on it, and our ensuing argument would often boil over into a full-blown wrestling match.

As fun as the trip was, the results did not go as well as we would have hoped. After big wins against Wales and Canada we faced Australia in a match that ended with us on the wrong side of an extraordinary 46–43 scoreline. It was the highest losing score ever posted by a New Zealand side and it put us on a collision course with South Africa in the semi-final. There were boys in that side who hadn't forgotten their loss to us at the previous year's under-19 world championship and they were to get their revenge in Mendoza. We were left to play for the bronze medal against France and Andy bagged a double that day as we won comfortably. None of us were happy with third.

We returned home in time to watch Dan Carter put on a clinic in the second test against the British and Irish Lions in Wellington (me wondering where would I be when they next came to New Zealand), and I slotted back into club colours and got my first outing in the red and black with the Canterbury under-20 side. It's weird but I was desperate to prove myself to the guys in that team. I think part of that could be down to the fact I didn't feel as if I had got to show what I was capable of in Argentina. This was another chance to do just that. When the season ended in October, I looked back on the last eight months of my life and realised how far I had come as a person and as a player.

Bridget and I had moved into a new home with Ti'i and his partner Frankie, and another friend, Anna, which provided for a much more domesticated set-up than the bachelor bungalow. We had made some great friends, my rugby was improving rapidly and we were enjoying our time in our adopted city. There was one thing missing, though. I was strolling down the road past Burnside Park a couple of weeks after the rugby season had finally finished and suddenly I realised what it was. I walked into the local cricket club — and signed up to play.

6

A RAPID ELEVATION

The 2019 season is about to begin and we are gathered at Rugby Park for our karakia and our season opening. In previous years we had gone to a local marae to connect with the people of Ōtautahi, but this year we have stayed at our headquarters and invited our people in. We share a kai together, taking the time to be grateful for what we have and the position we are in. When the meal is over, we board a bus — players and coaches — and head into the city to the cinema. Razor being Razor, he's made a film for us.

That surgery I was going to have? Yeah, that never happened, but we'll get to that later.

I'm a bit old-fashioned and I have never felt like I needed a visual theme to get me prepped for a season. I enjoy thinking about those mental cues and making sure we as a team have a collective purpose, but Razor has supercharged all of that. This had become our new normal in Crusaders land: season-long themes complete with multimedia extravaganzas and plenty of visual cues. For a lot of the younger guys it has been a massive boost, getting them in the right frame of mind and bringing them together. We are chasing the threepeat this season, a rarity in any sport. In the NBA, the Golden State Warriors are attempting to do the same. They are going to be our 'we'. Usain Bolt did it on the track in Beijing and London and Rio. He is going to be our 'me'.

I'm intrigued with the choice of Golden State. In the first couple of years we had themed the campaign around teams or individuals who had already achieved what we wanted to achieve. I can't help but think to myself, 'They better bloody win the thing or we could be looking for a swift thematic change.' I should have had a bit more faith in how Razor's brain works. The more I think about it, the more it works. In essence, if they win, we emulate. If they don't get a third title, we have a chance to go past them and do what they couldn't.

We sit in the dark as the film starts to roll. Razor and his team do such a good job producing the content. I look around the cinema briefly, catch the young faces in the squad transfixed by what they see. We take what we need to. Watching and listening to some of the most famous names in sport, interspersed with vision from our own matches over the last couple of years, there is a message that is slowly absorbed by the subconscious mind: we want to be considered as great as they are, and everything we do this year is going to ensure we are a part of that conversation.

I must admit, I always had my own internal motivation to get me through a year, but I understand the power of this collective buy-in as a team. Because of that I'll be as committed as everyone else to this message. That is my role as a leader, to help drive that enthusiasm, to set the standards, and to put the team above all else. A leader. Even the thought of being that once would have filled me with dread . . .

I flew into my work once the new season commenced in 2006. Rob Penney was still convinced that I should focus on playing number eight and stayed in constant contact after he was appointed to coach the Canterbury NPC team and Matt Sexton came in to take over the academy. I knuckled down, wanting only to seek continual improvement through my academy work and put in the requisite good performances for University that would put me in the right position to trial again for the New Zealand Colts team. I was growing more comfortable with my place at Rugby Park, though I was still a quiet achiever, concerned only with doing my job and pushing myself as hard as I possibly could.

I was rapt to be selected again for the Colts for the world championship that year in Auvergne, France. It was a stunning place to travel to, a countryside of gently rolling hills and forested parks, and towns showcasing six centuries of architectural style and elegance. We opened the tournament in the town of Riom before playing two matches in Vichy and a further two in Clermont-Ferrand. We were captivated by the surroundings, and by the hospitality of our French hosts. During our first week there we were invited by members of the local rugby club to dine with them in their homes. I was taken to a beautiful farm on the outskirts of the town and treated to one of the most sensational meals I had ever eaten. Dish after dish of perfect food was presented to me during the night, each more delicious than the last. My hosts spoke no English, and I spoke no French, but we were united by the common language of food, wine and footy. It was an evening to cherish.

As for the tournament, unfortunately it was a case of history repeating. Again, we were defeated by Australia in the pool stage and again we were beaten by South Africa in the semi-final. We got our asses handed to us by that colossal human Pierre Spies that day. If I needed a benchmark for where I needed to be, Pierre certainly provided it. Then again, I was only human. I'm not sure if Pierre was. I enjoyed getting the chance to start in every game bar the opener, but it was of small consolation considering the result. I didn't like ending my age-group career with consecutive losses to South Africa and I was left to wonder if we had fallen into the trap of believing we had the right to win simply by virtue of the fact we were wearing a black jersey. Even though I wasn't a part of the leadership team and hadn't put my hand up for anything other than a start, I could still see that there was a lot more that we — and I — could have done. I think in some ways that ignited within me a desire to be more actively involved as a voice, rather than just as a player.

Once I was back in New Zealand, Rob was always handy and willing to offer advice and technical tips to ensure I was doing everything to put myself in the frame for his provincial side, and he offered me plenty of reassurance that I was on the right track. At the conclusion of the club season I was named in the wider Canterbury squad, which was a massive moment for me. It marked the first time I was in line to play first-class rugby, and I was still just 20 years old. The pre-season programme featured two Ranfurly Shield defences, and I got the chance to travel with the team to Timaru for the first of them against South Canterbury.

Rob told me he wasn't going to play me in the game but thought I would get some value from being a part of the day. I understood his reasoning, but sitting on the bench that afternoon, fully kitted up, all I wanted to do was get on the field, especially as the man starting was Peter Nixon, the same bloke I had sat on the bench behind at the 2005 under-21 world championship. I had to wait another week to make my debut, in another shield defence against Wairarapa Bush at AMI Stadium. It was a touch one-sided (we won 96–10) but I relished every second, and it was superb to get that first taste of first-class rugby after having to settle for a glorified spectator role the week before. Suffice to say, from that point, I was hooked.

There were plenty of fresh faces in those pre-season Canterbury teams and none of us were under any illusions that we had cracked the code. The province was stacked with All Blacks and Super Rugby stars and I knew from that moment on that if I wanted more game time, I was going to have to work damn hard for it. I was thrilled to be named in the team for the first competition game of the season against Hawke's Bay and I managed to earn my first eight caps that season, seven of them as a starter and all of them at blindside flanker. So much for my move to number eight! I also scored my first try for Canterbury that year. The date was 10 September and I remember it so well because the opposition that day was Counties-Manukau, the province I had always dreamed of playing for.

Unfortunately, the season came to a premature end courtesy of a defeat to Wellington in the quarter-final, but that loss stands out for one significant reason: it was the first time I took the field alongside an openside flanker named Richie McCaw. It was a thrill to run out with a player like that. There was just something epic about the way he went about his work. He was an engine with no off switch. As much as I wanted to be in the team each week, I loved it when the All Blacks were back in camp and we had to run opposition plays against them. Everything lifted when they were there, and I was in awe of their skill level and intensity. I remember in one contact drill being absolutely cleaned out by Dan Carter and thinking to myself, 'I've just been hammered by a first-five. I have a long way to go.'

I understood in those weeks just why Canterbury rugby had become so successful: everyone was expected to operate at the level of the very best, and the very best never dropped their standards to make things easy. Moreover, those elite players would do everything they could to help you reach their level, once you had done enough to earn their respect. Even though, more often than not, their availability meant my demotion from the team, I thrived on being around them; they were the catalyst for my metamorphosis from fringe dweller to front and centre.

I didn't do a lot of talking around the environment, fully cognisant of the often-forgotten ratio of ears to mouth. I preferred to soak in every detail and suck up every tough lesson on the training pitch. I had a healthy relationship with the other younger guys in the team and knew that friendships with the veterans would be based, initially at least, on what I could produce for the team on the field. I was just enjoying the novelty of training every day for Canterbury, which was another of many incremental adjustments on my way to becoming a fully-fledged professional. I was technically still under the original academy contract, which came with a salary just north of $20,000, so Bridget and I led a frugal existence outside of our studies. That was just fine by us. We weren't the kind of couple who needed for much and, besides, the trusty Corolla was still going strong.

In years to come I would look back on those training weeks with a certain nostalgic fondness. Compared to modern professional loads with their highly diarised schedules and structures, reviews, previews, analysis sessions and various group meetings it seemed almost cartoonishly quaint. Not that we knew any better at the time. Lounging about on couches watching television in the afternoons seemed a perfectly legitimate way to earn a living for all of us then, as did golfing afternoons with Johnny Leo'o and Mose Tuiali'i, both of whom had a major impact on my development as a player.

While I was revelling in my opportunities at provincial level, there was one odd exchange during the season that certainly had my future ambitions on high alert. After the first competition game against Hawke's Bay, Reuben Thorne had returned to play for a couple of weeks and so I had dropped out of the team. I was busy working through one of Luke Thornley's gruelling gym sessions when Crusaders coach Robbie Deans casually sidled up to me. I hadn't met Robbie before, and he didn't exactly bother with official introductions. He simply asked, 'How would you like to be a Crusader next year?' I didn't quite know how to respond, but composure came to the rescue and I told him that sounded like a bloody good idea, or words to the effect. He looked at me for a few seconds with narrowing eyes and a subtle nod of the head, and then said, 'Get used to the idea.' With that, he walked away.

Maybe Robbie had seen enough of me to know I would go all right at Super level, or maybe he knew that Graham Henry's infamous All Blacks 'rest and rotation' policy was on its way ahead of the 2007 Rugby World Cup and he was desperate for cover. Either way, I was pretty blown away by what had just unfolded. As if the conversation with Robbie wasn't cryptic enough, after that I had absolutely no communication from him or anyone else in the Crusaders organisation for the rest of the season. I started to wonder after a while if I had imagined the whole thing, and it wasn't until the end of October that I finally heard from Robbie again. It was Super Rugby naming day, and this time he was calling to tell me I was in the squad. It was another typically wordy conversation. 'Congratulations,' he said. 'I want you to be a Crusader.' And that was about that.

I was just 21 years old when I was first signed for Super Rugby and still trying to add the necessary bulk to my relatively thin frame. I had played just eight games of first-class rugby for Canterbury, and I knew that I was some way down the pecking order in a province stacked with All Blacks loose forwards. I was yet to fully prove myself to the veterans of the provincial side, let alone to the stars of the Crusaders, but, and this is the funny thing, I still felt like I was ready for it. In fact, I had absolutely no doubt at all that I belonged in the Crusaders. If I was good enough for a coach like Robbie Deans, that was all I needed to know.

Bridget was absolutely thrilled when I told her the news. How happy we were now that we had made the decision to pack up our meagre possessions two years earlier and take the punt on a move to Christchurch. Mum and Dad were equally enthusiastic about me getting such an amazing opportunity. For my part, I didn't quite know what to expect or how to prepare for what would undoubtedly be a massive step up in class but, having received the invitation, I wanted to get to the party as soon as possible. When we gathered for the opening pre-season session in November, it became patently clear that trainer Ash Jones's idea of a party was not quite the same as mine. We got absolutely flogged, so much so that it was all I could do at the end of the day to crawl through the front door of the flat and flop onto the nearest soft surface.

In fairness to Ash, Luke and their team, the pre-season was actually an enormous amount of fun, even if it left all of us out on our feet. Every day was a different challenge and every exercise was a competition. It was instilled in us that the reputation of the franchise was founded upon hard work, and not just on the playing field. Tellingly, we spent many hours addressing our protocols, our behaviour, our personal and collective expectations, and how we could ensure every day that we were living up to the standards expected of us. Robbie had selected a young group of players to augment his All Blacks riches — riches he would have limited access to that season — and as such he invested as much time as he could tutoring us in the intangibles of the team. I had never met a coach so deeply passionate about team identity. There were many coaches who were good at telling you how to do something, few as articulate as Robbie was at outlining the 'why'. It was my first genuine taste of 'the Crusader way' and of the implementation of effective theming.

We began the year with a pre-season trip to Australia to play a couple of matches and it was a team largely comprised of the younger members of the squad. Our first hit-out was in Melbourne and after all my agonising about how quiet and shy I felt around Rugby Park over those first couple of years, I was named captain. I was blown away, really. I mean, obviously Richie was the captain of the team, but he was not yet back into training. Corey Flynn was likely to assume the role in the early part of the season proper, but here I was, on debut, getting the job. Robbie told me only a day before the game and I did not have a clue what to do. I decided the best course of action was to not do much at all, other than to run out onto the field first.

I think it was Robbie's way of saying he believed in what I was capable of, and this was a chance for me to believe in it too. It was surreal to lead the team in my very first game, and it summed up the kind of coach Robbie was: he was cryptic, certainly, but he knew exactly where everyone's button was. His ability to inject confidence into players was second to none, and I loved working under him. He had his work cut out in the 2007 season too, as with the All Blacks not available for the first seven weeks of the competition he had to draw on all his vast experience to get the rest of us up to speed — and quickly.

While the fans and media may have agonised over the absence of the All Blacks, I thought it was fantastic. Naturally, it gave me an opportunity to play — one that I would not have got under different circumstances. For his part, Robbie just treated his young team as he would anyone else. His message was a simple one: go out and express yourself. Robbie was so passionate about the team that it rubbed off on everyone there, and what we lacked in experience we compensated for with enthusiasm. We wanted to do well for ourselves, yes, but mostly we wanted to live up to the legacy of the club. We didn't always get that right during the season, but it was rare for Robbie to lose the plot with anyone. He was preternaturally calm before games and even at halftime, when things hadn't gone so well, he would work through the detail and the processes with an assured manner that made you believe you could go back out and right any wrong.

My first official Crusaders game was against the Blues at Eden Park on 2 February, and on a perfect Auckland night I became Crusader 110. I had to pinch myself all week. Just getting the start would have been special enough, but to get it against the Blues on Eden Park? I don't know how it could have been better, really. I ran onto the field that night with a big crowd in the house and a bigger smile on my face. I couldn't get rid of it, but I didn't care one bit. This was what it was all about — a big stage, two arch-rivals, my family and friends in the stands and a massive opportunity to show what I could do. It was the perfect debut, right up until the point we lost the match 25–34. It was the Crusaders' first loss to a New Zealand team since 2004 and the Blues' first win over a New Zealand team in two years. I hated losing, and losing my first one cut deeply. I didn't know it at the time, but 'milestone' games were going to become somewhat of a curse for me.

After bouncing back against the Reds, we took off for three games in South Africa and I continued to get the start. We played the Lions at Ellis Park, my first experience of rugby in that great cauldron of a ground, and lost 3–9 in the most boring game of rugby I had ever played. Louis Strydom kicked three penalties and we were left scratching our heads and hoping no one back home got up to watch. The Cheetahs were accounted for in Bloemfontein before we faced the Sharks at Kings Park. We had the game in the bag that day, leading by six points with time almost up. All we had to do was run it into touch and victory would have been ours. Instead we had a crack at them, knocked on, and let Odwa Ndungane cut us apart to score an 80-metre try. Ruan Pienaar kicked the conversion from the sideline and we lost by a point. It was a good lesson for a young team: express yourself but don't be an idiot when you do.

We stayed in the hunt that season, and I started the first seven games of the year before Reuben Thorne and Richie McCaw finally returned to action. Again, to my surprise, I wasn't completely out of the picture after that. In fact, I was named on the bench for each of the remaining games, earning 14 caps for the year. I hadn't played much, if at all, with some of those All Blacks, and wondered how they might perceive me when they came back in. I was relieved — or perhaps just glad — to find that I had obviously done enough to earn their respect during the first half of the year, and they were great at helping me develop further that season. It was *Boy's Own* stuff really: a 21-year-old kid getting to train and play each week with some of the biggest names in the game. If I couldn't get excited about that, there would have been something truly wrong with me.

I roomed with Richie on our first away trip following his return to the team and it was all rather nerve-wracking. I was on edge when I was told the news, and once in the room I duly offered him his choice of bed and generally went out of my way to accommodate him. Richie, as I would come to know over the years, was not the most chatty bloke and I, as the young fella, was certainly not going to be the one to instigate a conversation the All Blacks captain couldn't be bothered having. The upshot was, it was the quietest hotel room in rugby touring history, one with two beds and two mutes. It was an awkward start to a decade-long working relationship.

Mind you, it was a better scenario than the one presented by rooming with Chris Jack. Richie was quiet, sure, but only because he didn't have a lot to say. Chris Jack on the other hand just couldn't be bothered talking to anyone. I had the pleasure of the big man's company ahead of the semi-final against the Bulls that year in Pretoria — a match they only got to host courtesy of a 92–3 shellacking of the Reds the week before. We had lost our last game of the season against the Chiefs but still expected to host the semi-final. The Bulls needed to beat the Reds by 72 points, and what were the chances of that? You can imagine our surprise when we woke the next day to news that we were travelling to South Africa instead of playing in Christchurch.

It was a short turnaround, but we got acclimatised as best we could and made it through to game day with a genuine belief in pulling off a win against the odds. After devouring our pre-match meal, I had returned to the room to watch some television. I had just settled in when the door swung open and Chris stormed in. He went straight to the window and drew the curtains, picked up the remote and turned off the television, made sure every light was switched off, then climbed into his bed and promptly fell asleep. He had done all of this — all of it — without so much as a grunt in my direction. I was terrified. So much so I was even worried that the light from my iPod would be enough to invoke his rage. I just lay there in silence, in the dark, wondering if I could get out in one piece.

At least Jacko got his pre-match sleep in, and I hope he had sweet dreams because the game against the Bulls was a bit of a nightmare. Loftus was packed to the gunnels for that match, which was no surprise considering the team they had to support. That era of Bulls was something else with players like Derick Hougaard, Morne Steyn, Fourie du Preez, my old age-group nemesis Pierre Spies, Bryan Habana, Victor Matfield, Bakkies Botha . . . it was a roll call of South African rugby royalty. For all that, neither side could score a try in that semi-final, and the 50,000 fans had to suffice with eight Hougaard penalties and a dropped goal for good measure. They wouldn't have cared if the score finished 3-nil. Ellis Park had been an experience, but a trip to Loftus Versfeld when it's bursting at the seams with ferocious fans who take great pleasure in describing, in graphic fashion, each of the many ways you could be mortally wounded in the game is a memory that never leaves you.

The thought of being anywhere near an All Blacks conversation never once crossed my mind that year. I was engrossed in my Crusaders experience and dined out on every second I got to play. It was a surprise to me, then, when I was selected for the Junior All Blacks at the end of the Super Rugby season. In much the same way it was when I was picked for the Northern Region at school, I didn't even realise there was such a thing as a Junior All Blacks side, but once I was told I was in it, I was naturally delighted. The team was stacked with men who had been All Blacks, with the rest of us aspiring to get there. In some ways it was an elevator team — some of us were on the way up and some were on the way down — but the atmosphere that created had a cavalier edge about it, and there was plenty of socialising between matches in that year's Pacific Nations Championship.

I was fascinated by the renegade approach that team took. I had just finished a season in which everything about my preparation and performance had to be absolutely pitch perfect and now I was in a New Zealand team that operated like an invitational touring outfit. I guess the experienced guys knew what they were doing, and the results showed the gulf in class and resources between us and the rest of the Pacific, but it was an eye-opener for a young kid who took everything so seriously to be around a group who didn't want to let a little bit of rugby get in the way of a bloody good time. Coaches Ian Foster and Colin Cooper were happy to give the players the freedom to enjoy themselves, but I still thought it wise to be as diligent as possible. To me, a black jersey — any black jersey — was worthy of the utmost respect.

Unfortunately, the trainer for that tour was Nic Gill, who I had first come into contact with when studying in Hamilton. Nic would soon rise through the ranks to be an indispensable cog in the All Blacks high-performance machine, but for now he settled on treating me as his pet project. I sweated my way through that tour of the islands, on the rutted, rich, dark earth of Apia's streets, and on humid and storm-threatened Suva mornings, as Gilly set about adding some bulk and strength to my frame. 'You're skinny and you're weak,' he told me matter-of-factly. 'We're going to do something about that.'

7

THE CAPTAIN
AND THE ROOKIE

It's the beginning of March 2019, and it's the right time to make public my plans after the Rugby World Cup. It had been a long process getting a contract over the line and I am still yet to return to play for the Crusaders this year. The season is already two games down and I'm going to be sidelined for some weeks to come, but I knew that enquiries were being made about my future and that they were unlikely to stop coming. Right now, it was bad enough not being able to suit up with my teammates; I didn't want my post-New Zealand playing future to be a minor sideshow on top of that. Neither did I want to make a fuss — I had already announced during the end-of-year tour in 2018 that I would be leaving New Zealand — and so I was surprised when I was told that Scott Robertson, Steve Hansen and New Zealand Rugby CEO Steve Tew would also be a part of the media conference. I'm not sure I warranted that kind of attention, but that was out of my control.

Although I had envisaged a simple announcement, it was in fact humbling to have the big bosses there to offer their tributes and support. Not many players are afforded that level of respect when they make the call to leave New Zealand, and to be one of them meant plenty to me. I have never played the game for the plaudits, but while I listened to the coaches and Steve Tew talk I did take a moment to reflect on all I had been able to achieve during my time in New Zealand rugby. I couldn't help but think ahead to the point when this would all end. It didn't feel that long ago that I was ticking off firsts; now I was running a mental checklist of the lasts.

I thought back to 2011 when I had imagined that the 2015 Rugby World Cup may well be my swansong, yet here I was, hell-bent on making it through to the 2019 edition. It's funny how things had changed in terms of my career perspective. The carrot of the captaincy had certainly egged me on to continue through to a third world cup but the constant battles with the body had made the decision to make it my last year in New Zealand that much easier. It's a tough gig performing in New Zealand through the Super Rugby season, year after year. As much as I loved it, I knew there was no way I would be able to get through another one. The reality was I hadn't had a full, uninterrupted season in years and so by etching a clear finish line in my mind, I could repay the people who had supported me for so long by giving every last ounce of my effort to my club and to my country. On that mental checklist of lasts was one priority: my best.

My agent Simon Porter and his team at Halo Sport had worked for months to establish contract options in France, London and Japan, but Bridget and I had eventually settled on Japan and a two-season deal with the Toyota club. We had looked seriously at each of the options and thought long and hard about how each move would impact on our immediate and extended families. We also had to consider what kind of workload my body was going to be able to handle. The last three years had been brutal from a physical point of view and I didn't think I was up to the grind of the Premiership or Top 14 seasons. It's all very well to think you are indestructible but that's just ego, and the clubs aren't buying ego, they were buying a rugby player. We felt good about the Toyota offer and, as it transpired, I would have a familiar face alongside me at the club. Steve Hansen was also soon to announce that he would be joining Toyota as the new Director of Rugby.

We sat under the stand at Rugby Park, the table in front of us festooned with microphones and recorders, the cramped room filled with familiar faces from a thousand media stand-ups. Outside, the pitch hardened under a hot, late summer sun. A few stray decibels from the gym sound system danced into the room. Behind us, through a small doorway, John 'Foxy' Miles sat in his den, decorated with decades of Canterbury and Crusaders memorabilia, a hoarder's collection of jerseys and jackets hanging on a rail above the ripped brown couch and a dozen or two cold ones lying in wait in the beaten-up fridge. It had been home for so long, this place. Home away from home . . .

'Is this actually happening?' I asked myself aloud. 'This isn't supposed to happen. Not like this.' I don't know how long I stared at the television after the final whistle blew on the All Blacks' Rugby World Cup quarter-final defeat in Cardiff. It may have been most of the day. I had watched the last world cup in 2003 as a schoolboy, when the All Blacks were my sporting heroes. Now many of them were my Crusaders teammates. I saw Dan Carter's tears and Richie McCaw's despair, and Aaron Mauger's disbelief. I knew these guys. I felt their pain.

The aftermath was brutal. Never before had an All Blacks side been bundled out of a world cup at such an early stage and New Zealand fans were vociferous in their criticism of the team and the coaches. A very public battle for the coaching job ensued between Graham Henry and Robbie Deans, and very few of us at the Crusaders thought Henry would be reappointed. As far as we were concerned, the job was as good as Rob's. It came as somewhat of a shock to us, then, when Rob not only missed out on the All Blacks role but announced in December that he had accepted an offer to coach Australia. I can't say I saw that one coming.

I didn't see much of the Crusaders All Blacks until they returned to Rugby Park the following year. By that stage the visceral angst of the public had been replaced by a simmering resentment, which was an improvement of sorts, I guess. Those vanquished men who returned to our team in late January never betrayed how much that loss had stung them or how much it stung still. What we saw as a team was a group very much focused on giving their all to the Crusaders that year. They were hell-bent on winning the title — winning it for themselves and for Robbie Deans.

There was no need for extra motivation as we sweated through the dry January months and into the start of the new season. We all resolved to send Robbie off on a high note, even if the note struck by the Experimental Law Variations implemented that year was a bum one. We had a stacked team and, unlike the previous season, our All Blacks were available from the opening match. The drive they had to bury the demons of the year before was astonishing, and it was an empowering experience to each weekend run out alongside the likes of McCaw and Tuiali'i, Ali Williams and Brad Thorn. Dan Carter provided expert navigation at first-five and we claimed eight straight wins before suffering our first loss of the season against the Chiefs on a clammy April night in Hamilton.

We would suffer only one further loss that year, when the Highlanders came north and taught us a lesson in concentration. It was a timely lesson, coming as it did in the final game before the playoffs. Robbie let us know that he was none too pleased with our performance, and his words left welts in our eardrums. We defeated the Hurricanes in the semi-final the following week and the Waratahs in the final a week after that. Being named to start in that match was an incredible feeling, bettered only by the sight of Robbie and Reuben Thorne driving their swords into the pitch as the late evening mist descended into the concrete bowl of our half-built stadium. I had played in all 15 games that season, starting in 12 of them. As the champagne corks popped that night, Terry and Marilyn Read made sure they put one bottle aside. After all, the All Blacks team was being named the next day. They didn't tell their son, of course. They just thought it wise to keep a little something on ice.

It was one cork that never did get popped. When the team for that year's June series against Ireland and England, and the Tri-Nations, was announced, I wasn't in it. Perhaps I was getting a little ahead of myself, but I harboured high hopes that I had done enough to warrant selection. I had played well all season, had started in both the semi-final and final, and had been a part of a champion side. Although I knew I still had a long way to go, I did think I deserved a shot. Instead, the coaches had opted for Adam Thomson. Did I think I was a better option? Absolutely.

A couple of days later, after I had marinated in self-pity for about as long as was possible without pickling myself, I took a phone call. On the end of the line was Steve Hansen.

'Now listen, son,' he offered by way of introduction. 'We don't want to overload you. We think you are All Black material and we'll pick you for the end-of-year tour, but you've played a lot of footy and it'll do you well to have some time out.'

I listened intently and said 'yip' a lot and while I was no less gutted about missing out on the team for that year's Tri-Nations, at least I now knew I was on the right track. Before that phone call, I hadn't heard anything at all from the All Blacks; to receive that encouragement from Hansen over the phone afforded me some perspective. I still watched the All Blacks play throughout that June series against Ireland and England, and a tough Tri-Nations with Australia and South Africa, but I could never quite rid myself of the itch to be out there playing for them. There was some irony in being told I hadn't made the All Blacks because I'd already had a big playing workload for the Crusaders. When the provincial season came around I played all 14 of Canterbury's matches, starting in 13 of them.

Casey Laulala and I were given the chance to be Canterbury's co-captains for 2008. I was still just 22 years old, had played only a couple of seasons and was completely blown away by the offer. We had met Rob Penney for a coffee before the start of the pre-season programme and Casey and I had a couple of weeks to talk about how we were going to make it work. Casey had a lot more playing experience than I did but, like me, was new to the captaincy role. We looked at what we both could offer, figured we would be best to drive our own departments — forwards for me, backs for him — and let me take the lion's share of the on-field chat. We had guys like Corey Flynn, Ti'i Paulo, Hayden Hopgood and Bubble Hamilton in the team, so there would be no shortage of able lieutenants to lean on when we needed a wise shoulder. We thought we had struck upon a great plan for the season. And then Casey broke his arm before the opening match.

I pushed myself to be more of a presence around the team and even though I was in no way a genuinely vocal person, I tried to initiate more conversations than I usually would. It was my belief that having the loudest voice does not make you the best leader, and it was in those tentative first months that I hit upon my own style of leadership, one based around many small and — if necessary — private chats with individuals in the team. Those personal connections become the mortar between the bricks with which I built my captaincy. Just taking the time to share a coffee and a chat was so much more rewarding for me than barking instructions at the team and, hopefully, that was also the case for the other people involved. I knew when the riot act needed to be read, but I had guys in the team who had memorised the appropriate clauses.

Being thrust into the leadership role as I was, I found the space in which I was most comfortable to operate — I tested the water by dropping small pebbles into it, in the hope the ripples they made became waves that swept through the team. I also realised that my effectiveness would be based on my ability to communicate with everyone in the group, and no two people in any team respond to a single message in the same way. Only by getting to know the individual can you build a solid collective. I was blessed to have had two full seasons of Super Rugby which gave me some kudos with the senior players, and I was still very much one of the young brigade so could identify with the new blokes. In many ways, I was a bridge between two distinct worlds, a captain by virtue of a generational twist of fate.

I probably could have done with some coin-tossing practice. On my first crack at the time-honoured art I attempted to flip the coin with my thumb, only for it to slip off onto the floor and roll under a doorway. I was embarrassed as it was, but my humiliation was made complete by the fact my opposing captain that day — a pre-season meeting with Wellington at 'the mudbox', QEII Park — was none other than Piri Weepu. He started laughing at me, and it was one of those laughs of his that started in his toes and worked its way up his torso until manifesting itself in uncontrollable shrugs of the shoulders. I at least got to have the ultimate revenge on him later that year when, in one of the most dour finals in provincial history, we defeated Wellington on their home turf and gave Rob Penney the swansong he deserved. Final score: 7–6.

I was absolutely thrilled to win the cup that night, especially as we knew the Wellington team could create points from any place on the park. They had been our chief tormentors over the last couple of seasons and played the game as if they operated in a heretofore unknown dimension. Winning a final against them was going to take courage, heart and a ruthless intensity in defence. We had to shut down the space and time for a team that existed in a completely different physical realm. I didn't help myself; all season long I had worn headgear that was at least two sizes too big and invariably slipped down over my eyes. The Wellington runners were elusive enough without me chasing them blind.

We could all see the joy that win brought to Rob, not least because he had been personally responsible for the development of so many of us in that team. He was a relentlessly upbeat coach, a man who only ever wanted to see his players reach their true potential so as to give the team the best chance of success. We had spent many a morning chewing the fat about captaincy and the finer points of loose forward play. And we had spent many an afternoon discussing and practising the role of number eight. Rob's early vision was right on the money. That season I had been given the chance to play at the back of the scrum, just as he said I would from the moment I arrived in Christchurch.

I was intent on celebrating the win with the team that night, but after I had downed a couple of drinks in fairly rapid fashion Richie McCaw gave me a small tap on the shoulder and, with a barely perceptible wink, quietly said, 'Don't have too many tonight.' Then he wandered away, leaving me to ponder my choices. I didn't have to ponder for long to be honest; Richie hadn't given me any choice in the matter. I would learn from experience that he had delivered that message on behalf of the coaches, but even if I didn't know that then, Richie was the All Blacks captain and the team for the end-of-year tour was being named the next morning. I was not about to jeopardise any chance I had of hearing my name read out. I enjoyed the next few hours with the team, careful not to overdo the refreshments, and then Bridget and I called it a night. On the way back to the hotel we chatted about what tomorrow might bring. Were we ready for this? Would this change anything? Neither of us really knew. What we did know was that this crazy adventure we'd signed up for just a few years earlier showed no signs of slowing down.

The All Blacks team for a potential Grand Slam end-of-year tour was named at ten o'clock the next morning, which just so happened to coincide with our arrival at Wellington airport for the flight back to Christchurch. It was 2008, of course, a time before everyone's face was glued to a smartphone. The selection news that morning rippled with rising excitement through the bags and the bodies lined up at the counter and reached me by way of a pat on the back. I didn't know how to feel. I was excited, certainly, but that initial rush of adrenaline soon dissolved under an attack of anxiety. I barely had time to land in Christchurch and get home to Bridget who, like me, was wondering just what came next, before I was on my way back to the airport, to Auckland, and into an entirely new world. I sat uncomfortably on the plane, clammy and panicked. I may have just led a team to a national title, but now all the old uncertainty returned, the recollections of childhood trial matches and the sabotage of self-doubt. Was I really cut out for this?

At the heart of everything was one overwhelming thought: don't mess this up. From the moment I arrived at the team hotel in Auckland, the day became a blur. I was handed an appointment sheet and sent on my way: outfitting, nutritionist, team manager, coaches, trainer — each allotted session requiring an awkward, sweaty hustle through unfamiliar corridors. That night we gathered in the team room and Richie McCaw addressed us for the first time as a group. He delivered an impassioned talk on what it meant for us to be there and what was expected of us now that we were. It was a surreal experience sitting in that austere conference room, surrounded by the best players in the country. I had no idea how the other new boys were feeling. I suspect they were just as nervous as I was.

I may have been in the All Blacks, but I knew I wasn't an All Black yet. There was little time to dwell on that fact, though. We had barely 48 hours in Auckland before we departed for the first match of the tour, against Australia in Hong Kong. A logistical quirk meant we were all given our own rooms for the week, which only added to the underlying feelings of stress. I was so fearful of missing an appointment or meeting that I would traipse back and forth to the team room at least 10 times a day, just to check and recheck the schedule on the wall. It was some comfort to note that I wasn't the only one doing so.

I was not required for the Hong Kong test and sat in the stands that night along with the 40,000 others who had poured in for their first taste of an All Blacks test. Ostensibly, I felt like I was one of them, a spectator like everybody else. I had only been to one test in my life, and that had been a decade earlier when England had played the All Blacks at Eden Park. Now here I was, in the heart of So Kon Po, still watching but acutely aware that the next time the team took the field I might well have a very different perspective.

The All Blacks defeated Australia 19–14 and I revelled in being in the changing rooms after the game, celebrating the victory as a part of the team. I couldn't wait now to get my shot and was thrilled when I was named in the team to play Scotland the following week. Normal service had resumed and we were back to sharing rooms — in this case the smallest rooms in Edinburgh — and I was fortunate to spend the week with Rodney So'oialo, albeit with approximately five inches between our beds. Rodney wasn't the most vocal man, but in the brief gaps between long silences he offered me words of encouragement and advice. I knew it was my first All Blacks tour and as such I found a comfortable standing among the other rookies, but I was there to play rather than to make up the numbers. Being selected for my test debut was a reflection of the faith so many people had shown in me and when I thought about them and what they had done to help me, I felt a calmness descend in what was otherwise a nerve-wracking week. 'Take this feeling and run with it,' I thought. 'This is exactly where you are supposed to be.'

It's a funny thing to be part of a young All Blacks side. We all knew that we weren't the top dogs — they were the guys holding the pads opposite us in training — but it was not the time to trip over a bottom lip. In essence, we were being given an opportunity and regardless of how many stars were missing, it was our time to shine. I was motivated to show the coaches exactly what I could produce for them, as I am sure everyone else in that team was. I had been given an interesting choice by Steve Hansen that week. Liam Messam and I were both making our debut in the Scotland game and Steve had asked if I wanted to play number eight or on the blindside. I jumped at the chance to play at six, given that was where I played for the Crusaders. Liam had at least started a couple of Super Rugby matches at the back of the Chiefs scrum. I figured he would be much more confident there than I would have been, even though I had just finished a provincial season in that position.

The redoubtable Keven Mealamu was named captain for the match and in his own humble way he instilled in us a belief in our ability and an awareness of what was expected. Yes, we lacked experience, but there would be no asterisk next to the result. We were the All Blacks and we had to prepare and play like it. Kevvy was a man that every single person in the team respected. He did everything off the field with an effortless grace and a massive smile yet played the game with a fearsome aggression and an intensely physical edge. He was the archetype for the modern All Black. It's fair to say we all loved him.

The day of the game dawned fine and cold, Edinburgh's grey streets bracing themselves for the winter ahead. I busied myself finding a spare All Blacks jacket for my dad who had made the trip with Mum to watch my debut. Their bags had gone missing in transit so I begged our own bagman Errol 'Poss' Collins to provide some spare kit for them, much to my dad's delight. After a walk through in the morning, the team filed one by one into Manager Darren Shand's room where all the playing jerseys, socks and shorts were laid out in neat piles. Darren handed me my kit, shook my hand and wished me well. I walked back to the room cradling that jersey and once inside I placed it on my own bed and stared at it. I thought back to that car ride to the Goldfields trial with my father. 'If you make the team, I'll buy you an All Blacks jersey,' he had told me then. For the second time in my life I had been given an All Blacks jersey, only this one had the number '6' on the back of it.

The pipe band awaited as the bus pulled into Murrayfield, the stadium surrounds thronged with fans, its sweet shops and food vendors doing a roaring trade in the cold night. We were piped around the back of the towering west stand, travelling at walking pace behind the band, and cheered on by the supporters stacked above us on the stairwells as we exited the bus and made the short, purposeful march to the sheds. I thought that was an unforgettable experience, but it was later topped when it came time to run out for the match. The field was in complete darkness, with a lone piper on the roof of the stand, a solitary vigil in the wash of a single spotlight. It was quite the scene indeed, though

I was more concerned with not tripping over in the darkness. My mum was devastated that she never got the chance to see me actually run out onto the field. So much for pageantry.

The scoreline would read 32–6 that day, but it was by far and away the toughest game I had ever played. Every second in those 80 minutes was hard fought and brutal, and played at a pace no amount of pre-game chat can prepare you for. I managed to grab an early nerve-settler for myself when I stole a Scottish lineout and Anthony Tuitavake scored from the resulting attack, but no matter how positive that play was and how many points we added to the tally, the physical demands of the Scottish pack never diminished. By the end of the game I was beaten and bruised but absolutely elated. It was only after I sat down in the shed, boots off and tape torn from tired legs and arms, that I allowed myself a moment to think, 'Now I'm an All Black.' I was absolutely touched when Jason White, my opposite that day, came to the shed and handed me his Scotland top. He knew I would find it hard to give away my first test jersey and he asked for nothing in return. It was a gracious and incredibly kind-hearted gesture, one which I have mused on many times since.

The Scotland test would be my only start of the tour, but the next week I was named on the bench for the Ireland encounter at Croke Park. It was an unbelievable atmosphere at Ireland's largest sporting ground and home to the Gaelic Athletic Association. More than 81,000 fans descended on the park on that crisp Dublin evening, their collective roar deafening. It was a completely different experience to be watching knowing that I would have a part to play, as opposed to sitting in the stands as I had in Hong Kong. That Ireland side was stacked with legends — Quinlan, Best, O'Connell, O'Gara, O'Driscoll, Kearney, Bowe and Heaslip among them — and, buoyed by their passionate, partisan crowd, scrapped and fought for the entire match. By the time I replaced Rodney So'oialo in the 71st minute, the score was 22–3, which is the way it would stay, but nothing came easy that night, and it was a nervous watch, waiting to get out in the middle.

I was more nervous at the after-match function when, much to my surprise, I was presented with my test cap and asked to make a short speech. I had no time to prepare anything and managed to bluff my way through it, but the Irish team and guests were most gracious and everyone in the room stood as my cap was handed to me. It was a touch of class from our hosts that night, and for the second week in a row, a classy gesture had left a lasting impression on me.

A lasting impression was left on all of us who attended a stage show in Limerick two days later. We were facing Munster at Thomond Park in a midweek match, 30 years after their famous 12–0 victory over the All Blacks on the same ground, and we had been invited to a play about that historic occasion. It was Wayne Smith's idea to go along to the theatre, to give us an idea of just how impressive that win had been against the first Grand Slam All Blacks side in 1978. I'm not entirely sure it had the desired effect because the next day we were completely under the pump. Munster were absolutely possessed for the clash, and by the time I got the chance to get on the field we were behind on the scoreboard and completely on the back foot. Never before had I felt so much pressure; composure had become a foreign concept to us and everything we tried was served with the sour taste of panic. In the end, a Joe Rokocoko try saved our bacon and broke Munster hearts.

My relief was off the charts. It just so happens that when Piri

My family have always been my biggest supporters. Here we are in 1990: Mum, Dad, Gareth, Mark and me.

Where it all started: the Drury JB1 team was the first official team I played for. I'm on the far left, ready to get amongst it.

There from the beginning. Bridget was part of a big support crew that travelled to Wellington to watch me play my first game for the New Zealand Secondary Schools team in 2003. This photo was taken after our win against Samoa. Inset: Bridget and I pose for a photo at the Rosehill College Ball, 2002.

Head in the clouds. Leaping tall at lineout time in my test debut against Scotland at Murrayfield in 2008.

Above: A proud moment for my ever-loyal parents, Marilyn and Terry, at Murrayfield following my test debut at the end of 2008.
Below: I shared my test debut with Liam Messam (left) and Jamie Mackintosh.

November 2009. We retained the Hillary Shield after a typically tough contest against the English at Twickenham. I'm all smiles with Beaver, Conrad and Andy.

I spent my childhood idolising this man. Jonah Lomu was one of my all-time favourites and I used to love watching him play for Counties and the Blues when I was a youngster.

The full complement of All Blacks loosies pose with the Webb Ellis Cup after our victory over France in the final of the 2011 Rugby World Cup at Eden Park. From left: Adam Thomson, Jerome Kaino, Richie McCaw, me and Victor Vito.

With Jerome Kaino in the team bus after the World Cup final in 2011.

Celebrating with Bridget and the Cup after the final.

The haka ... and a proud moment for me against Italy in Rome, 2012. It was my first game as All Blacks captain. We got up for the win and, left, I topped the day off with a try.

The season of the trophy — 2013. Clockwise from top left: With the Dave Gallaher Cup (France), the Freedom Cup (South Africa), the Bledisloe Cup (Australia) and the IRB International Player of the Year trophy.

Weepu was subbed in the 62nd minute, physiotherapist Pete Gallagher had run onto the field to tell me that, in my second game for the All Blacks, I was taking over the on-field captaincy. It was the biggest hospital pass thrown that day, and we threw plenty of them.

Some years earlier, the great All Black Sir Bryan Williams had offered his reflection on that 1978 loss. He had said, 'When you are not totally focused for the game, that's when things go wrong.' There is no doubt that we as a collective had not been totally focused. Perhaps it was because a subconscious, corrosive apathy had crept into the side, that some players thought their selection for that match was more a slight than an honour. I do know there was some soul-searching in the changing room afterwards and that we were embarrassed by that performance. Take nothing away from those Munster men, they deserve enormous respect for how they played that day, and they deserved more respect than we had shown them before the game and during it.

I was back on the bench the following weekend against Wales in Cardiff and, while I didn't take the field, I savoured every minute of the Millennium Stadium experience. It would later become my favourite place to play outside New Zealand and I would bet there is not a single player who has stood out in the middle and not got goosebumps listening to that massive crowd sing their climactic anthem. They sang and roared and screamed and cheered and booed for 80 minutes that evening, their ferocity and fanaticism on full display in every corner of the place. I would have done anything to feel that from out on the field.

We had talked before the tour about the opportunity to claim a rare grand slam and everything came down to the final test against England at Twickenham, for which I was once again named on the bench. I operated over those last couple of weeks of the tour as a bit of an in-betweener; I enjoyed the company of the 'Munster Crew' for whom the tour was pretty much over, while on the other hand I was still trying to press my claims as a regular test selection. It was as if I existed at the intersection of two sets of an unofficial All Blacks Venn diagram. Make no mistake, there were All Blacks, and then there were first-choice All Blacks. We all knew it, and the coaching team, led then by Graham Henry, did not seem to be concerned about it. The only thing that mattered was the next game, and who was playing in it. Right now, that was England, and I was in the team.

I replaced Jerome Kaino with 25 minutes of that test remaining, a test in which Alain Rolland dished out yellow cards to the English with all the gusto of a casino dealer. Four England players were sinbinned in that game, and the 82,000 fans at Twickenham fell quieter with every card shown. A Mils Muliaina second-half double settled things, and with a 32–6 victory we became the first holders of the freshly commissioned Hillary Shield, and the first visiting grand slam-winning team to have not conceded a try. It was incredibly satisfying to be on the field at the final whistle and allow that soon to be familiar set of emotional waves to pass over me: relief, joy, pride — and in that order.

I reflected later that night on what had been the adventure of a lifetime. I had worked hard during the tour, on and off the field, but it hadn't been at the expense of all the fun. I had loved the excursions we had taken as a team, tasting the bitter richness of a Guinness straight from the factory in Dublin, and visiting the towering National Wallace Monument atop the forested Abbey Craig in Stirling. I had played in some of the greatest stadia in the world, seen the sights and seen the Queen. Now it was time to go home and eat something. Steve Hansen had told me I needed to put on some weight. More specifically he had told me that I was going to be a 112-kg number eight for the All Blacks who had the potential to play 100 tests. That was more than enough motivation for me.

8

THE NEW NORMAL

I'm still weeks away from making a comeback and I know that people are talking about me. It was good to have made the official announcement about my plans for Japan next year, but I am starting to get itchy feet. I just want to be out there playing with the Crusader boys. I know there is no rush. I have to be patient and give my back the best chance of healing. Having been days away from surgery last month there was a last-minute intervention. I talked with the medical staff at the Crusaders and All Blacks one final time and re-evaluated everything. Although I knew there would be no second chance, I had to believe that if I could just get a few more weeks of rest, the disc would settle down and the need for surgery could be avoided.

It had been a fraught 24 hours making that final decision but having committed to a non-surgical recovery route, I was glad. It is starting to bug me that I can't get out there, though. It's the middle of March and I know there is an ongoing conversation in the public about my form, and whether I am past my best. I know that talk is out there because people bring up those stories when they talk to me. It saves me the trouble of watching it and reading it. I knew there had been a lot of chat about me during the end-of-year tour, especially after the Ireland match. Did that concern me? No. It's a fickle business, professional sport. To be honest, I was feeling great at the end of the year. To be able to play through the end of the Super Rugby season and into the northern tour was outstanding. Then again, I am the one wearing the skipper's armband and when the team loses, a lot of that is naturally going to rest on the shoulders of the captain. I understood that burden and I had long ago made peace with that aspect of leadership because it will not change. What I can change is the public perception as it stands right now, but I need to be playing. 29 March. That's the date with the ring around it for my return.

It's easy for me to be focused on the team and not the media. I can't say the same for the family. As every professional player knows, your family does read every-thing, and watches the news and listens to the radio, and they are the ones left to flinch in the face of some of the more ferocious comments. Bridget is always my barometer in these situations because she rarely talks about rugby. When she starts asking me questions about my game I know immediately that she has heard or read something about me that she didn't like. People are wondering when I am coming back to play, and whether I am going to be fit for the Rugby World Cup this year. They doubt it. In some quarters it seems I am yesterday's man. I see it as part and parcel of what I do, and I have been through it many times before. Unfortunately, the people closest to you are the ones more profoundly affected by it.

I am lucky, really. Over the course of my career I have seen many guys close to me take an absolute hammering from the press and the public, and every time that happens I have felt for them. It is really a case of 'there but for the grace of God go I' but you always have to be mindful of the fact no one gets through their career without being critiqued. We are fortunate to live in a country in which our sport maintains a place of such importance that it is central to so many conversations. Accepting that you are occasionally going to be the subject of a conversation you don't like is key to enjoying your limited time in the spotlight. I have been in the spotlight for a long time now and I think it's a privilege. I always did, right from the moment I got a chance to cement my place as a starter in the All Blacks . . .

Bridget and I were married on 10 January 2009 in her family church in Papakura. We were pups, really, young by modern standards to be getting hitched, but we didn't care. We were high school sweethearts for whom the sparks had flown right from the moment we had locked eyes around the bonfire seven years before. I had only been back from my first All Blacks tour for a few weeks, long enough to decompress and to absorb the enormity of those weeks and the life-changing experiences they had afforded me. Long enough, too, to be schooled in matters Catholic by the local priest, who seemed more interested in talking about footy than the Holy Trinity, which was just fine by me. I loved our wedding day, surrounded by family and friends and excited for our future together, one that promised to be filled with adventures, but the days and weeks that followed flew by too fast and by the end of the month another season was calling, one that would take me away for ever-longer periods of time. We both knew it, and accepted it, and making that commitment to each other on that gorgeous summer day was an acknowledgement of the fact that as much as my career was important to me, our relationship was the most important thing.

I had a new wife, and I had a new boss. And no, they weren't one and the same. Back at the Crusaders Todd Blackadder had been appointed head coach after Robbie Deans' ascension to the Wallabies job. He was certainly no stranger to us, having been around Rugby Park on many occasions since returning from Scotland to coach the Tasman Mako. Of course, he was also one of the greats of the club, its success synonymous with his tireless play and unassuming captaincy. He was a good man, lanky and slow moving with a shock of messy grey hair and a permanent twinkle in his eye. Just as it had been for Robbie, his chief concern was to ensure every one of us worked as hard as we could for our mates and for the team. As one of the chief architects of the Crusader ethos, Toddy was very much invested in enhancing his legacy.

In many ways, Toddy coached exactly how he had played. There was no bullshit and no short cuts. He believed wholeheartedly in the notion that hard graft would garner the results we were after. He didn't share detail with us in the same way Robbie had, and he was much more collaborative with his assistant coaches, but we all enjoyed the fresh calm voice and the variation on what we had become accustomed to. If anything, Toddy would likely accept that, like many of us, he was learning on the job, but he knew what he wanted and let us know what was expected without the need for long emotional speeches or complex designs.

Robbie had been a man for whom season themes were critical and he had a knack for making us feel like we had helped to shape that imagery as a team. We would all throw ideas around the team room for a few days before settling on a concept that resonated with us. Robbie would then distil that concept, extracting the essence of the idea and adding a drop of it onto everything we did. It was his way of holding us accountable all season long. Toddy didn't much need that. For him the Crusader values — integrity, hard work and honesty — spoke for themselves. Being a 'Crusader Man' was our job, our theme, our aspiration and inspiration. I really enjoyed that about Todd. Like me, he didn't need extra motivation to push for high standards.

The All Blacks experience the year before had only heightened my desire to play well for the Crusaders and now that I was beginning to feel at home in the team, with solid friendships formed over many hours of training, touring and playing, I felt a massive responsibility to deliver each and every week. There is no doubt that having had a taste of test rugby I was hungry for more, but I willed myself to stay fully focused on the job at hand, knowing that if I played to my potential, I would be in with a shot when the All Blacks were named on 1 June that year.

Playing to our potential as a team was something we failed to do that year. We got a good start, grinding out a win against a tough Chiefs side at home, but over the next four weeks we were beaten by the Brumbies, Hurricanes and Highlanders, and we scraped our way to a 23-all draw with the Force. We were missing a couple of stars through injury, but we all believed we were better than what we were showing. All the soul-searching and hard work in the world just couldn't seem to get us out of an attacking rut, and even though we started to rack up the wins, they were hardly convincing. We ran off four straight victories, all by margins of four points or less, with a high score that month of just 17.

Somehow, we stayed in the hunt for the finals, but it still took a Leon MacDonald dropped goal in our last game of the season against the Blues to keep us in it. We limped into the semi-finals in fourth spot by virtue of a superior points differential to that of the Waratahs. We knew we were lucky to be there, but our luck ran out at Loftus Versfeld a week later when the Bulls turned on their traditional 20-minute momentum shift and 50,000 fans shouted us into submission. They would go on to savage the Chiefs the following weekend in the final, showcasing just what a sensational team they were. It would take me a few years to figure it out, but I would later understand what made that team so tough to beat: they forced you to think more about what they would do than what you could do.

From a team point of view, we were more disappointed in the fact we had left ourselves with such a tough assignment when, with a bit more creativity throughout the season, we could have had home advantage or at least an easier pathway to the final. It was a comedown from the year before when we had felt destined to win the title, but there was no shortage of resolve within the squad. We knew we were better than that, and we would show it next season. As sad as I was to come up short, I didn't have to wait too long to find something to smile about. A week later I was named in the All Blacks for the June tests against France and Italy and subsequent Tri-Nations. For the first time I would have a chance to play a test match on home soil.

It was an All Blacks side well and truly down on experience. Richie McCaw and Dan Carter were both still injured, as were Andy Ellis, Corey Flynn, Rodney So'oialo and Sitiveni Sivivatu.

Tanerau Latimer, Wyatt Crockett and Isaac Ross had all received their first call-ups to the national side, and Mils Muliaina had been named skipper in Richie's absence. It felt like something was missing in the first week of training, preparing for a French side we were all wary of after what had unfolded in Cardiff two years before. I could sense the tension around the team during that week in Dunedin, even more so because in the absence of so many veterans I was elevated to the leadership group. The voices we had come to rely on just weren't there, and ours weren't strong enough. As a result, the coaches took it upon themselves to take more of the wheel than they had previously needed to. In other words, we didn't do enough as players in the build-up to that first test to drive ourselves. When the pressure came on in the match, we couldn't control the outcome.

It was not the way I had envisaged my first home test panning out, a 22–27 defeat on a cold and dewy Carisbrook evening. The game was 80 minutes of mistakes and growing frustration. We lacked clarity and combinations and made a season's worth of elementary errors. Steve Hansen would later famously quip that we would just 'flush the dunny and move on', but that's not how we felt inside the team. The changing shed, under that dilapidated old grandstand, was a depressing place to be after that game, and the public and the media had a field day over the performance, which certainly got under the skin of the coaches who needed no reminding of the pain of 2007. We hunkered down the following week in Wellington with a siege mentality and vowed to win the next one, at all costs.

On Monday I was told I would be playing number eight. I was already feeling the pressure, and the decision to switch me to a new position filled me with dread. I had only had one provincial season at the back of the scrum and had reverted to blindside for the

Crusaders. I knew there were many similarities, but with conditions predicted to be grim I would need to be disciplined at scrum time and schooled up on the subtle shifts in running lines and defensive positioning. I don't know if I would have been more comfortable had I not just experienced my first loss as an All Black, but as things stood I was as nervous as I had ever been in my career. We won the test — and won it ugly. France took the Gallaher Shield on a countback. None of us had any idea about that before the game and to be honest we didn't give it much thought afterwards. The only thing that mattered that night was that we had won.

We won the following week too, against Italy in Christchurch. Graham Henry rolled the selection dice for the one-off match and, down on confidence after the French fortnight and playing on a miserable, murky night, we managed to win without convincing anyone — not least of all ourselves — that we were improving. I started again at number eight, against the formidable Sergio Parisse, and was set to nab my first test try until George Whitelock came flying out of nowhere and caught the pass that would have put me over. In the end we claimed a 21-point victory, but it was never easy; certainly not as easy as the fans expected it to be. It was a good reminder for us as a team that test matches are not supposed to be easy.

In seasons to come I would reflect on that first home series and think about the calibre of men I had got the chance to match up against — guys like Thierry Dusautoir, Louis Picamoles, Sergio Parisse and Mauro Bergamasco were all outstanding loose forwards and incredibly tough men to play against. To be honest, at the time I was simply too naive and too focused on my own game to give it much of a thought.

Our thoughts soon turned to the Tri-Nations and we welcomed

back Richie McCaw and Rodney So'oialo. Having the skipper back especially was a shot in the arm, a signal that normal service could now resume. Rodney's return meant I dropped out of the starting team for the first test against Australia at Eden Park, but I was still happy to have a spot on the bench and to be a part of the action. We brawled our way to a 22–16 win that day but so much for normal service; we lost our next two against the Springboks in South Africa, setting up a must-win test in Sydney in late August. The starting loose forward trio for the All Blacks that day would be Jerome Kaino, Richie McCaw and me. It was the first time the three of us had started a test together.

We never really had to talk too much about our combination. Sure, there were conversations at training about aspects of the plays we were working through, but it felt from the very start like we each complemented the other's play. I knew Jerome from back in the Counties days and obviously I played with Richie on a regular basis at the Crusaders, so most of all I trusted and respected them. That meant I was free to focus on nailing my hand while still having faith that we would naturally get to know when each of us could have the biggest impact in a game.

We also learned quickly how to push each other's buttons in tests. I loved getting Jerome fired up on defensive scrums — not that it was hard. All I would need to say was something like, 'Righto mate, let's get round the corner and smash someone', and Jerome would do just that. He loved living in a mindset of hurt. We were also aware of the need to spread ourselves across the park so we never got caught in one area. In that way at least one of us could be in a position to make a big play at any one time. For his part, Richie just ran as far, as fast and for as long as was necessary. His button was permanently pushed.

Our biggest problem as a team was making the necessary adjustments to the way the game was being played. It was a defence-dominated era, a hangover from the introduction of the Experimental Law Variations that favoured big kicking teams with big mauling packs. In other words, it was perfectly suited to the South Africans and punitive on sides like us who liked to dominate possession and attack at all costs. In Sydney we wanted to introduce some changes to the balance of our structure, and I was a beneficiary of those changes. My days as an All Blacks blindside flanker were officially behind me. From that test on I would only ever start in the number eight jersey.

By some miracle — specifically Dan Carter's left boot — we won the test against Australia 19–18 and I ran on one leg for most of it after taking a massive smack on the knee early on. I did briefly mention my discomfort to physio Pete Gallagher but thought it wise not to make a big deal of it. In some ways that game felt to me like my first genuine test start — the Bledisloe Cup on the line, with 80,000 people at ANZ Stadium there to watch — and I didn't much fancy being taken off the field. I gritted the teeth, dug deep and got on with it.

In an interesting switch, Graham Henry had taken charge of the forwards after the losses in South Africa and he would soon ask me to do the lineouts for the team. From that year it became my job. I came up with the moves and the calls, revelling in my newfound responsibility. I always enjoyed the lineouts, but I had never had to think so hard about that aspect of the game. Before I knew it, lineout analysis and planning had become my own little side project, and it would remain that way throughout my career. What made the role so fascinating was that we hadn't been considered a great lineout team in recent years and to me that was an opportunity —

a chance to do something that was truly transformational. There was no real discussion required; I would turn up to Ted's room on a Sunday night and show him what I had come up with. He would look at it with a frown, and say, 'No worries, I'll back you.'

We focused our lineouts on two things: pre-calls and tempo. In the case of pre-calls we would know exactly what our first five lineout jumps and throws of the game would be and in what areas of the field we would use them. That naturally flowed into tempo. By knowing exactly what we were doing without having to wait for the call we would get to the lineout as quickly as possible and complete the throw before the opposition had a chance to get set against us. One simple word would signal an overcall, in which case the throw would go straight to whoever was free and we could get on with playing at pace.

Having that job made me feel valued and that made a world of difference to me in what was proving to be a tough season. I was still desperate to pin down a regular starting spot and welcomed any chance to have an impact. Being wanted, as they say, boosts the ego but being valued fills the soul. What didn't fill the soul was being steamrolled by the Springboks at Waikato Stadium three weeks after snatching that win in Australia. Frans Steyn may as well have been kicking penalties from Huntly that night, such was his range, and we were still exorcising the errors that had plagued us all season long. If we took anything from that match, while we stood watching Victor Matfield raise the Tri-Nations trophy (something that provided plenty of motivation over the next few seasons), it was that our last 10 minutes had been probably our best period of play all season. If we could somehow take that positive away with us, we might just be able to turn things around.

A week later, in Wellington, we thrashed the Wallabies.

There was a great deal of relief and satisfaction among the team as we sat chatting in the shed after that match. Cory Jane had been superb for us, diffusing kicks and launching counterattacks in combination with Mils Muliaina and Joe Rokocoko, and as a team we had played with an attacking verve that had largely been missing from our repertoire all season. There had also been the ongoing sideshow of the Graham Henry–Robbie Deans rivalry to deal with in the week leading up to the match, a rivalry which had threatened on occasion to become the main event, at least from a media point of view. It may come as a disappointment to find out it was never a conversation among the players, but we could all sense that the external pressure certainly got Ted's back up. We were stoked to do the job for the boss because we understood how much was riding on it for him.

With my 2009 All Blacks selection, my time as a provincial player had ostensibly come to an end. I had won 35 caps for Canterbury in my three seasons in red and black and had been given the honour of captaining the team to a title win in 2008, but in the next decade I would play just twice more in provincial colours. I had relished the opportunity Canterbury had given me and was greatly indebted to so many people within the union for turning me into a player worthy of international honours. It was a time of change, though. Fewer and fewer All Blacks were now available to their provincial sides as the risk of burnout and the increasingly brutal toll of heavy playing loads became more widely understood. I was deemed to be in need of a breather ahead of the end-of-year tour, and even though I loved playing, I was thankful for some respite.

The tour would prove tough but enjoyable, starting with a fourth win over the Wallabies in the bonus Bledisloe Cup cash game in Tokyo. It was not the greatest spectacle for the Japanese fans — Dan Carter and Matt Giteau kicked 10 penalties between them in an ill-disciplined and depressingly flat contest. I sat on the bench that day, replacing Rodney So'oialo with 30 minutes of the match remaining. I wasn't to know it at the time but a few weeks later Rodney, who had battled a debilitating neck injury that season, would play his 62nd and final test, against Italy in a Milan scrumfest. The Tokyo test would prove to be the last one I would ever start from the bench.

We battled past Wales in the opening test of the European leg on a Millennium Stadium pitch that was more akin to a farm paddock than a professional sporting ground. Italy were eventually subdued but not before a couple of reputations — my good friend Wyatt Crockett's among them — had taken an absolute beating, and all evidence that a test took place at Twickenham should have been instantly destroyed lest anyone got the idea that was how rugby was supposed to look. While we hadn't conceded a try in three games, we hadn't exactly set the world on fire with our own attack. A week later, against France in Marseilles, things finally clicked into gear. Revenge, as it turns out, is a great motivator.

Marseilles was a great escape for the team, and we soaked up the sights and sounds of such a beautiful destination, exploring the marina with its cafés and restaurants serving the day's fresh catch to outside tables, the Mediterranean sun, softened and subdued by the coming winter, a welcome change from the London gloom. We walked the pedestrian malls, marvelled at the cobalt-blue waters of the ancient port and admired the way the city's terracotta tiles tumbled down from the hillside home of the grand Basilique Notre-Dame de la Garde, its famous tower topped with a golden statue of the Madonna and Child.

We enjoyed the spectacular location, but we worked damn hard that week on our game preparation. We knew that we were still to hit the highs of the Australian win in Wellington and we had some unfinished business with the French. I think the danger they posed was by now deeply ingrained in the All Blacks psyche. There was the Battle of Nantes and the 1994 tests in New Zealand, and the enduring thrill of the Rugby World Cup final victory in 1987 had been somewhat tempered by more recent semi-final and quarter-final defeats. It had become a clichéd question, 'Which French side will turn up?' We never bothered asking it. We prepared as if we were about to face the greatest French side that ever lived. We were driven to start the game well. If we could knock them down early, we had a chance to pull away and inflict some real damage on the scoreboard.

The Stade Vélodrome was already heaving by the time we arrived for the game. It was a warm, windless night, and the fans were in a festive mood, stacked high in the open-air Tribune Ganay and packed into the hospitality boxes of the Tribune Jean Bouin. Behind the goal-lines, the Virage Sud and Virage Nord, each rising three tiers into the still black sky, were filling fast. The atmosphere was incredible, and nervous glances were exchanged between us as we tested the surface and began our warm-up. Had there been a roof it would have been blown off at kick-off time. The noise was more than deafening; I felt like I was swimming through sound.

It was the French, rather than us, who got off to a fast start, pressuring us in the scrum and drawing a penalty to earn the first points. We responded with a try to Sitiveni Sivivatu which had been created through a simple lineout play, but the French kept going up in multiples of three and had their noses in front at quarter time. At that point I felt as if the stadium fell silent. A change came over us as a team, a calmness. I think we realised then and there that the French weren't going to beat us by kicking penalties. From that point on, we were away. Sitiveni started tearing the French to shreds and Mils Muliaina scored. Then we roared into life at scrum time and Jerome crashed over for another. It was 22–12 at halftime, and France troubled the scorers no further that night. We added two more tries and claimed a 39–12 win to finish the test year.

It was a cracking night, one spent celebrating a job well done. To end a challenging season on such a high was just what we had needed for our own confidence, and having Bridget there to share that moment with me was fantastic. It was the first time she had been to Europe and things had almost gone pear-shaped when she got lost trying to find her hotel after a late arrival and made a panicked 1 am phone call to me. It was a tough way for her to start her touring life, but luckily when the morning came she was able to see a different side to Marseilles.

We thought we'd shown a different side of ourselves as a test team in that boiling cauldron of the Stade Vélodrome. We had played with intuition, instinct and a belief in what we were trying to achieve. The defensive structure, one that was designed to allow swift and surgical counterattack opportunities, was beginning to feel like second nature to us, and Wayne Smith, our assistant coach and master tactician, would help us perfect it over the next couple of seasons. I lay in bed the next morning, before packing up to leave for London, and thought back through the last couple of years, recalling that feeling I had of being in the All Blacks but not quite an All Black. Well, I felt like an All Black now, I really, truly did.

9

RATTLE AND SHAKE

How do you ever come to terms with something like this? How does a community and a city and a country process the senseless massacre of so many kind and gentle people? Friday, 15 March 2019 has become yet another date on a calendar of pain for the people of Christchurch and I have spent the afternoon on lockdown at Elle and Eden's school. We are the lucky ones. We'll go home tonight and have dinner and bedtime stories, and the next day we will wake up and there will be five of us in our family, just as there was when today began. Fifty-one people will not be coming home tonight. Many more will return home in the days to come, changed forever.

We'll get together in the coming days. We'll sit down as a team and we will digest what has happened here today, but we will never accept it, and we will never forget this act of savagery and cowardice. We represent our people; we play for them. When you play for a tightknit team you know how to respond when the times get tough, and in times of loss . . .

It is easy to think that the extended break given to the All Blacks before the start of the Super Rugby season is some kind of perk, but after playing every game for the Crusaders and 13 of the 14 tests for the All Blacks in 2009, my body and mind considered it nothing short of a necessity. As much as I delighted in every opportunity to play, I was beginning to gain some sense of the price to be paid, physically and mentally, at the highest level of the sport. There was no way to hide from the ongoing maintenance, though, not even over those few holiday weeks.

I kept my training up over those summer days, fully aware that Todd Blackadder expected his All Blacks to deliver for him the moment we arrived back at Rugby Park. In his view, we were the standard bearers for the entire team and as such we had no excuse for not performing at our very best. I was highly motivated to keep pushing my own levels to new heights. Yes, I had secured the starting job for the All Blacks in 2009, but I never once believed I could rest on my laurels. I had made a pact with myself in high school that if I was going to be an All Black, I wanted to be a great one. The great Barbara Kendall had said it would just be something to make the team, but once that had been achieved I wanted more and more from the experience.

Todd always wanted what was best for the Crusaders, but I could sense he struggled with the jigsaw puzzle that his All Blacks presented him. He would have much preferred to have us back earlier, but if we didn't have that off-season there was simply no way we would have been able to get through the longer seasons. Then again, although we hadn't been there for the pre-season work, we were still going to be the players he wanted in the side come competition time. It was a challenge to strike that balance for the betterment of the team, and although he accepted it as a reality of the professional landscape, I doubt he ever fully made his peace with the situation.

The reality is there are natural peaks and troughs in any athlete's season and regardless of how much you put in to training and to preparation, there will be times when form and reputation are poles apart. I am sure Toddy knew this as well as anyone, but the fact was he would invariably pick his All Blacks to play when they were available. I think he could have shown a bit more faith in the wider squad at times, driving more internal competition which, perhaps counterintuitively, can be one way to ease the pressure on individuals. When there is full, squad-wide trust, no one player has to carry a burden greater than the one he is capable of bearing. Expectation is shared more evenly.

For all that, I was not complaining about being named to play each week. I had not missed a game since my debut for the Crusaders in 2007, and my run continued as the 2010 season began. It pays to note that the central ethos of the team had not changed at all as we approached the opening game against the Highlanders at AMI Stadium. At the start of every season we had one overarching, simplistic goal: to win the title. I'm not suggesting for a minute that was some kind of original concept. I mean, every team had the same goal, after all. I think the critical difference between the Crusaders and many other teams was that we didn't just want to win the title, we expected to win it.

After the battles to find our attack in 2009, we started the season with our outside backs in full flight. The Highlanders couldn't live with us on that February night, and Zac Guildford, Jared Payne and Sean Maitland all crossed for tries in a 32–17 win. It was a great opening shot, especially from the backline. We ran them ragged that night on a hard track with a big crowd in the house and our tails up. It was the kind of performance that sets up a season while simultaneously shaking off all the nervousness that clings to you in the week leading up to the first real test of where you are at as a team. After the disappointment of the semi-final loss the year before, this was the game that was going to kickstart our ride back to the winner's circle. A week later, the Reds put 40 points on us in Brisbane.

All the hand-wringing in the world won't help you find consistency, nor will soul-searching, or palm-reading for that matter. Truth was, we never felt as if we had a handle on why some weeks we played like world-beaters and on others we looked like a dog's breakfast. We certainly took our medicine after our capitulation against the Reds and strung together a series of wins — some impressive, some not worthy of dwelling upon — until by early April we had established a 5-1-1 record, a draw with the Hurricanes being the only blot on an otherwise satisfactory copybook. The squad was in great heart, and I felt as though my own form had been worthy of my new status as a starting test All Black. I had played 49 consecutive games since my debut and was all set for a milestone 50th appearance when the team suffered a loss far greater than any of us knew how to deal with.

Luke Thornley, my friend and my first trainer when I had arrived at the Canterbury academy as a gangly kid with a burning ambition and none of the muscles to match it all those years ago, was an ever-present, effervescent fixture at Rugby Park where he had continued to work closely with players of all levels. We all loved him, the way he went about his work and the standards he set for all of us in terms of our approach to strength and conditioning and nutrition. He seemed like the sort of guy who always had time for everyone, and whose relentless positivity would always take him places. On 11 April that year, he took his own life.

I was devastated by the news, as so many others in the organisation were. Luke had been an inspiration to me during my time in Christchurch; the guy I could rely on when I needed a push or just a side serving of extra encouragement. We thought of ourselves as a family at Rugby Park and Luke was our brother. How had none of us been aware that he may have been suffering his own problems away from work? Had we simply been too focused on what Luke could do for us, rather than what we could do for him? These questions, warped by grief, tormented me over the subsequent days. I couldn't wait to get out there the following week and honour his memory by playing the game of my life. Toddy knew better. Taking me aside, he told me that I didn't need to play. He realised that I was in no head space for rugby, and that the best way to honour Luke would be to take that week to process his death. It was a kind gesture, perfectly illustrative of Toddy's perceptive capabilities, and it was a relief. There's no way I could have played that game.

As it was, the boys went out that weekend and hammered the Cheetahs. Luke would have loved it.

We had our chances that year and never quite took them. There were things I could look back on with all the 'if onlys' in the world but that wouldn't change the fact that we once again blew our hopes of a home playoff and boarded the plane for yet another semi-final against our old friends, the Bulls. The game was to be played at Orlando Stadium that year, built beside the railway line that carried Johannesburg's workforce to and from the narrow streets and compact homes of the Sowetan sprawl, the famous cooling towers of the world's most famous township visible across the tin and tile rooves to the south, and in the distance Johannesburg's skyline glinting in the afternoon sun. We had little time to take in the views. We were stuck in a traffic jam, and the clock was ticking down to kick-off.

We eventually made it through the logjam, but we had been inextricably thrown by our late arrival, and nothing went to plan after that. The Bulls came out and did to us exactly what they had done the year before, and we were left to sit in the sheds afterwards, comparing bruises and reflecting on the lack of resilience we had shown that afternoon. It was a timely lesson in the power of adaptation and the need to be able to deal with changes in conditions. Yes, we had a process for our game day, a routine. But if we could be derailed by something as minor as being 20 minutes behind our perfect schedule, then we weren't going to be winning competitions any time soon.

It was frustrating because as gutted as we were, there was still so much about how we trained and played that we knew was absolutely right. We couldn't afford to throw everything out. If we kept our faith in the system, in each other, and in how we played, we would find a way to win a title. Surely we would . . .

The international season rolled around and regret was jettisoned in favour of revenge as far as emotional anchor points go. Motivated by the South African shut-out of the previous season, we spoke at length when we assembled about making amends that year. First we had a June series to contend with, Ireland first followed by back-to-back tests against Wales, but it was clear that every last detail of the off-season planning had been undertaken with the express purpose of beating the Springboks — mindset, moves, tempo and tactics. I sat in that first session as Richie McCaw stood before us all, delivering his now familiar considered and composed address. I leant forward in my seat, my feet bouncing up and down on the carpeted floor. All I could think about was how I was going to have to toughen up.

Wayne Smith had obviously spent the six months between the end-of-year tour and the June series doing little else but refining his game plan. I could see the many cogs in his big brain click into place one after the other as he ran through his theory on how we could play to win against a team like South Africa. Much of it centred around diffusing high kicks, which was nothing new to us. What was innovative was his belief that the entire team had a role to play in the kick receipt because the kick receipt was not an outcome but an opportunity to launch our own attack. We were going to take South Africa's trusty weapon and turn their own gun on them.

And we had a new term: click plays. In simple terms, if South Africa turned the ball over, we clicked. Again, just like kick receipts, forcing an error was only the beginning of the play, not the result. We had to think about swooping on the smallest mistake and being ready, no matter how long we had spent on defence, to swing onto attack. Wayne referenced the San Antonio Spurs, specifically a key stat that looked at the number of passes per basket and the speed of their transition from defence to attack. We couldn't believe what we were hearing. Wayne Smith, along with Graham Henry and Steve Hansen, had devised a strategy of playing that could best be described as 'have a bloody go'. It was music to our ears, and we ate it up.

We ate up the Irish as well. On 12 June in New Plymouth, on a spongy and waterlogged Yarrow Stadium field, we went ballistic. All up that night we scored nine tries on our way to a record 66–28 victory. Everything we did seemed to come off, and the harder we worked, the more we were able to do and the more that worked too. It certainly helped our cause that my opposite, Jamie Heaslip, was shown a red card after just 15 minutes, but the control shown that night by the likes of Jimmy Cowan at halfback and Conrad Smith in the midfield, and the way we were able to express ourselves without second guessing the play, would have been enough to defeat any team by a handy margin.

The sceptics were not as convinced of course, and as a team we knew that Jamie's sending off meant the result would forever have an asterisk beside it. We kept that in mind as we headed to Dunedin to prepare for the first test against a handy Welsh side. If we really were on the right track, this was the chance to prove it. It was also a chance to farewell Carisbrook, with Dunedin's new stadium well on the way to completion and the famous old ground rusting and creaking under the weight of 102 years of test history and spilled beer. It was a sell-out on a cold, still Otago night, with the terraces heaving as they had done for decades and an All Blacks side fit to bust before emerging from the confines of the concrete-block sheds and out onto the famous pitch.

It was a fraught display in the first half as we tried to push the play against a determined Welsh defensive line, but we got our noses in front and turned for the second half with a 15–9 lead. During halftime there was not a single note of panic in our discussions. We knew the plan, trusted in what we were doing and believed wholeheartedly that if we upped the pressure, Wales would struggle to live with us. I had seen Dan Carter take control of games before, and in that second half he did it again, expertly guiding us around the field and taking every chance he created. It was a peerless display from him, and the outside backs feasted on everything he dished up. By fulltime we had added a further 27 points and shut the Welsh out.

The Welsh improved the following week in Hamilton, but we still managed to post a scrappy 29–10 win. They did us a massive favour in the way they exerted defensive pressure because it allowed us to understand what underpinned our playing strategy. We could only express ourselves on attack if we filled the field. In other words, it only worked when we had numbers across the park at every moment in the game. That was how we worked ourselves into position to outmanoeuvre the defence. In Hamilton we had been too bunched, too eager to use our numbers in situations when it simply wasn't necessary. We took that lesson away from the game and readied ourselves for South Africa.

In the weeks between All Blacks games we would each return home, but it was imperative during these short breaks that we stayed on top of our conditioning work. For most of us that involved running, and plenty of it. Because we were both loose forwards and therefore had similar programmes to follow, and because we both lived in Christchurch, Richie McCaw and I would meet at Rugby Park and work out together. The sessions were tough, and here's what I discovered: if I could keep up with his shadow, I knew I was fit. His mindset, the way he could push himself to places no one could follow, was one of the most extraordinary things I witnessed.

I'm naturally a hard worker, at least I like to think so, but to see what he could do was absolutely inspirational. I sometimes turned up for our running sessions more nervous than I would be for a game. As gruelling as those hours were for me, I knew I was in a privileged position to be able to test myself against the fittest guy in the team, if not the sport. The sessions themselves were based around intervals on time and plenty of shuttles. The longest distance in one interval might be 300 metres, but we would absolutely smoke ourselves while we were doing it. I came to realise that Richie could somehow run the tenth repetition as fast as the first and I marvelled at his capacity to do that. I could live with him for a few, but I knew that if I went too fast too early, I would be totally blown out for the last few reps. Not him. He was a machine.

That time spent together away from the team built our camaraderie really, and it added to our on-field relationship. It also helped me to understand what it was going to take to have a long career in the game. Working with Richie taught me so much about applying myself to a task and pushing my body through its natural aerobic threshold. It amazed me to realise how quickly that became second nature, and because we had spent that time together, we knew exactly what each other could do on the field and how far we could push each other.

The Springboks arrived at Eden Park for the first test of the Tri-Nations intent on bashing us into submission. We lined up for kick-off ready to run them off the pitch. We had stewed on 2009's 3-nil drubbing for long enough. Now it was time to put things right. Seven of our starting forwards that day would go on to start in the Rugby World Cup final the following year, and we had made a pact that we would not take a step backwards all day. That was the mindset we had spoken about before the June series. We needed to bully the bullies. It worked early too, when Bakkies Botha let his frustration overflow and was handed a yellow card for being Bakkies Botha.

It was an intensely physical game, but we felt as if we had the edge right from the opening minutes. I was particularly proud of the way we attacked their lineout and we did our best to compete for everything. We were up against the undisputed king in Victor

Matfield, but it was our job to take his crown. Tom Donnelly, who had only been given limited minutes in a test jumper, had a great night for us, but all across the park there were standout performances. Mils Muliaina carted the ball up from the backfield all night long, and South Africa's limited tactics were exposed for everyone to see. By taking away their ability to maul, and turning their kicks into threats, we broke their belief. We could see it evaporate before our eyes. Suddenly, they realised that what had worked for the Bulls for two straight seasons was not going to translate into the international game. The following weekend in Wellington, on a brutal and blustery winter's night, it was more of the same.

All I wanted to do was to win battles all night long and I set my sights on winning them against Pierre Spies. This man had been my nemesis from colts level through to the pro-leagues and it was time to draw the line. I tracked him all game long, stalking him around rucks and charging him in the open field, taking myself back to those days in Papakura as a kid when I would rush out of the line to put a spot tackle on the biggest boy on the opposition. The Springboks were ideologically predisposed to talismanic worship. If I could take down one of those pillars of strength, I could help undermine their faith. I think everyone in the pack thought the same way I did, and it was as a pack that we nullified that traditional Bok threat.

The following year's Rugby World Cup, though by now a germinating seed of thought in the back of my mind, had not yet entered the team conversation. The only things that mattered to us over those few months were beating South Africa and retaining the Bledisloe Cup. The combination between Richie, Jerome and me, which had gelled so well the year before, now felt as if it had settled, a dish in which every ingredient complements the others. We were incredibly focused on working together and we had a game plan that suited us. It was a perfect storm of motivation and situation.

Those first-up wins were a great stimulus for the team and was a great confidence boost for coaches and players alike. As for me, I was loving the way I was expected to perform and the way I had been able to utilise my key attributes in games. There was no doubt that the way we played suited me down to the ground and because of that I was given every opportunity to build my mana around the team. I still had no official leadership role and didn't feel the need to push my case for one, but I was day by day earning the respect of the older, more senior players and setting an example for the younger boys to follow. I had found my place, and it was starting to feel like home.

A two-week break before the first Australian match of the series did much to replenish the tank after two bruising encounters, and the Wallabies could not keep pace with us in Melbourne as we racked up 49 points in a game that felt a lot closer than the scoreline suggested. They were much improved on the return leg in Christchurch, but still we did enough to emerge victorious and to reclaim the Bledisloe Cup. It was a bit of a comedown to be so unconvincing in our play, but perhaps it was indicative of us getting a little bit ahead of ourselves. Over the next two matches, in Soweto and Sydney, it was the opposition we let get ahead. A Ma'a Nonu break and Izzy Dagg finish were just enough to claim an unlikely 29–22 win against South Africa, while I managed to crash over late in Sydney to snatch a 23–22 win against the Wallabies.

We didn't think too much about it at the time, but those two wins would be crucial to our ethos over the next few seasons.

They kickstarted a belief within us that if we kept playing right to the final whistle, we could come back from anything and prevail. The self-belief that gave us was on a level I had never experienced before. Sitting in the sheds in Sydney after that one-point jail escape, Bledisloe Cup filled to the brim, we all buzzed with a boyish joy at what had just transpired. Winning was great but winning when the chips were down — with skill and execution and stamina — that was the best feeling of all. Our mental game was growing stronger, and the leaders were adamant this was to be our new way of thinking: winning from anywhere.

Those wins represented a seismic shift in our approach to creating winning outcomes, but it was seismic activity of a different kind that we concerned ourselves with once we returned home. In the early hours of 4 September, a day before we were due to depart for the Sydney test, a magnitude 7.1 earthquake had struck Canterbury. I had sat bolt upright in bed when the rumbling began, not knowing quite what to do. Bridget was heavily pregnant with our first child, Elle, and had managed to get herself under the doorframe in the bedroom. We were both rocked by the experience, but we were pleased to know the damage to our house was minimal and superficial at worst. I didn't really have much of a clue how much damage had been wrought that morning, and after some reassurances from Bridget I was happy to board the plane and head to Sydney.

We weren't to know what was to come a few months later. How could anyone have?

10

CARNAGE AND CHAOS

We have talked for hours at Crusaders HQ about what happened last week at the Al Noor Mosque and the Linwood Islamic Centre. Our team has become part of the broader conversation, which we are all aware of. It is understandable at a time like this — a time of great sadness and anger — for people to question all that they know and all that they believe in, but what can we do to make a positive contribution? That is what concerns us most. I look around the room. There are young people in this team and in the wider organisation who can't even begin to process what has unfolded in Christchurch. There are others — fathers, mothers, sisters, brothers — who can only imagine the heartache that the victims' families are suffering. We care, deeply.

The game against the Highlanders the day after that grim terror arrived was called off. It was exactly the right decision. How could anyone have taken the field that night after what had happened? Now the season would go on, though. We knew we would be criticised if we didn't publicly discuss the events of that terrible day, but we did not feel it right to add to what was already an emotionally charged dialogue. I had been asked repeatedly to make comment as the All Blacks captain. I chose to post a personal message to the people of Christchurch, instead. I wanted it to come from me. I wanted it to be personal.

There were calls from many quarters for us to change the Crusaders name in the wake of the March tragedy. We discussed that at length, not in terms of whether we agreed with those calls or not, but to better understand the motivation behind them. It felt good to have those talks as a team; they were conducted in an incredibly supportive space and central to all of them was how we could best represent the victims and the city. There would be decisions made at much higher levels in the organisation, but it was our job to get out on the field and perform to the best of our ability.

I have already mentioned the theme for our season. Because the deeds of Usain Bolt were a great source of inspiration for us, each week our man of the match was presented with a gold baton, symbolising his willingness to help the team. The baton was then placed on a rack in the team room to inspire the rest of us. Two days after the shooting we walked into the team room to find a red baton hung on the rack, next to the date of the attack. It would stay there all season long, to remind us of who we represented. Beneath the rack of batons, the score of each of the season's games was printed. In the box for the Highlanders match, a simple red heart.

Regardless of the public's perception, we resolved then and there to play every game with the victims in our hearts. A few years earlier we had also been driven by a city's grief . . .

It was a cash game in a foreign city with no trophy on the line. We all understood why it needed to be played — the money has to come from somewhere — but bare economics did nothing for our head-space heading into the fourth 'Bledisloe test' of 2010. We had already played Australia three times, had now defeated them in 10 consecutive tests and, to be honest, we would have much preferred to get to Europe and begin our quest for another grand slam, rather than play an exhibition test in Hong Kong. We could have done with a kick in the ass over that attitude. We lost, 26–24, after Australia scored late thanks to a questionable kick and some woeful defence. Then they celebrated like they had won the lottery.

The condemnation came swiftly from the public back home. They — and Graham Henry for that matter — made Stephen Donald the scapegoat. We could tell people were angry about the result, but their reason for disappointment was a little different to ours. Apparently, in the eyes of the public, we were on a mission to set a new world record for consecutive test wins. That record stood at 17 and we were just two short of the mark heading to Hong Kong. This loss had scuppered any chance we had of that, which was perceived to be a major malfunction in the universe. What they didn't realise is that we weren't motivated by that because we already wanted to win every game we played. Instead we were motivated by the fact we had finally talked about the Rugby World Cup before we departed, and that this tour was going to replicate, as closely as possible, everything we wanted to do come that tournament the following year. That's why it hurt us so much: at the very first hurdle we had fallen.

I felt for Stephen Donald that night. He had been really good for us in the team over the last couple of seasons and it was a big chance for him to cement himself in the side. It didn't pan out for him, or us, but he copped far more grief than he, or anyone, deserved from the public. Worse, he was cast aside by the All Blacks coaches and we all knew it. Ted didn't exactly make a secret of the fact that he had pretty much washed his hands of 'Beaver' for the rest of the tour and it is tough to see a teammate go through what is ostensibly a humiliation. We all understand that we operate in a cut-throat space and no sooner has fulltime been called on one game than planning starts for the next one. If we have a loss, we hope we get a chance to put it right the following week. Beaver never got a chance to do that, playing only once more on that tour as a replacement against Scotland. He deserved better than that.

Funnily enough, he probably deserves a bit of credit too. The way Australia celebrated that win on the field stayed with us for many seasons after that; the image of them carrying on like they had just won a title rather than a pick-up game was etched into our minds for future inspiration. Losses can be timely, and that one, while unpalatable to many, was one of them.

After the Hong Kong setback, we pretty much ran the same test team for all but the Scotland match. The coaches figured that was how it would be come the business end of the Rugby World Cup and so we knew what was at stake. We were all desperate to play those games because we knew we were in a live audition, and the coaches wanted to see if we could still perform in the final test as well as we had in the first. We rebounded from the Australian game with a solid win over England, put Scotland to the sword and were 20 points better than Ireland in Dublin. Three down, one to go: Wales at Millennium Stadium. Before that match more bad news came from home.

On 24 November, after a second catastrophic explosion, it was reported that 29 men had been killed in the Pike River Mine on the West Coast. The Pike River disaster, as it became widely known, was one of the worst industrial accidents in New Zealand history and rocked the small, tightknit communities of that rugged, wild province. The Pike River Mine was situated deep in the heavily forested hills on the edge of Paparoa National Park, just north of the town of Runanga, home to one of New Zealand Rugby's most endearing and treasured men, John Sturgeon. 'Sturge' had been a manager of the All Blacks, a stalwart of the West Coast Rugby Union and a champion for his community and many other charitable causes. He was President of New Zealand Rugby that year, and he was devastated.

We were deeply moved by the address Sturge gave us at the team hotel. A tall and distinguished man with a gentle manner and a firm handshake, he was stooped and sullen that evening. This was not a story about a faraway tragedy for Sturge. These were his people — friends, and the sons of friends. They were familiar faces, boys he had watched grow into men, and their loss would never be fully recovered from by those left to deal with the enormity of their grief. When he was finished, we sat in silence and absorbed what he had told us. That night, those people became our people and we vowed to play for them. Before the game we observed a minute's silence — if anyone could relate to a coal-mining tragedy it was the Welsh — and we played the game with those 29 men foremost in our minds, and later auctioned off our jerseys.

Death and life: Elle was born on Christmas Day, delivered fit and healthy at Christchurch Women's Hospital and transferred with her beautiful mum to St George's the same evening. I briefly headed home once Bridget and baby were settled and Bridget's mum Helen packed some ham sandwiches to take back to the ward in lieu of our Christmas dinner. Aftershocks from the September quake were a part of daily life in Christchurch, but the next day a particularly violent one hit, just as I was heading back to see the girls at the hospital. I had been warned that the birth of your first child changes your outlook on life. Up until then it had been just me and Bridget. I knew we could cope with the constant shakes. Now I fretted about Elle. Would she be safe living here?

Home life changed for ever, and for the better, but rugby continued. I spent my summer break around the house, doing what I could to give Bridget a break and fitting my training around Elle's broken sleep. I drove across town to train on the hard grass running track at the university, cooking myself in the Canterbury sun and doing all I could to keep as fit as possible for what shaped as the biggest year of my career. There was no escaping the thought of the Rugby World Cup. I let it percolate in my head as I ran laps of the track, as I ran towards the challenge.

The Blues gave us a wake-up call in the opening game of the season; the earth gave us a bigger one four days later. On Tuesday, 22 February, Christchurch was torn apart. Richie McCaw and I were sharing a sushi lunch at a mall in the suburb of Merivale when the shaking began. We instantly knew this quake was different to the many aftershocks we had experienced. It was a violent, malevolent crack of a quake and it ripped through the building sending us and everything else in the place flying. Richie was in a moonboot and walking with the aid of crutches and he was thrown from his chair. I leapt to my feet and tried as best I could to hang on to the table, as the ground beneath me rippled and waved.

I don't know how long it lasted, but when we regained our composure we only had one thought: let's get out of here. We moved as fast as we could to the entrance, merchandise strewn across shop floors and alarms blaring. My car was parked just a few metres from the front doors, on Papanui Road. Water gushed along the footpath and flowed into the stormwater drains. People poured out of buildings in various stages of shock. Less than half an hour after we had left, the building frontage fell onto the road, on the exact spot my car had been parked. I couldn't reach Bridget on the phone. All around us was chaos.

I dropped Richie back at Rugby Park, the usual two-minute drive seeming to take forever. From there to our home in Shirley, on the north-eastern edge of the city, the roads were completely under water. I couldn't understand how an earthquake had caused flooding like that. I was yet to be schooled in the science of liquefaction. I drove as fast as I could to get home, but the water concealed every crack and hole that had opened in the roads, and the short journey took close to half an hour. I finally arrived to see Bridget standing in the driveway holding Elle, looking determined to get out of there as quickly as possible. She had already packed a bag for the baby and sorted a plan.

It was bad enough to see the damage inside, but as we surveyed the interior I looked out into the backyard to see geysers of mud erupt across the lawn. This was liquefaction, the earth beneath us quite literally turned to liquid mud by the reverberation of the quakes. A lake of silt and water was spreading across the section, with no sign of abating. We were transfixed by the scene and by the time the flow was over, almost a foot of fresh mud covered the entire lawn, and it seeped through the sunken corner of our living room. There was no way we could stay in the house. My aunty and uncle lived in Burnside, close to the airport on the other side of town. Bridget and I packed a bag and headed straight there. Amazingly, it was like there had never been an earthquake at their place.

We watched the news in disbelief that night. Like so many others who had spent the afternoon dealing with their own set of circumstances, it was the first chance we had to see the scale of the damage. There was a numbness in the room as we tried to comprehend the loss of life — a toll that would increase in the coming days. I wanted to get Bridget and Elle out of there as soon as possible, but it would be a few days before they were on a plane to Auckland. The following afternoon I phoned a couple of lads to ask for a hand to shovel the mud out of my backyard. We carted wheelbarrows of the stuff out of the driveway, following the neighbours' lead and tipped it in a growing pile at the edge of the road. Mounds of mud formed all the way down the street. Bridget kept us fed and watered and in good spirits.

Having cleaned up my joint we just kept going around the neighbourhood, shovelling mud from other houses and backyards. Eventually, the senior players gathered at Todd Blackadder's house to discuss what we were going to do. It was clear that playing that weekend against the Hurricanes was going to be a big ask, and we were relieved to be told the game would be called off. What wasn't so clear was what happened after that, and if we did go back to playing, where on earth were we going to call home?

Every earthquake starts the same, that's the problem. After 22 February, I could never tell when an aftershock was going to end. Like so many people in Christchurch, I felt my nerves fraying further with every shake. It was hard to watch the nightly pictures of lives and property destroyed, harder still to fully comprehend the fact that so many people had been killed. Most of us just wanted to keep busy and so we kept loading the shovels and wheelbarrows and tried to be of use. Some guys had to get out of town for a few days, just to decompress after what they had been through.

On the Friday, a bunch of us gathered at the local pub and shared a couple of beers. It was good to talk about our experiences and to take time to care for each other. On the Sunday we again headed to Toddy's. We had to think seriously about footy again. Were we going to commit to the season?

What we knew was this: if we decided to get back into the swing of things, we had no ground, no certainty and no real idea of how things were going to pan out. What we did have instead was a quandary: we could take some more time out to regroup and to recover, but we would have to forfeit those competition points while we did. Would it be two rounds? Three? More? And then what? What would be the point of returning to play at all if by the time we did we had no chance of winning a competition? Our city was broken, our people had suffered unimaginable loss. Maybe what they needed right then was a team to represent their strength, not magnify their vulnerability.

It was clear after that what needed to be done. We were going to get back on the horse and do what no team in professional sport had done before: we were going to win a title without a home of our own. From the moment we committed to that course of action we felt like a band of brothers, ready and willing to rise to the most unique challenge in the history of the competition, if not the sport.

With Rugby Park off limits, we trained for the next few days at Lincoln University, on the browned-off plains south-west of the city, and prepared to face the Waratahs in a round three clash at Trafalgar Park in Nelson. The match doubled as a symbol to the people of Christchurch that we were going to carry on regardless, and as a tribute to the 29 men who had lost their lives in the Pike River Mine disaster in November. As a small gesture to the families of those men, and to the tightknit West Coast communities they came from, we wore commemorative jerseys complete with the famous red and white hoops of that proud province. The people of Nelson were superb. Their support meant so much to us that weekend.

Having set for ourselves such a worthy challenge, we felt like we were ready for anything that week. Ready for anything, that is, except leaving our families while we travelled. Elle was not yet three months old and Bridget, for all her formidable independence and bravery, had been genuinely spooked by the earthquake and by the constant aftershocks. There was no escaping the chaos for the people we left behind, and given the awful human toll of that February day, we all lingered that little bit longer when we said our goodbyes, fearful that if something happened while we were away we would be powerless to help. Earthquakes had become the everyday language of the city, and we were able to track the thousands of tremors on our phones while we were away. We toured in a constant state of anxiety.

When we saw the schedule for the season we felt as if we were like a travelling carnival pitching up in regional towns and putting on a show for the locals. Nelson, Timaru and Napier all got matches that season and then there was the scarcely believable idea to take our round six game against the Sharks all the way to Twickenham. In for a penny, in for a pound, as they say. So, we hopped on a plane to London bound for a historic first. When I say hopped on 'a plane', I mean several. Such was the late decision to go that the team had to split up, each group finding a different flight, route and airline. It was a logistical triumph.

That week was without doubt one of the highlights of the year. We had become so accustomed to touring the UK in the depths of autumn that to be there in spring was a revelation. On top of that, we were blown away by the level of media and public interest in the match. We all knew London was teeming with Kiwi and South African expats, but Super Rugby had long been breakfast fodder for the local fans and they too descended on Twickenham in great numbers. I know there were costs to cover and money to be raised, but if I had one regret about that week it was that the tickets were priced at test-match level. I would have loved to have seen 80,000 people in the stadium that day, even though the 40,000 who were there created a sensational atmosphere.

Everything was different about the Twickenham experience that day. My only experiences of that grand stadium had been as an All Black, running out in the cold and dark in front of a packed hostile house. Here I was now, in the home changing rooms, leading a side out onto that famous turf with a crowd very much behind us and the occasion. We put on a show that day — both teams did really — and I was so proud to have been a part of that match. I think I was prouder still to be part of a professional sport that still had some soul.

We were well looked after in London and glad for the bye week after the Sharks match, but once back into action we managed to put together a month's worth of solid performances before the Highlanders handed us a hiding in round 10 — our first loss since round one. New habits die as hard as old ones it turns out, and our recently perfected penchant for dropping games we really shouldn't drop was on show against the Cheetahs a few weeks later. A one-point loss to the Reds at Suncorp a few weeks after that had us scratching our heads. Worse than that, it would end up costing us a chance to 'host' during the finals series.

Four days before our last round robin game against the Hurricanes in Wellington, Christchurch experienced another large aftershock. I had only just got the section back in order and watched out my window as the mud and water began oozing up through the ground again, just as it had in February. I don't know whether I was mentally and physically exhausted from the travel and the grind, but as I picked up the things that had fallen off walls and watched the earth swallow my lawn, I broke down in tears and started to sob. For the first time in my life I felt like I was having a breakdown. I sat there, crying, steeling myself to shovel mud for the next few days. It was only a call from Dan Carter, asking if everything was all right and if a few of his Southbridge Rugby Club boys could help me out, that snapped me back out of my funk.

The chance to head back to Nelson for what was potentially our last 'home' game of the season was eagerly anticipated, and once again the city came alive for us. It would have taken a great side to beat us in that quarter-final, such was our desire to end our time in Nelson on a high note. As it was, the Sharks were never in the hunt. As if we hadn't already clocked up enough miles that season, we were straight back on a plane that week to Cape Town for the semi-final. I think by that stage we were almost completely out of juice, but we found something special that afternoon at Newlands thanks to an overwhelming level of support during the week and at the stadium, and we managed to beat the Stormers 29–10 with an epic second-half performance led by the senior players. We had been to Nelson, Timaru, Tauranga, Auckland,

Napier, Wellington, Dunedin, Cape Town, Bloemfontein, Perth, London and Brisbane so far that season. What was one last three-leg trip to Queensland?

Apparently, it was a bridge too far. On a humid night at Suncorp, the year caught up with us. It shouldn't have, as we were better than we showed that night, but with the finish line in plain sight we just didn't have the legs to get us there. Had we allowed ourselves to buy into the hype surrounding that match? It seemed everyone was already talking up what an achievement it would be to win the title, but we hadn't won anything yet. Maybe we had thought about the outcome rather than the process. That was something we had promised as a team we wouldn't do, but it would have been hard not to after the season we had endured. All those moments that we would back ourselves to win, suddenly became 50:50 propositions. We hammered their scrum but found no reward for the effort. We created chances but could never quite finish. Will Genia ran 60 metres to score the winning try.

There is no way I can ever look back on that season without thinking it remains one of the most extraordinary achievements in the history of rugby. To start a season with a loss, to play every game on the road while dealing with the stress of leaving loved ones in a city on the edge, to cover that many miles and to make it all the way to a final was a remarkable story. But victors write history and so that year will always be a footnote to someone else's success. It would take a long time to be able to rationalise that defeat. We stood on that field and watched James Horwill lift that trophy and then we wandered into the sheds and sat in silence. We were broken men from a broken city.

We boarded the plane for home the next day in a miserable mood. We felt as if we had failed our people, that was what hurt us the most. All we had wanted to do was to give them something to cheer about, but we were now on our way back to Christchurch and we were coming empty-handed. We were all thinking how different things might have been had the trophy been strapped into a seat beside us on that flight. When we landed, we braced ourselves for an apologetic walk through the terminal. What we walked into was something none of us will ever forget. The arrivals hall was absolutely packed with fans and all of them were cheering for us. To be in a losing team coming home to that was the most surreal experience of my career. I think half the team was in tears. I certainly was.

The All Blacks coaches recognised what we had been through and made it clear to us that most of the Crusaders contingent wouldn't need to spend a lot of time around the camp in the initial weeks of the international season. There was a hastily arranged game at Carisbrook against Fiji (the T-shirt said 'The final test — again') which I was not required for, either. It was a kind gesture from Graham Henry and his team. They knew how much the Super Rugby season and the daily stress of Christchurch's new and uncertain reality had taken out of us that year and they were more than happy to trust us to spend that time at home and do our training there.

I missed the opening game against Fiji and the next test against South Africa, only spending one day with the team before returning, refreshed, for the Bledisloe Cup test at Eden Park. It was a Wallabies side that had been upset a few weeks earlier by Samoa and it felt as if they had still not recovered. We were maniacal in our defence that day with Richie McCaw possessed and Brad Thorn at his damaging best. We were still smarting from the events in Hong Kong the year before and in no mood to experience that kind of loss again. A massive crowd of more than 50,000 ensured we were pumped up for the entire game and that Quade Cooper felt about as welcome as a rodent infestation. I don't think I had ever heard a New Zealand crowd that hostile to a single player before. Then again, he had put a knee into McCaw's head in Hong Kong. Kiwis were hardly going to forgive him for that transgression.

When the team left for South Africa, Dan Carter, Brad Thorn, Richie McCaw and I were left in New Zealand. The plan was to link up again with the team in Brisbane the following week, by which stage the Rugby World Cup cull was to be complete. It was a strange feeling to meet with the rest of the lads knowing that some had already been sent home, their Rugby World Cup dreams in tatters. The team still hadn't officially been named, which added a strange and unsettling dimension to the build-up. In any event, the Wallabies came out and pumped us in the first half and, although we came back with a vengeance, did enough to hold us off and to claim the Tri-Nations title. For the second time that year, James Horwill lifted a trophy on Suncorp Stadium.

I would happily take some responsibility for the loss, but I lasted all of 12 minutes in that game before my foot was caught in a ruck and I heard my ankle pop. Dr Deb Robinson took me off the field straight away and I had to sit on the sideline and watch the events unfold on the field, all the while not knowing if I was going to be fit for a certain tournament that was now just two weeks away. My mind took me to some dark places during that game as I contemplated the potential ramifications of the injury. That night Doctor Deb put my foot in a moonboot and the next day sent me straight back to Christchurch while the rest of the team boarded a plane for Auckland and Monday's World Cup assembly.

It was a tough flight, on my own with a special brand of post-injury pessimism for company. The next day I went straight to hospital for scans and the prognosis was not good. The imagery had revealed a syndesmotic or high ankle sprain, and Doc Deb called to say that it was likely to be a six- to eight-week recovery time. The opening game of the World Cup was less than two weeks away. It was then that she told me I was still in the squad and that they would give me as long as I needed to come right before taking the field. It was the most extraordinary call from them, and I pinched myself to make sure I wasn't dreaming it up.

I had to look on the bright side. I had been thrown a lifeline by the coaching staff, and Doc Deb reassured me that she and the medical team would be doing all they could to get me right well ahead of schedule. We looked at the dates ahead of us and put a ring around the final pool match against Canada. That was five weeks away. I could be ready in five weeks, surely . . .

11
ON TOP OF THE WORLD

It feels so good to put on the jersey again. Sitting under the stand at Westpac Stadium in Wellington, feeling that energy of a team on a mission. This is what makes it all worthwhile. There is nothing but excitement in this room, the clatter of sprigs and the slow, steady individual rituals in those brief minutes before the door opens and the action starts. Back slaps and clearing throats and deep inhalations of air tainted with the smell of anxiety.

The boys are coming off a loss. They have been rare since Scott Robertson took control of the team and found the winning formula. Last week in Sydney the Waratahs had got the better of the boys, but how could anyone in the side have had their minds completely on the game after what had happened just eight days earlier? We had to reset ourselves, find the steel within and get back to playing rugby. That's the only thing we could do now.

I pace slowly around the room, thinking of what I have to do in the next 40 minutes. Shut down their space. Give them nothing to work with. Attack at all costs. Keep it simple. Do what you know best. It will all come back, I tell myself. You have been here 145 times before. I have to trust that the back is ready to go. I have had the break I needed and I am ready. This is going to be where my 2019 season truly begins, and I know the final destination.

I look around at the leaders in this team, men I have played alongside for so many years. How fortunate I have been to take the field with them season after season, to know that they are on my team. Sam Whitelock brings us in close and we lean in to listen. He has grown into one of the best captains in the game, a no-nonsense talker with an acute eye for aggressive leadership. The team take in his words; they drop like stones in a lake and ripple through the room.

It's time to go do what we do. It's time for us to get back to winning. I want to be sitting in this room after the game with a victory in my pocket and a smile on my face. I love winning. There's no better feeling . . .

I walked into the All Blacks' team hotel in a moonboot and for the next four weeks I was able to get a true sense of what the Rugby World Cup meant to New Zealand. I wasn't playing and I wasn't training with the team, and so I got to experience a side of the event that very few in the team did. If there was a silver lining to this injury cloud, I had found it. I really loved sitting in the hotel on the opening day, watching the fanzones build up on the television coverage and having a chance to feel that atmosphere descend in a way that as a player I never would have. I got to sit in the stands at Eden Park that night and watch the opening ceremony, all the while absorbing that patriotic fervour and feeling the excitement electrify the stadium.

We all knew that our fans loved footy, but I never quite comprehended how closed off we are from that game-day vibe. We have our own emotional triggers as a team, but we are in our own bubble in those hours and minutes before kick-off, completely oblivious to the things I was now seeing. Sitting there among the Kiwi supporters that night reminded me of why we play this game, and who we are representing when we do. It was a great boost for me, and I wanted very much to bottle that feeling and to keep it with me the next time I ran out to play. I got plenty of chances to think about that while spending my days at the Waitakere Aquatic Centre, aqua jogging to keep fit. It must have been a heck of a sight for the rest of the swimmers: here was the All Blacks number eight in the slow lane, jogging along with the septuagenarian women. I can assure you I looked like a complete goose.

When I wasn't frolicking in the public pool, I was thrashing myself on a grinder. There was little else I could do to keep in shape, but there was one other thing that Doctor Deb was keen to try. It was called platelet-rich plasma (PRP) therapy, which involved being injected with a concentrated dose of my own platelets to help speed up the recovery process. It was a relatively new therapy from a New Zealand sport point of view, and I was sworn to secrecy. It was a completely legal procedure but none of the All Blacks had ever tried it. Deb asked if I was happy to give it a go and I was 100 per cent on board. So it was that twice a week I was a real-life Secret Steve, heading over to North Shore Hospital to have my blood taken out and the platelets injected back into my ankle. I kind of enjoyed the whole clandestine nature of it all.

I still had a role to play within the team, especially with my lineout plays work, which I fed into the trainings each week, but being on the periphery was hard because all I wanted to do was get out on the field and play. The team had no problem accounting for Tonga and Japan in the opening two games and it was the day after the 83–7 win against Japan at Hamilton that physiotherapist Pete Gallagher drove me and Mils Muliaina to a nondescript football field in the middle of suburban Hamilton and let me have my first run since the injury. Getting through that session was a hell of a good feeling and I was able to slowly build through my work that week and through the next. By that stage France had been taken care of at Eden Park and only Canada remained before the quarter-final. If I was going to be ready to play, it would have to be in that game.

We headed to Wellington for that final pool clash and trained at Rugby League Park, home of the Hurricanes, on the Tuesday before the match. I knew in the back of my mind that I had to push myself to see if the ankle could handle the pressure, but I was terrified that it would give out again and my chances of playing would be ruined. Eventually, I had to do what was right for the team and I knuckled down and got into a pretty tough session. I was about 10 minutes deep and was forced to make a tackle off my injured foot. I heard a loud bang first, and then the pain followed. I got up and walked off the training field. All I could think was, 'That's that. I'm not playing.'

Deb and Pete followed me into the physio room, listening as I outlined what I had just felt on the field. When I was finally done whingeing, Deb explained that there were plenty of reasons the ankle could have responded the way it did. Then she told me in no uncertain terms that I was going to be fine. I didn't believe her until I woke up the next morning, pain-free and able to walk without any problem at all. It seemed as though things might just work out after all and the next day I trained with a newfound spring in my step. Everything was looking good for the weekend. And then Dan Carter crashed to the ground in a heap, and the world closed in on us.

It was an eerily quiet team room that evening when Graham Henry told us all about Dan. His World Cup was over, and we all knew how big a loss that was, but Ted was adamant that we were going to bring the next man in and he was going to do the job for us. 'Get around Dan,' he told us, 'but we are carrying on so let's keep our focus.'

I was crushed for Dan. I had got to know him over the past few years and understood how much he was driven to perform on the biggest stage. Yes, he was a big part of the team, but that was beside the point. At that time all we were concerned about was our mate. Having had my own World Cup thrown into disarray I was well placed to feel his pain acutely, but at least I was now getting the chance to be part of it. I can't possibly understand fully how he must have felt in those first few hours and days. What we did appreciate was that we were all going to have to step up to fill the gap. That meant the forwards had to take charge. We didn't make a big deal of it, didn't bring it up at team meetings either, but we decided there and then that we were going to win the World Cup through the forwards.

'It's going to go bang, and it's going to hurt like hell, just so you know.' That was my pep talk from Pete Gallagher before my first Rugby World Cup game on an overcast, drizzly Wellington afternoon. I was well short of the recommended recovery time and wracked with doubt about my chances of getting through the game, but I was thankful to Pete for his advice. I knew it was coming and so I was prepared for it when it happened, in the first ruck of the game. The pain was excruciating, but I willed myself back to my feet and kept going, hoping that over time it would subside. All I could do was get into my work and ignore whatever agony I was in. Be positive, play the game.

I got through 51 minutes of the match before being replaced by Anthony Boric. Sitting on the sideline as the boys put on a good display, the pain began to ease. 'Bugger it,' I thought, 'I am good to go.' From that point on, it was full noise and back to a full training load. It felt great to be back in the bubble with the team, slipping back into my normal game-week routine and shutting out the world again. My days of aqua jogging with grannies were behind me and ahead was a quarter-final against Argentina, a game none of us were taking lightly. There is just something different about the Argentinians. For some reason it always feels like you are playing against a team made up exclusively of men who look your father's age.

The week got off to a rocky start when Israel Dagg and Cory Jane decided to mix sleeping pills with energy drinks and found themselves in a Takapuna bar at some crazy hour of the morning. I was back on a self-imposed media ban so certainly didn't know what the public reaction to their shenanigans was. What I did know is that we thought they were absolute clowns, but they were dealt with, made their apologies, and we all moved on without much fuss. There was no point dwelling on it — what was done was done and Cory certainly had a chance to put it all behind him by playing the house down that weekend. He did exactly that. Israel would get his chance a week later, unfortunately because Mils Muliaina's tournament would come to an end in the Argentina game, his 100th test for the

All Blacks. Colin Slade's tournament also came to a premature end that night, opening the door for the most unlikely recall of Stephen Donald.

We were under no illusions that we had a massive opportunity in front of us, nor were we unaware of the significant weight of history that was piled on our collective shoulders. For all that, we managed to find ways to ease through the weeks of the playoffs. We had families around us, and I would sometimes catch a ride out to Papakura with Keven Mealamu and spend the night with Bridget at her parents' house. In camp we just enjoyed each other's company, playing cards or catching up for a coffee or the occasional dinner out. We tried to stay as relaxed as possible, embracing the moment, and the fact we were training well certainly helped us stay in the right frame of mind. After a 33–10 win over Argentina, we knew the Australians were up next. We couldn't wait to play them. We wanted to play them badly.

We had no doubt we were going to win that game. We didn't doubt it once during the week, nor on game day. Arriving at Eden Park that night and feeling the energy of a partisan home crowd just fuelled our desire even more. I doubt I had ever been that keyed up before a game — not by nerves but by a sublime sensation of unflappable confidence. As soon as the ball was kicked off, we knew we had them. Quade Cooper kicked it straight into touch. We settled into our work and did not let up for 80 minutes. I thought it was one of the best games Richie, Jerome and I had played as a trio — Richie covering every blade of grass, and Jerome putting in big hits at key moments. Our back three were sensational, with Wayne Smith's master plan coming to fruition in full glory that night.

It was odd to look up at the scoreboard at fulltime and realise it was only 20–6. If I am honest, I thought we were worth a lot more than that on the night. It was as dominant a performance as I could ever remember being part of, if not on points then certainly on momentum. We walked back into the sheds that night beaming, knowing that we had one more week to play, one more game to win the ultimate prize. We made sure we celebrated winning a semi-final before we knuckled down and thought about what lay in wait.

We recovered well on Sunday and I spent the early evening trawling French game footage to find all the telltale signs in their lineout defence. Did they two-pod? Were they looking at the jumper or the hooker? Where were their feet on every play? I made my notes and headed to Steve Hansen's room where he and skills coach Mick Byrne were waiting. Ostensibly we were meeting to discuss what special lineout moves we could use in the game based on what my research into their defence told us. What I had found was that they committed to the jump in two distinct pods which took out six of their players and created an opportunity for us to use a move we called 'the tea bag'. Between the three of us we figured how best to open the gap between their two pods to allow our runner to get through. We always took a special lineout into our games, but for one reason or another the game dynamics rarely gave us the chance to use them. We put this one in the playbook, just in case.

The rest of the week took care of itself. We all knew the routine, and we trained well on Tuesday before gathering for our club night that evening. The club night had been instigated the season before as a way to keep us connected to the roots of the game. We would all turn up in our club jerseys, have a couple of beers if we wanted to, eat a few chips and set up some raffles. There were prizes given for our player of the day and defensive player of the day from the last game and there was always a 'dick of the day' award for someone who had completely screwed something up. No mistake was too small to put yourself in the running for that one. It was always a relaxed social night and it set us up well for the rest day on Wednesday during which I spent some time wandering the waterfront with Bridget and Elle, soaking in the buzz around the city.

We were always upbeat as a team, but in those hours when a small group of us would slip away for a cuppa or a quiet game of cards, we would certainly discuss the pressure we felt and talk openly about our fears of failure. I found it healthy to do that, to acknowledge that it was a massive game with high stakes and that there was some fear in our hearts. It would not have been good to hold that all inside during the week. If we all agreed that fear existed, we could work together on ways to keep it in check. We had done plenty of work on the mental side of our game, the mantra of staying in the blue rather than seeing red, and this was the time to show what we had learned.

I had my own room during the week of the final and I loved that. I had my own routines in terms of sleep and how I liked to recover, and just having that space was a welcome relief from the chaos of the week. I enjoyed the company of the boys, but having been someone who had spent a lot of time working on my own, it always felt restorative not to have anyone else to worry about during those evenings. I didn't need to watch the television or read much of the coverage. The questions being asked in the media conferences always gave me enough of a hint about what was being discussed and written, and any time I left the hotel I was imbued with the fizz and pop of the city as it counted down to kick-off with us. That energy seeped through the walls of the hotel and filled the public spaces.

As much as we knew it was not just another game, it was interesting that not much needed to be said during the week. Richie wasn't training at all because of his foot, and so I had taken up a bit of the slack around the talk in those situations. But by and large we all knew our jobs, and as a forward pack we were tight and trusted each other to do what was necessary. Steve Hansen and Mike Cron were blunt at the best of times, and there was nothing they needed to add in terms of expectation for the week. The coaches were likely feeling the heat because of their increased exposure to the externals of the contest, but they were outwardly calm as game day fast approached. The hardest part of the week was whiling away the hours before kick-off.

It wasn't until we walked out of the hotel and boarded the team bus that the nerves kicked in. I had done my best all day to keep a lid on things, spending time with Bridget and Elle, taking a few of the lads out for a coffee and some cards, having a walk through with the team in the afternoon. As we walked outside, the multi-storey car park opposite the hotel was jammed with fans, all leaning over the rails to see us on our way. The sight of that flicked a switch for me, and it stayed full on for the entire bus ride to the stadium. Thousands walked the route to Eden Park that night, and our bus had to slow to a crawl just to part the crowd that gathered around to bang on the side or catch a glimpse of us through the window. I had never seen anything like it, especially not in New Zealand. I was transfixed by the scene, as was everyone else on that bus. None of us could quite believe what we were seeing.

It was almost a relief to pull into Eden Park and walk into

the changing room. Once I was inside, things felt normal. This is what I knew, and where I belonged. Outside may have been a swirling, chaotic mess, but this was our zone. This was where we played. We knew it was on and Richie simply said, 'Do your job.' As far as team talks go, it was short and sweet. As far as challenges go, the sight of the French marching towards our haka in a flying 'V' on our turf was nothing short of exhilarating. All the nerves disappeared, and hunger flooded in to take their place.

The game was a tussle from the outset, and it was clear that we were in for the long haul unless we could spark that little bit of magic. Thierry Dusautoir, France's sensational skipper, took a long lineout throw and I tracked across to make the tackle. Before I knew it, Piri Weepu was in on it like a duck dog and duly earned the penalty. He had already missed a shot and I looked at Richie. 'Tea bag,' I said. Richie pointed to touch and we set the lineout about 10 metres from the French goal-line.

We set up and looked at the French pods. It was on. Brad Thorn went up at the front and I sat in behind for the back lift. Jerome Kaino took a step back, committing the pod opposite him before quickly shifting forward for the jump. Piri Weepu tracked wide, shaping to take the ball off the top and dragging his opposite out of the pocket. Keven Mealamu threw the perfect dart, and Tony Woodcock took the ball, ran straight through a giant hole and scored. We all swarmed him in the in-goal, absolutely losing it. It is a thing of pure joy to see a special move put into practice, especially one so contingent on the opposition doing exactly what you expected them to do, and we were over the moon.

The elation didn't last. From that point on, everything got hard. Neither side gave an inch and I felt every tackle and every collision. It was a monumental contest, one that was going to take all of our power and skill to prevail in. And we were going to have to do it with first-five number four. On the 32-minute mark, Aaron Cruden's night came to an end. Onto the field ran Stephen Donald. I remember feeling for Aaron, but we loved Beaver, were stoked to have had him back in the team with us, and we trusted in what he could do. The public may have drawn a collective breath, but we just got on with the job. If we couldn't deal with an injury now after everything we had been through, we were bloody slow learners.

I began to shake as soon as I sat down in the shed at halftime. I had no idea what was causing it but my whole body was in a kind of shock. We had a 5-nil lead and 40 minutes left to end a 24-year-old curse. Was I nervous? Hell, yes, I was. For the moment, though, I was just trying to hide the fact I was a giant jelly. I was so focused on trying to stop shaking that I heard not a word of the halftime talk, and as soon as I ran back down the tunnel all the symptoms disappeared, never to return again.

The second half was an object lesson in brutality. Beaver kicked a penalty to give us an 8-nil lead, which evaporated when Thierry Dusautoir scored adjacent to the posts after France cut a move across the face of our defensive line. There were 30 minutes left to end the curse and we were ahead by a solitary point. The game was a heavyweight slugfest, every punch met with a counterpunch, two tough competitors out on their feet but running on survival instinct and little else. Twenty minutes became 10 minutes. France missed a chance to kick a go-ahead penalty, while we made our tackles and tried to conjure ways to come up with the ball. Five minutes became three minutes. Richie went down in back play, his eye socket bleeding. We had a scrum, but we needed a plan. The three men closest to the play were Andy Ellis, Stephen

Donald and me, none of us leaders, one of us the reserve halfback and the other the fairytale story of the century.

We needed to keep the ball, that much we knew. I made a call to take the ball off the back and run blindside. From there we could set a ruck and keep the ball close. I had no jurisdiction to make that call, but neither did I have a choice. It was my call and my responsibility and in that moment I felt empowered to own the decision. I felt something else: complete calm. Two minutes later, Craig Joubert blew his whistle for a penalty to us. There has never been a sweeter sound. I raised my fists in the air, the crowd roared back to life, and Andy kicked the ball into touch.

We were world champions. We were out on our feet. That's the way we stayed for the next four days, parading the cup around New Zealand, pretty much three sheets to the wind, elated, tired, relieved and ready for a break. On the final night of the celebrations in Wellington we sat around as a team for one last night, sharing beers and laughs and friendship forged in the fire. It would be the last time we would all be together, and we savoured every second of it.

12

BACK TO WORK

It's the middle of May and I have missed back-to-back games for the Crusaders. Last weekend's game against the Blues was always one that I was scheduled to sit out due to the All Blacks rest protocols, but I had also been forced out of the previous weekend's fixture with the Stormers at Cape Town, which had ended with a 12-all draw. I had taken a hell of a neck stinger in what had been an otherwise incredibly satisfying routing of the Bulls at Loftus Versfeld. There is probably no better feeling in a Super Rugby regular season than silencing the fans in that vast stadium. It's only a neck stinger, I tell myself. After everything else I can get through this.

The back has been great. And until the layoff I was feeling fantastic to have strung together a run of games for the Crusaders. I had got through 40 minutes against the Hurricanes and another 60 against the Brumbies. I could feel myself grinding through the gears as I took full part in the home wins against the Highlanders and the Lions. Considering how close I had come to missing the season entirely, I'm savouring every chance I get. I've also been able to bring up another milestone: 150 games for the Crusaders.

I think about all the great men who have been, and still are, a part of this club, and what it takes to reach the 150-game mark. Considering the history of the Crusaders, only a handful of names adorn that list — in part because so many of those synonymous with Super Rugby success here also had All Blacks commitments or required extended breaks. I think of guys like my great mate Wyatt Crockett who became the first man in history to reach 200 Super Rugby caps in 2018, and that competitive little bastard Andy Ellis who was capped 154 times by the club before heading overseas. Corey Flynn, the epitome of a team man, had given his all for us 151 times. Now I had joined them, one of four to have surpassed the mark.

I loved walking out onto the stadium that night, down the tunnel to the sound of 'Conquest of Paradise', the red flags waving in the terraces, a cold wind blowing in from the east. To have my children with me was the most special thing of all. Elle and Eden took it all in their stride, of course, adorned in their own jerseys happily walking beside me. Reuben once again stole the show when he burst into tears in my arms. It wasn't the first time he had been overawed by such an occasion. As always Bridget was there to save the day and we had some saving of our own to do as the Sharks came out biting. Curwin Bosch did his best to kick his team to victory. Mitch Hunt did his best to live up to his reputation for clutch plays and converted his own try to secure a 21-all draw.

Milestone games were never a strong suit of mine. We took it in our stride. Some points are better than none, after all. I sat in the shed afterwards and still shared a beer with the boys, my specially monogrammed jersey another for a growing collection of very special mementos. On the walls in the shed are the bronze plaques of Canterbury and Crusaders legends, screwed in place on simple boards above the benches that sit either side of the room. I was getting closer by the day to the time I would be handed my own plaque and when I would stand there with three of my best mates and we would take a screw each and attach it beneath the others.

For now, though, we are two games from the playoffs and back to winning ways. We will be in Fiji this week, to take on the Chiefs in Suva. Looking to extend our victory march. Every win is crucial. Every win is earned . . .

There's only so much sitting on the couch I could cope with over the summer following the World Cup victory. I knew it would take a little time to readjust to home life again, just as it always did after long tours and longer seasons, but it was far more pronounced after the elation of such a big moment. It's a constant challenge to not get too wrapped up in the job, but everything about the week of World Cup celebration had been on a different plane, and we had all willingly lived at that level for as long as we were able. Now it was over, and I didn't really know what to do with myself other than play with a 10-month-old baby and go to bed early.

It was still a thrill to be out around town and to have conversations with people about the win and what it meant to them. It seemed as though everyone wanted to shout me a beer or a cuppa, or put a dinner on the tab, and for that I was always grateful. I caught myself thinking back: the memory of seeing

Bridget when we had finally got back to the team hotel after the final and the celebration under the stand at Eden Park; the hug my mum gave me, the one that seemed to last forever; the smile on my dad's face that would not go away, his firm handshake and the fact nothing needed to be said; a walk to a burger joint with my mate Andy Ellis at whatever hour it was by then. Typical, really. That's where the night ended for two world champions, in a bloody Wendy's restaurant.

The memories I knew would never fade, but the euphoria would, and soon enough it had. It was time to get back on the grind and by the first week of January I was more than ready to hit the ground running at Rugby Park. It was good to have had a long spell but also great to be able to get in with the team earlier than I normally would. We felt like we had some unfinished business after the marathon 2011 season. Christchurch was still a shattered city, and there was more pain to come for many of the people most affected by the quakes, but we had a new 'temporary' stadium and a job to do. It was the same job we had every year: to win a title.

There was a fresh buzz around rugby that year. New Zealand had been captivated by the Rugby World Cup and the success of the All Blacks and we wanted to make sure those of us who had been a part of it gave as much back as we could. The Canterbury boys had also won the National Provincial Championship in 2011, and they too were buoyed by their own success. For my part, I already had my sights set on the next world cup, and the road to Twickenham started at Rugby Park, Christchurch.

As had become customary, we began the season proper against the Blues at Eden Park, clinging on for a one-point win in a torrid affair that never reached any great heights as a spectacle.

We played the game with a little more than a third of the ball and tactically we were all over the show. Dan Carter was out injured after the World Cup and Tyler Bleyendaal was finding his feet as a first-five, but we had more than enough experience in the side to help him drive the game and simply didn't use it. We kicked the ball away as often as we got it and spent most of the game tackling. We took the victory, but none of us were convinced that we were on the right track. The following week we were beaten by the Highlanders and deservedly so. We had played exactly the same way as the week before. I could tell the season was going to get niggly.

It proved to be another one of those inconsistent years. The team was in great heart under Todd Blackadder, Daryl Gibson and Dave Hewett, but at key times we seemed to fade as if we were a poor facsimile of the team we knew we could be. We could string together runs of solid wins and then inexplicably come unstuck in a game we were heavily favoured to win. The nadir came with a 19–28 loss to the Rebels in Melbourne during which I was dropped in a lineout, sustaining a painful pelvic injury. I don't know what it was for me that season but as the June test window neared, I was beginning to feel every bump and niggle, and began to find myself forced from the field or missing out on selection. I was hoping that the high ankle sprain I had suffered the year before wasn't a sign that my body was beginning to feel the effects of long seasons and the rigours of test-match footy. I don't know if hope really has anything to do with it.

When the June test window opened, I assembled with the All Blacks in Auckland ahead of a three-test series against Ireland. Steve Hansen had been elevated to the head coach position and Ian Foster had been brought in to be an assistant. Steve wasted no time in stamping his mark on the team, and I received my first invitation to join the leaders' group. It was a confirmation for me that I had earned my stripes as an All Black. Over the last couple of seasons, I felt I had grown in confidence with every passing week in the team, but to be given that extra responsibility was a massive honour and one I took very seriously. I wanted to make sure that I was a voice for everyone in the team, and Steve wanted everyone in the team to have a voice.

That was one of the noticeable differences between Steve and Graham Henry: their approach to the squad dynamics. I had got on with Graham well, but much of our relationship was built upon the fact I had quickly become a starter in the side and therefore had the chance to communicate with him daily. Graham was a ruthless competitor with a steely focus on what was important for the game at hand. Therefore, if you weren't necessary for that week's job, you could find yourself on the outer pretty quickly. It can be a lonely place for a player, standing on the fringe of the All Blacks, never quite knowing where you stand. Graham was not the greatest at keeping the guys on the edge completely involved with the team. I think some of those guys resented the way that made them feel, even though it was never through any malicious intent on Graham's part.

It's an easy trap for head coaches to get caught in, even the most experienced of them, and as the players have changed it has become imperative for coaches to be ever-more inclusive. That was certainly obvious when Steve took the reins. The 'All Blacks within the All Blacks' mentality needed to change, and he was going to change it. Steve was not without his idiosyncrasies of course. He could be deviously manipulative when he wanted to be, painfully cryptic too, and needed his people to know that ultimately he was in charge. For all that, though, there was an awful lot of softness underneath, and we could tell that he genuinely cared about all his players in a way that Graham could never fully express.

We had a great mix of guys in the team for that Irish series with the experienced core augmented by the addition of youngsters such as Beauden Barrett, Brodie Retallick, Sam Cane, Aaron Smith, Julian Savea and Luke Romano. We could all see the collective talent in that rookie group, but few of us could have known how crucial those players would become in the years that followed. For those of us who had been there for the World Cup victory, Steve had a simple message: Yes, we were the current world champions, but why should that come as a surprise? You worked for it, you earned it, and now it's time to go and play like it. In other words, a World Cup win was the starting point. His ultimate goal was for us to become the most dominant team in sport. And that started with a new style of play.

Up until 2011, rugby had been a pretty simple game for the forwards, and that's where we believed we could evolve the game to all new levels. There had been no real set plays for the pack, instead we had used simple calls about where the ball was going and where we might need to get ourselves to in order to be involved in the next play. We were simply chasing the ball rather than using it in a meaningful way. We wanted to put some genuine structure in place: our locks in the middle of the field, our props running in pods, and our ball-running loosies working their way to the edge or running directly off the halfback. Essentially, we wanted to create overlaps and opportunities across the width of the park.

The rush defences that were to become common practice were still in their nascent stage and teams weren't then coming at us the way they would learn to. On the flipside, very few teams were using the structures we were putting in place and even if they were, they perhaps didn't have the variety of ball carriers that we could muster. We wanted to use the ball to beat the man and to run square, and we wanted everyone in the team to be able to do it. It was perfect timing for the redevelopment of our game. We had an injection of exciting talent who all wanted to be at the forefront of a revolution, and we had the experience to pull off the experiment.

Suddenly, I found myself with plenty of space to express myself. I had the opportunity through the new structure to have a crack, and to use the skills that I had developed over a long period of time. The real joy in the plan was that the opportunities were all born from the positioning rather than pattern learning. Many of the plays were ad libbed, but they were only possible because we were getting ourselves set in the right parts of the field. Everything was designed to stress the defensive line so that as soon as a team overcommitted, we would have the extra numbers to hurt them.

Unfortunately for Ireland, we unleashed the beast in the opening test at Eden Park, with Aaron Smith and Brodie Retallick outstanding on debut and Julian Savea stealing the show with a hat-trick in his first test. I was gutted not to score a try of my own after regathering a restart and tearing off down-field, only to be dragged down just before the line. It didn't matter in the end as we cruised to a 42–10 victory. A week later we were brought back down to earth. On a cold and miserable night in Christchurch, Ireland found their defensive venom and the scores were locked up at 19-all before a 78th-minute dropped goal saved the All Blacks blushes. I watched the moment from the bench where I had been sitting since taking a head knock late in the first half.

I would be teased for years after my halftime chat with Luke

Romano and Sam Whitelock during which they were trying to tell me about our attacking lineout positioning, holding up fingers to indicate where we were all supposed to stand. I could barely follow what was going on and ended up asking where our hooker was supposed to be. Of course, he was throwing the ball! It was at that point they told Doc to pull me out of the game. The effects of concussion would keep me out of the final test in Hamilton, which was a pity. The boys got back on the horse that night and destroyed the Irish 60-nil.

Injuries would continue to dog me once Super Rugby restarted, and a few weeks before the playoffs I broke a rib in a rugged and fiery match with the Chiefs. My Super season was over at that point and I could only watch on as the boys went down to the Chiefs in the semi-final in Hamilton. Another year and sill no cigar.

Injury disruptions may have become part of my life, but it was a disruption of quite another kind that was the standout moment of that year's inaugural Rugby Championship. We had started with back-to-back wins over Australia in Sydney and in Auckland and were in preparation for the first test against Argentina in Wellington. Right after the captain's run on the Friday I received a text from Bridget telling me she wasn't feeling the best. Bridget was due to give birth the following week, but she assured me that baby wasn't coming right then and there. An hour later she called me. The baby was coming.

All I could do was find the next available flight and try to get back to Christchurch on time. The next plane was leaving at 6.30 and I managed to get myself on it. All I knew at this stage was that Bridget had gone to hospital. I was seated in the rear of the plane and I explained to the service manager what was happening and asked if there was any way I could get off before the other passengers. More than a few had already turned their heads to look at me, wondering why on earth I was leaving Wellington the night before a test there! The inflight service manager was kind enough to ask everyone to stay in their seats so I could get off first and I ran to the taxi stand and headed for the hospital.

I missed my second daughter Eden's birth by 10 minutes.

Bridget was staying overnight at the hospital so I went home for a sleep and brought Elle back the next morning to see her new sister. She walked in and saw a baby on her mum and immediately burst into tears. It was the start of a healthy sibling rivalry. I still had the test to play that night and was booked to fly back to Wellington at midday. A couple of hours before my scheduled departure, I got a call from the team. No propeller planes were landing in Wellington. I was now scheduled to catch a flight to Auckland and another back to Wellington. I kissed my baby and girls goodbye and hightailed it back to the airport.

In the guidebook on good preparation to play a test match, landing at 4.30 pm after three hours of plane travel, having missed every single second of team routine, will not be high on the list. Fortunately, I still went out and played all right, and we got a satisfactory if not overly impressive win. The next day I was back home to my family and our new addition, before heading to Dunedin, La Plata, Johannesburg, Brisbane and the end-of-year tour. I vowed to work on our family planning after that. And to make sure I showered Bridget in gifts for life.

I was in the leadership group now and very keen to build my leadership profile within the team. We were challenged to grow ourselves as leaders and to use our position to be demanding of ourselves and of others. We met each Sunday to work out a clear direction for the week ahead and made arrangements to instigate any conversations that needed to be had with guys in the team. I had grown increasingly comfortable with doing that and it was nice to be able to hone that style in an official capacity.

Richie was great at utilising me to be more of a voice for him on and off the field. He would look to me if something needed to be said so he could focus on the bigger picture. I loved the role, and during the tour I got the chance to captain the side for the first time, against Italy at the Stadio Olimpico, the scene of some of New Zealand's most memorable Olympics moments. It was good to feel nervous again before that game, but I was ready for the honour and privilege of being an All Blacks captain. We won the match and I had a cheeky thought to myself: I can now call myself an undefeated All Blacks captain.

Heading into the last game of the year against England at Twickenham we were yet to taste a loss. The closest we had come was an 18-all draw with Australia in the third Bledisloe Cup match in Brisbane and so we had a chance to become the first team to get through an international season unbeaten. We were excited by the challenge ahead and went out for a team dinner on Tuesday in great spirits. By midnight I was vomiting, among other things, in my hotel bathroom. I called Doc to say I was no good. She simply said, 'You're not alone.'

Whatever I had went through the entire team over the next 72 hours and by game time everyone was shattered. The English were terrific that day and had obviously done a lot of research into how we played. They were able to put enormous pressure on our attack and we just couldn't find a way through. It is folly to make excuses for a loss. We should have been better than we were that day and we couldn't hide from that fact. Steve Hansen called it our 'rock under the beach towel', which was the perfect metaphor for how we felt.

I hated losing. It didn't matter what team I was playing for, every loss felt the same. I never wanted to go out in public after being defeated because I always felt I had let the fans down. Maybe I overestimated the importance of these things to other people, but I couldn't help the way I felt. In saying that, the after-match functions in the UK were, by and large, great affairs and I did enjoy being part of an old-school tradition that had long ago lapsed in our part of the world. I liked the fact we could finish a game and, win or lose, at least share a beer with the guys we had played against. The speeches after the England game, however, almost turned me off for good.

There is a time and a place for a good gloating, but it's probably not in an official function while the team you just beat are standing there. I have no idea who the fish-head was who delivered that night a masterclass in inane prattle about England now being officially the best team in the world, but he provided a lifetime of motivation. It was the end of the season, we were hurting from a loss and we were in no mood to celebrate anything, but after listening to that speech it's fair to say we got serious value from the RFU bar tab.

The rock under the beach towel became my rallying call for the following season. It was another frustrating year with the Crusaders, one that ended in yet another semi-final defeat to a Chiefs team that would go on to defend its title. We had begun to struggle against New Zealand teams, or maybe they had sensed some vulnerability in what we were doing and had sniffed blood. They were definitely arming up on us, and none more so than the Chiefs who had changed the way they played, hitting more players around the rucks and throwing bodies into breakdowns with genuine venom. Sam Cane and Brodie Retallick were massive for them in this department, but they had great depth and power right across the park.

The Chiefs had a sensational coaching group, with Dave Rennie, Tom Coventry and Wayne Smith all master craftsmen in their particular areas of strength, and they were bloody smart in the way they played. About the best thing about that semi-final defeat is that we learned plenty from it and implemented that knowledge the following year.

I somehow managed to wreck my big toe during the Super Rugby season, which was a crazy injury really and one I felt slightly embarrassed about, given it kept me out of action for a much longer period than I imagined it would. It turns out that a big toe is quite important when you're trying to run. I should have thought of that before I ripped all the ligaments out of it. I was happy at least that the recovery time wasn't long. I had been told that in the absence of Richie McCaw I would be the captain of the All Blacks for the June series against France and wanted desperately to stamp my mark with the skipper's armband on.

Being that little bit older, and entrusted with the captaincy, I probably felt that it was my time to dominate — not just to be the best number eight on the park but to be the best player on the park. Injury setbacks aside, I had become so familiar with how much my body could handle and how far I could push myself mentally and that was the question that was circulating in my head every week — how could I go out and be the best? Through that year I think I found the recipe. The way we were playing was giving me opportunities out wide, and chances for offloads, and the freedom to do all the things that give a team a competitive advantage. I felt during that All Blacks season that all the work I had put in over the last decade was now paying a dividend.

It was an unbelievable thrill to captain the side in an official capacity for an entire series. I knew that I had a chance to showcase my leadership skills across the four weeks and to have a greater impact on the team than I had previously. I leapt at the opportunity, hell-bent on doing it justice. The captaincy was much more than a symbol to me; it came with a massive obligation to be the best I could be for myself and for everyone in the team. It had a rejuvenating effect and, combined with the forced layoff during the Super season, helped me to go out and play well. It was never a question of holding back for me, no matter who I was playing for, but this opportunity felt akin to being let off the leash.

France came to play in the opening match at Eden Park, just as we had expected. Before the match we had been very calm about what we had planned to do and how we were going to execute, but the French are nothing if not unorthodox and they found new and interesting ways to unsettle our structure and slow our ball down. It was a perfect night in Auckland and we never quite made the most of the conditions, fighting our way to a narrow halftime lead and failing to score a second-half try on the way to a 10-point victory. The following week, all the things that went wrong for us in Auckland suddenly went right. Our defence led the way in Christchurch that night and Aaron Cruden was sensational at first-five. It's hard to know whether our pressure or France's seeming indifference was the biggest contributing factor in the 30-nil win, but we were happy enough to know we had shaken at least some of the rust from the opening week.

The biggest message from me to the team ahead of the final

game in New Plymouth was to stay focused on our game. There is always a risk against the French that you can spend too much time thinking about what they might do, and not enough thinking about what you have to do. We had locked up the Gallaher Cup, but there was a bigger goal in mind, one that had been percolating since the England defeat in November. Now was not the time to slip up.

A little Rene Ranger magic came in handy on that cold night in New Plymouth, and a try to hometown boy Beauden Barrett iced what was until then a half-risen cake. The final score read 24–9 but, crucially, we had wrapped up the series 3-nil and could look ahead with some positivity and zero complacency. The loss against England the year before had not been spoken about in the June series, as much as some of us may have harboured the hurt for a dose of personal inspiration. To us, the 2013 year was just another chance to go out and win games. That is what we wanted to do, and during that year's Rugby Championship that's exactly what we did.

The most memorable match of the championship was undoubtedly the South African clash at a packed and feral Ellis Park. I loved playing there in front of a raucous and partisan crowd. It was an intimidating place, made even more so by the thin air and the thick history of All Blacks heartbreak. Everything about the game had a real sense of occasion. A jumbo jet flyover, reminiscent of that famous Rugby World Cup final in 1995, left us in no doubt we were in for a test for the ages, and so it proved to be. The equation was a simple one: win with a bonus point and we win the championship. We all knew what we had to do.

What unfolded that day was 80 minutes of the most pulsating rugby I have ever been a part of. Despite the lead changing often in the second half, I felt completely in control of my own game and was certain the rest of the guys felt the same about theirs. Down 17–24, it was Beauden Barrett who scored a late go-ahead try and, moments later, Richie McCaw added another to put the game out of reach of the Boks. At fulltime we had prevailed 38–27 and claimed the Rugby Championship. There is a series of photos taken at fulltime showing us strewn all over the pitch, absolutely spent and with no energy to even celebrate the win. We would use those photos many times to remind ourselves of what absolute commitment looks like.

At what point did the perfect season enter the conversation? I'm not entirely sure. It must have been on the end-of-year tour, but it was like one of those stories that has no source. Somehow it just became a talking point. We had already had a year of learning new structures to lay over the top of what we had absorbed the year before, and we were only just beginning to bed in how we wanted to play the game over the next couple of seasons. No one had wanted to add any more complication to what was already a big-thinking itinerary.

The tour itself had been split to factor in the workloads of the players. Some of the squad headed to Japan for a one-off test against the home side in Tokyo while the rest of us departed for Europe and a return test against France in Paris. Paris was one of the great destinations for us, a place steeped in history and haughtiness, and the Stade de France always felt as if it were only ever a moment away from turning into a riot. We accounted for *Les Tricolores* in front of 81,000 rambunctious French fans and headed to Twickenham to avenge the previous year's loss. It was mission accomplished, but not without a struggle. A lineout special for an early opening try had given us some hope that we could really make a statement to silence the buoyant crowd, but we never quite earned the breathing space and settled for a 30–22 win.

The plan had been to send a number of players home before the last test against Ireland, but there was no longer any chance of that. We had amassed 13 wins that season and had one test to go. There was no getting away from it — the perfect season was on the line and not a single player wanted to miss out on being in Dublin for a tilt at a special piece of history. It was probably the best decision we had made as a team that year. Off the field at least.

Nothing can truly prepare you for a test like the one we played on 23 November at Aviva Stadium in Dublin in front of 51,000 passionate fans. Or maybe everything you've ever done prepares you for just such a game. We got absolutely blown off the park in the opening 40 minutes. We were outmuscled, outrun, outthought and outplayed. After 18 minutes the scoreline read Ireland 19, New Zealand 0. The Irish forwards, inspired by veterans like Rory Best and Paul O'Connell, Cian Healy and Jamie Heaslip, took us to school in every facet of play. They were three tries up by the time we realised we were actually in a test match. Rarely had any of the team experienced that kind of blitzkrieg. We were shellshocked and in desperate need of divine intervention.

Instead, we had a bus. When Julian Savea crashed over before halftime we started to come to our senses. Johnny Sexton kicked a penalty before the break to take the score to 22–7 at the turn, and inside the sheds we just took a long hard look at each other. It wasn't about perfect records or other feats of history. It was a game that presented opportunities just like any other. All we had to do was crack the code. When we came out for the second half, we were at least halfway transformed, but it took 25 minutes before we managed to get Ben Franks across the line. That took the score to 22–17 and once we got within striking distance, I could tell that the entire team believed we could win.

I mean that genuinely. At no point did I look around the faces in the All Blacks side and see anything other than sheer determination, but it would not be until the 80th minute of the game that we got a chance to show what we could do when Jack McGrath copped a penalty on our own 10-metre line. What happened next was this: we all said play it. Aaron Smith tapped and passed to Ben Smith who made 10 good metres to the halfway line at which point we recycled and Aaron Cruden passed to me on the right for another 5-metre gain. We stayed to the right with Beauden Barrett just making the gainline 6 metres in from touch, from where two passes got us back to the midfield through Sam Whitelock for a loss of 5 metres.

Ma'a Nonu then hit a flat pass on the left and tipped on for Ben Smith who cut back into midfield and set just short of the Irish 10-metre line. Aaron then hit Owen Franks two wide on the right and he tipped on to Ben Franks who set the ball again just short of the Irish 10-metre line. After that five of us stacked on the left and Aaron Cruden took a wide pass from Aaron Smith and passed to Ben Smith who passed to me. I ran as hard as I could and slipped an inside ball back to Ben Smith who finished 15 metres in from the left-hand touch, and 2 metres short of the Irish 22.

Ma'a Nonu then appeared out of nowhere and took a short ball on the left, which he in turn fed back inside to Ryan Crotty who was tackled 10 out from the Irish line. Aaron Smith then went right, and Owen Franks settled things with a hit-up in the middle. Aaron Smith got to the ball quickly and headed right again where Julian Savea fed Liam Messam who was dragged down 5 metres inside the right-hand touch and 5 from the Irish goal-line. Aaron Smith threw a wild pass to the left that went behind the front-running Franks brothers and was scooped up on the bounce by Ma'a Nonu who pulled off a trademark diagonal run to the left and was caught 15 metres from the goal-line and 20 metres inside the touchline.

At that point Aaron Cruden made the decision to hit the left where he took the pass from Aaron Smith and fed Dane Coles who ran down the tramlines and slipped an offload to Ryan Crotty to score. It was the most beautiful try I have ever seen. Made even more so when Aaron Cruden got a second crack at kicking the conversion after an early Irish charge and sent it through the middle for a 24–22 win and a first-ever perfect season. I can guarantee you that while we were jubilant, we were also feeling for the Irish. Had we been on the other side of that equation, I would have been distraught.

There was not much that could top that Irish game, nor an undefeated year, but there was one last bit of good fortune for me personally: I was named International Player of the Year by World Rugby. There was no glittering ceremony or reception, but I didn't need that. I think someone chucked me a trophy at a Crusaders game the following year. That seemed perfectly reasonable to me.

13

OFF BALANCE

Winners are grinners and we are grinning from ear to
ear. It is 6 July and the Crusaders are champions
again. The changing room is filled to the brim with our
loved ones and the people who make all this possible.
Luke Romano is spraying champagne all over the place.
Every one of us is in a pair of ski goggles and in high spirits.
I can see Shane Fletcher handing a cell phone to George
Bridge and then to Sevu Reece. Each takes it and wanders
out the back door. I know who is on the line, and I know
what the message will be: enjoy tonight but take it easy.
We will need you to be ready when the All Blacks assemble.
I chuckle to myself. It feels like a long time ago since Richie
McCaw gave me the shoulder tap.

The Jaguares were tough out there tonight. The body
knows it has been in a scrap. It's amazing to think of how
far that team has come in just four years. We all thought
they had added a new dimension to the tournament, but
their rise has been nothing short of phenomenal. They took
us all the way in the game, made us work for every single
point. I respected that. It made this feeling even better.

It's the last time for me, I know it. Tomorrow I'll be back

to attach my name to the wall. Tonight, though, I am going to celebrate every second. Dad is here, standing in the corner saying not much. Gareth and Mark are here too. All the Read boys together for another special night. I don't want this night to end, to be honest. For 13 years this has been what I have strived for, to win titles for the Crusaders. Now I have four of them. I couldn't think of a better way to end.

The families eventually leave and just the team remains. We shower and change, all the while the music stays loud, and the boys laugh their way through the beers and the fried chicken. We will meet the families again soon, but this is a time just for us. When we are ready Sam calls us all to attention. There is one last thing to remember tonight: we are a team and we look after each other. We all know what is expected of us, and no one wants to ruin this night for the club or for anyone else.

We will enjoy it, though. Of course we will. And I will enjoy it as much as anyone. You have to when the times are good. Especially when you have lived through the bad . . .

It was late June 2014 when I finally broke down in front of Bridget. We were alone in a beige-carpeted hotel room. Outside, a drizzling mist cast the colours of city lights and clung to the windows. It was late in the evening after the third All Blacks test against England. I had played just 40 minutes. For 20 of those minutes, against all my natural instincts, I had been afraid of facing contact. I was tired of the headaches and the dizziness, and the constant, menacing fear. I couldn't do this any more. I stood there with my wife, and she held me as I sobbed.

This was not how I had envisaged the year panning out. Whoever imagines their life sliding off the rails in a nondescript Hamilton hotel room? No, this was supposed to be the best year so far. It was my second year as captain of the Crusaders, and we had plenty of work to do in order to improve on the semi-final defeats of the last two seasons. When Todd Blackadder had offered me the captaincy of the Crusaders at the beginning of 2013, I did not hesitate to accept. Richie McCaw had led the side for eight seasons, lifting the trophy on three occasions — a feat matched only by Todd himself — and I dreamed of following in their footsteps, to be the man who got to stand on the podium on behalf of the team and raise that trophy high above my head in triumph. It had been five years since a Crusaders captain had felt what that was like, and that was long enough.

The Rugby World Cup was visible now, a destination on the near horizon, and planning had already begun in earnest. There were guys knocking on the selection door of the All Blacks, all of them gifted athletes who had the same aspirations as those of us already inside. It felt as if many of the senior members of the team were at a career crossroads, where desire intersected with the harsh reality of professional rugby's physical toll. There was positive competitive tension in the team, one that the previous year's historic run only served to heighten. I loved knowing that others were coming for the jersey I wore, and that I was prepared to do anything I needed to do to keep it. Continual improvement was the catch-cry for the year.

For all our talk as a team about hitting the ground running, it was not the start we were after. I missed the first game against the Chiefs at home and returned for the round two match against the Blues at Eden Park. We lost both, the second in worse fashion than the first. We were then able to claw our way to wins against the Stormers and the Rebels. We never panicked as a team. Instead we dug in and trusted that our roster was more than capable of rediscovering something of the magic that had deserted us. We doubled down the following week preparing for a home match against the Hurricanes. Having already shelled points to two New Zealand teams, we were not keen on helping out a third. There was a bit of personal zest to enliven the build-up as well: the match was set to be my 100th for the Crusaders.

On 28 March, I walked down the tunnel leading from the changing sheds out to the floodlit pitch of Addington Stadium. Memories of the first time I played for the Crusaders came flooding back as I emerged into the light and broke into a jog, the team holding back to give me a chance to enjoy those few seconds. I soaked in the sound of the crowd as I waited for the others to join me, exhaling all the nervous energy that had built up inside the shed in those minutes before the knock on the door. I was ready for this one.

And then, I got hit by a bus.

Julian Savea knocked me out cold. The game was barely 25 minutes old when I attempted to tackle him and that is all I remember of the action. I was taken from the field, but there was no requirement for a head injury assessment — there was no way I was going back on after that collision. After fulltime I was presented with a commemorative mere pounamu (greenstone club) by the Rugby Union President, Ian MacRae, but I couldn't answer any questions about the game so I bluffed my way through the television interview after the presentation. We had lost, 26–29, that much I knew. The curse of the milestone was alive and well. I, on the other hand, was not well at all.

I'd had bad head knocks before but never had I endured any real lingering concussive effects. It was a foreign feeling to me to wake the next morning feeling queasy and disorientated. I shook it off, to be honest. We were boarding a plane for South Africa that morning and I figured a good, long-haul rest would help me feel normal again. Protocols demanded that I not suit up for the game the following week against the Lions at Johannesburg so I had plenty of time to let things settle before facing the Cheetahs. Sure enough, I improved over the following days and trained and played without issue in the Bloemfontein game when the locals got their first taste of a left wing by the name of Nemani Nadolo. That giant Fijian carved up all day long, scoring a hat-trick in just his second start. It's fair to say we had found our magic — all 130 kilograms of it.

I never took a win in South Africa for granted, and securing two on the bounce gave us great heart as we returned to New Zealand for a date with the Chiefs in Hamilton. I would tell you how much I enjoyed the one-point win that night, but I copped a swinging arm in the head and was knocked out again. I sat in the changing shed, without any recollection of leaving the field or walking inside. I was more pissed off than anything as the night went on — annoyed that I had received another head knock and was now likely to miss more of the season. That annoyance soon turned to concern. This time the symptoms did not dissipate as quickly as they had before. I spent the next week suffering from intermittent headaches and haziness. One minute I would be fine, the next in a daze.

The following week was no better. Neither was the week after that. All the staff at the Crusaders agreed that we should just take things easy, let the head settle and then slowly come back to play.

I stayed sidelined for four weeks, the symptoms still coming and going. Mainly I suffered them in silence, which had been my way. I would share details of how I was feeling with Bridget — largely because she was starting to wonder why her husband was taking afternoon naps instead of helping with the girls — but I never liked to burden too many people with my problems. There was also a part of me that didn't want to jeopardise my season, or to show weakness. I would learn the hard way that when it comes to the head, silence is not the best course of action.

We played the Force in the last game before the June break. I was eager to get some minutes given the first test of the England series was now just a week away. It was a Friday-night game in Christchurch and it was good to be back out there, until I took another knock. It was not as serious as the others had been, and I didn't lose consciousness, but I spent the remaining minutes worried about it, thus reducing my effectiveness in the game. The next day the symptoms — the headaches, the fogginess, the sudden onset of drowsiness — all returned with a vengeance. We had driven to North Canterbury for a family lunch during which everything hit me at once. I had to wander away from the group. I was having an anxiety attack. I thought I was going mad.

When I arrived at the All Blacks team hotel on the Sunday, I had to discuss my state with Dr Tony Page, but I didn't tell him everything. That was pure stupidity. We decided that we would reset the concussion protocols and that I would sit out the first two tests in Auckland and Dunedin. I hated missing out on playing. I had already missed out on five games for the Crusaders and now this. Weirdly, I was passing all the baseline tests — a fairly standardised practice in which players answer a set of questions at the start of the season to record a 'baseline' for cognitive function.

After a head injury, answers to those same questions will show if there has been any functional deterioration — and the symptoms came and went without explanation. I wanted so badly to be out there playing, yes, but I didn't want to risk long-term damage. That is a quandary many modern professionals know all too well.

Whether I had just convinced myself of it, or whether it was fact, by the third test in Hamilton I felt as if I was good enough to get back into training and playing. The plan was for me to play just half the match. The series had been decided in Dunedin the week before and the pressure on the boys was off. That showed in the first 10 minutes as Julian Savea crossed for two of his three tries that night. Then, at the 20-minute mark, it happened. It was just a freak contact in the tackle, an awkward collision that whipped my head backwards. It definitely rang my bell, but my one thought was, 'Man, I can't come off here!'

I knew I only had to get to halftime so I didn't tell anyone about it. I didn't want anyone to know. Selfishly, I eased off through until the break and when the boys went back out for the second half I stayed in my seat in the shed. It was a low point for sure. Outside, the crowd noise rose and fell with the action — action I wasn't a part of. Was this the reality for me? One little knock was enough to put me out of the game. That hit wasn't anything I hadn't experienced a hundred times before, and yet here I am, moping in the shed. I eventually pulled myself together, went outside, and sat with the boys to watch the rest of the game. Later I talked to Doc Page. This time I told him exactly what was going on.

That night I saw Bridget, and crumbled. I didn't want rugby to be the end of my life, but I didn't want this to be the end of my rugby. I feared the worst.

I eventually got to sleep back at our team hotel and the next morning put on a brave face for the boys as everyone said their goodbyes. Once back in Christchurch I had a heart-to-heart with Dr Deb Robinson who sent me to a concussion expert at Burwood Hospital. For close to three hours I was subjected to a battery of tests — puzzles, counting quizzes, mind games and myriad other examinations. The session reconfirmed that my brain function was fine, which was why I was having no trouble passing the baseline tests. The bad news was my vestibular system, which comprises the inner ear balance organs and the parts of the brain that coordinate and process balance information, was, well, a bit knackered.

Things started to make sense. I had been getting headaches while driving, just from the act of looking left and right, and even innocuous pursuits — watching my girls bouncing on a trampoline for instance — would cause me to lose focus and feel dizzy. Now I could see why. In short, my brain didn't trust the signals it was getting from my ears and eyes. Those spatial orientation signals from the inner ears — the ones providing information on motion and equilibrium — were no longer equal and opposite so the brain interpreted the difference as constant movement, hence the vertigo-like symptoms and the headaches. There was also an impact on the vestibulo-ocular reflex which maintains clear vision during movement. That accounted for the intermittent haziness.

The reason all of this came and went was that the brain, being the remarkable thing that it is, realises it can no longer trust the information it is getting and works to reduce the signals. When it does that, many of the symptoms go away. It is the brain's way of turning down the television during the annoying ad breaks.

While we were searching for a diagnosis, Doc Deb had also suggested that I go to a psychiatrist. There was a concern that being so wound up was only making things worse. At first, I baulked at what I thought she was implying: that I was manifesting my problem through worry. Yes, I was worried all right, but I wasn't making any of this stuff up. I soon realised that wasn't the point she was making and I was right into the idea. I was in a fragile state, and having been living with the fear of potential brain injury, I was ready for some outside assistance. I was glad I went.

I now had a choice to face with the Crusaders. I was captain of the team and we had just three rounds left to secure a playoff spot. I wanted to get back out there and lead again, so I devised a plan with the medical staff. If I took any knock that concerned me during the upcoming Hurricanes game, we would instantly pull the pin on the season. If I got through it without a worsening of the symptoms, we would plan ahead and make sure all the help I needed was there to work through the balance issue. I agreed to the scheme and, while I didn't feel great, I got back on the field against the Hurricanes at the end of June.

I got through the game and vowed to carry on. It was not the easiest period of my career. I would have to sit in the car for a few minutes after driving to training, just to let the headaches pass, and I would pop up out of breakdown work on Rugby Park and need a moment to gather my thoughts. I was also having to nap most afternoons just to shut out all the stimuli that sent my brain into overdrive. I began a course of vestibular rehabilitation therapy (VRT), designed to desensitise the balance system to problem movement, and to enhance the brain's ability to compensate. The programme was based on repeated small exercises, like walking down the hallway placing one foot in front of the other, or moving my head side to side while keeping my eyes on an 'X' taped to the wall, or even flinging myself backwards onto a bed. All of them made me feel worse which was, funnily enough, exactly what they were supposed to do as the brain figured out a way to cope.

I fell into a weekly routine of VRT, psychiatrist visits and team training, all accompanied by the ongoing symptoms I had now endured for more than two months. I would have to stop the VRT on Thursday to give me a chance to feel half decent again by the weekend, and it was tough on Bridget and the girls as I just couldn't take full part in family life. My mood was greatly affected and those closest bore the brunt of that. The joyful things, like picking up the kids or chasing them around the house, was out of the question. All my physical capacity was saved for training and playing. I didn't tell any of the team about what was really going on. So much so that I would remove all the tape 'X's on the walls if we ever had guests over. I didn't need anyone asking what they were for.

It was only after the Super Rugby final in Sydney — a harrowing loss to the Waratahs who were awarded a last-minute penalty on halfway when Richie misjudged a breakdown play — that I could feel a genuine abatement of my symptoms. I had the week to replenish the tank before the first Bledisloe Cup game of the season. By the time the All Blacks assembled again I was feeling like things were settling down. Maybe I had just found something else to feel sick about. That Super Rugby final loss was one of the most deflating experiences of my rugby career, an elevator drop moment of horror, made worse for us because the Waratahs coach was Daryl Gibson, himself a former Crusader and teammate of Todd Blackadder's — not to mention an ex-assistant coach of ours. Todd never let us know how much that result cut him, but he didn't have to for us to know.

Mentally, I had been rocked by everything I had gone through and there was no doubt my performances had suffered as a result. Yes, I'd had my share of injuries, but this had been different. For the first time in my career I was playing knowing I wasn't bulletproof, that this game could have consequences far greater than broken bones. Bones heal, ligaments can be reattached and cuts can be stitched. Months of missing out on the fun of being a dad can never be replaced, and shutting out the world is no way to live in it. Actually, no, it wasn't that I was waking up to my own mortality. It was just that I was starting to more accurately count the cost of what I did, and I didn't like adding it up.

I did enjoy being back in the All Blacks environment, though, as I always had done. We all knew what was at stake and how few chances there were left before next year's big tournament. That year's Rugby Championship was a battle royale, starting with a 12-all draw in Sydney against the Wallabies. There were some harsh words for the team on the Monday after that. Eye contact was at a premium in the review session. We knew we were in the firing line and atoned for such an insipid showing when we hosted the return leg at Eden Park. It was a rebound for the ages, with Aaron Cruden playing one of the best games of his international career and Brodie Retallick and Sam Whitelock foreshadowing what they would produce a year later at the Rugby World Cup. It was probably my best game of the year too, but my job was made much easier by a front five that savaged the Australian forwards. By the end of the match we had posted our highest-ever score against Australia at home, recording a 51–20 victory.

Things didn't always go to plan that international season. In Wellington against the Springboks it felt as if we had run them off the park all night, but in reality we could only deliver a four-point win. At Ellis Park we thought we had them at 25–24 with just over a minute left on the clock. It had been an epic test, the fortunes of both sides ebbing and flowing on a bright and warm afternoon. Turns out if you replay something enough on the stadium screen, the referee will eventually take notice, and action. In those final moments of the match, the Television Match Official ruled a penalty against Liam Messam for an illegal shot on South African legend Schalk Burger, and Pat Lambie kicked a goal from somewhere near Pretoria. It was an amazing kick, one worthy of my eternal admiration had it not won the game for the Boks. It was the end of a 22-match unbeaten run, but we could only take our medicine and move on.

We at least got to experience the other side of that coin against Australia in Brisbane in the final Bledisloe Cup test. Down 22–28 with time up on the clock we once again found a way to work ourselves into a scoring position from which Malakai Fekitoa crossed for an injury-time try. Colin Slade then clutch-kicked the conversion for the win. That comeback belief was so central to our ideology, and I think of all the tricks in our book, that was the one thing that always put the most fear into the opposition — they knew we could take them well past the 80th minute.

Variety, as they say, is the spice of life, and November's northern tour kicked off in Chicago. None of us really knew what to make of the venture, but we were all excited to touch down in the windy city and to experience something new. We all loved it immediately, and the week was spent sating our appetite for all things American. So many of the team are huge US sports fans, so to get the chance to head to a Bulls game or get to see the Blackhawks live was a genuine thrill. Many of us just marvelled at the scale of that great city, walking across the DuSable Bridge as the tour boats chugged underneath, down Michigan Avenue past the Tribune Tower and the Wrigley Building, along the magnificent mile. Running out onto Soldier Field, home of the Bears, and seeing 68,000 people in those towering stands, sent chills up my spine. I was stoked to captain the side that day and to see how many people came from all over the US to watch us play the Eagles.

I had grown in confidence each time I had been given the chance to captain the All Blacks and after the USA experience it hit home that I very much wanted the job after Richie McCaw finished up. I did have a wee chuckle, thinking I was on the verge of leading the team, considering how quiet I had been when I first arrived and how desperate I had been to keep my head down and just work. I guess it was a philosophy that paid off for me. I was the same at Canterbury and had been offered the chance to lead that team; the Crusaders was no different. I wasn't the young, quiet bloke in this team any more. By the end of that season I had amassed 72 caps for my country and was signed with New Zealand until the end of 2017. The British and Irish Lions would be coming that year. How good would it feel to captain New Zealand in a series like that?

I let that thought percolate for the remainder of the northern tour, during which the team came through tests against England, Scotland and Wales, and was happy to have formulated another goal to keep me going through the off-season and beyond. Losing the Super Rugby final still pissed me off. Over the last couple of seasons I had ticked off some scarcely believable achievements — being a part of the unbeaten test year, the World and New Zealand Player of the Year awards, the chance to captain the All Blacks in a series, and the elevation to the captaincy of the Crusaders. Yet there was one thing missing: I still hadn't had a chance to raise that Super Rugby trophy over my head. I visualised that moment so much that I could see individual faces in the imaginary crowd and taste the celebratory bubbles. Next season we would give it a crack. Definitely.

Thinking big was a powerful tool for me. I finished the season still suffering from the ongoing vestibular issues but knew that a decent break and a chance to rest the brain as much as the body was going to be crucial heading into what shaped as an epic season. We finished in Wales with a win and with a message from the coaching staff: the campaign for the 2015 Rugby World Cup had very much begun.

I went home for the summer vowing to keep up my rehabilitation. The symptoms would never completely go away and even to the present day I still have moments where things send me off, or the occasional week when I have to get back into some of my old VRT exercises. It's never as bad as it was, but it's there, lurking in the background, putting me off balance once in a while. Most of all I promised to get back to being a dad, and a better person to be around at home. Bridget had carried so much of the burden for me that year. I needed to do what I could, to be there for her. That was the balance that most needed to be restored.

14
BACK TO BACK

It's Friday, 24 July and Wellington has turned on a stunner. Tomorrow we play the Springboks, the last time we get to face them before our opening match of the 2019 Rugby World Cup. It's my first test of the season and I can't wait to lead the side out there tomorrow night. We all know what is expected of us, but it will be the first time we have all played together this year. Most of the Crusaders contingent stayed in New Zealand as the team travelled to Argentina. Now it is our turn to play.

It was strange to be at home watching the test on the television like everyone else. There is a feeling of helplessness when you can't be there with the boys. I'd had the chance to address the entire squad before they left, but I would have loved to be there, even if I wasn't playing. On the Thursday before they departed, we had come together in our team room at the Heritage Hotel in Auckland. I had spoken about our past, our legacy, what we stand for as All Blacks. I reminded the guys who had been there before just why they are there, and how they got there. I outlined the expectations for the new players, watching them inch forward in their chairs, just as I had done when I was a rookie.

I always try to prepare well for that first address of the season. I only get one chance to get it right, to set the tone for the entire year ahead. It's a big year, no one needs reminding of that. I look for that subtle shift in body weight when the guys lean forward just a little bit and you can tell that they are just itching to be a part of it. That's the reward for the privilege of leading. We have a chance to finish a decade of dominance this year, to do something unprecedented. If we can't get excited about that, we shouldn't be in the room.

We have discussed the opening test this week. We accepted that there was going to be some rust. All the calls are different, we're trying new things and, while there were plenty of mistakes, ultimately what worked for us was that Beaudy made line breaks through the middle and guys were putting their hands up for action. We need that baseline to work from, to say 'these are the things that worked and these are things we need to stop doing'. I just want to make sure we are focused around the rugby because with a big squad, that is where the connections all begin.

The coaches are calm. They've created a way we want to play the game in attack. We've changed the way we set up. It's not enough any more to run square off 9 and 10. We need to run hard lines off those players, and to run more of our game out the back and off our midfield rucks. We have been able to shovel the ball in the past across the line, but it doesn't work now. We have a much broader range of plays, but they will take time to bed in.

The nuances are difficult to master because in training

you have everyone available, but in a game you lose guys who are caught in a ruck or tangled up in another part of the field. So much of rugby is now pre-empted. Hesitation can kill us. We are on edge more about our own game than we are about the Boks and that is a very different feeling to what I am used to. I talked about that on Monday with the guys. Yes, we will build during the week, but we have to get our heads into the match early. The one thing about playing the Boks is that you have to be in the right mental space to put your body on the line. It will be a big game as a lot of the guys haven't played since the Super Rugby final.

We have an expectation to win and to look good doing it. We've been guilty in the past of losing games because we've worried about that. When we nail our game, we know there are not many teams in the world that can live with us. I have experienced days like that with this team. I sit back in my hotel room now and think about how good those times felt . . .

Losing my balance had helped me discover my balance. That's the easiest way to put it. After what I had gone through the year before I began to understand just how much pressure I put on myself and how many other people were affected by that. I had a family, my health was important to them as much as to me, and there were things that defined me more than tackle counts and winning percentages. Did I care about rugby any less? No, and winning was just as much of a driver for me as it always had been. I just began to care about everything else more, to gain some perspective on what I did for a living.

Above left: In the naughty chair against Tonga in the final pool match of the 2015 RWC. Not a great look for the match captain. Above right: Only a few minutes into the final and I have fractured my ankle. There was no way I was going to quit. Below: Richie and I make a statement tackle on Wallabies captain Stephen Moore. We wanted to set the tone that day, and did.

Richie and I hold the Webb Ellis Cup aloft after the World Cup presentation ceremony at Twickenham.

Left: Family time — with Eden, Bridget and Elle . . . and the spoils of victory.
Right: Sam Whitelock and I pose with our Cup winners' medals in the changing room after the final.

Leading from the front. Charging over Wales' Gareth Anscombe during the international series opener at Eden Park in 2016. I had been named captain of the All Blacks that year.

Back to the winner's circle. Jack Goodhue congratulates me after scoring a try in the 2017 Super Rugby final against the Lions in Johannesburg. It would be the Crusaders' first title in 11 seasons. A great start for coach Scott Robertson and new captain Sam Whitelock.

I'm not looking terribly impressed as French ref Jerome Garces issues a red card to Sonny Bill Williams in the second test between the All Blacks and the British and Irish Lions in Wellington, 2017.

Smiling through it. Lions skipper Sam Warburton and I hold the trophy aloft after splitting the 2017 series 1–1. The final test draw, and the controversy that went with it, was a bitter pill to swallow. Inset: Keven Mealamu presenting me with my 100th test cap after the drawn match at Eden Park. Milestone games were always complicated for me.

With Sam Whitelock after I'd presented him with his 100th test cap following the 2018 Rugby Championship/Bledisloe Cup match against the Wallabies at ANZ Stadium in Sydney.

With Prime Minister Jacinda Ardern and partner Clarke Gayford in the changing rooms after our victory over Australia at Eden Park in 2018.

The whole family was at Rugby Park in Christchurch as we celebrated the Crusaders' Super Rugby three-peat in 2019. From left: Bridget, Elle, Reuben, me and Eden.

Kapa O Pango rings out at Yokohama Stadium prior to kick-off against South Africa in our first pool match at the 2019 World Cup. We got the result we wanted.

The dream is over. Steve Hansen consoles me after our semi-final exit at Yokohama. It was gutting . . . we gave it all.

Some perspective was probably required when it came to the Crusaders results under Todd Blackadder too. While we hadn't won a title in the last six years, we had been to four semi-finals and two finals, and both finals had turned on one solitary play. There were few teams in the competition who could even dream of a record like that, but even so there was no satisfaction at Rugby Park. We understood the expectation to win — we played for the Crusaders because we loved having that legacy to look back on and to emulate. One of the hallmarks of those champion Crusaders sides was that they all knew how they wanted to play, and how to play like they wanted to. The wins reinforced that thinking, the titles proved that the plan was working.

We weren't winning titles and because of that our plan kept changing. We had great players on the roster, but we were no longer able to count on them week to week. Injury, age and the need for longer return to play protocols for the All Blacks meant there was more onus on the entire squad to deliver, and the younger guys coming in needed more detail and more clarity on their roles. The new generation was different, but not in a negative way. They just wanted to be guided by more than simple work ethic. They were coming through from school programmes that were operating with semi-professional efficiency. They were visual learners who wanted instant and constant in-depth feedback. While guys of my time had been happy to sit back quietly and watch, these boys wanted to be engaged with from the moment they walked in.

The environment was still fantastic to walk into, and we were still attracting excellent talent which showed me our off-field game was definitely on point. Guys like Scott Barrett, Codie Taylor and Mitch Drummond would have massive parts to play in the future success of the team, and more like them would join us under Todd's watch. Just as tellingly, the senior tranche of players remained deeply committed, albeit with a growing sense of frustration that we just weren't nailing the big moments. Again, that is where the detail was so important, and the messaging just needed to be clearer. Aaron Mauger, Tabai Matson and Dave Hewett were all ex-Crusaders and each of them had aspirations to be a head coach. I don't know if four such ambitious coaches in one group was the answer to the title puzzle.

We had matches that season during which we could put 50 points on a team without breaking a sweat, and others after which we just wouldn't know how we had lost. Every time we thought we had cracked the code, we would come thumping back down to earth. It was by far the most inconsistent season I had ever experienced in the colours, and of course I took it personally. I was the captain of the team and I asked myself every week what I could do to get the club on a more even keel. Ultimately, I don't think I was vocal enough when I needed to be. As it was, we missed the playoffs that season. It was a first for everyone in the team. Our final game was in Canberra where we scored a hearty victory over the Brumbies. We sat in the shed afterwards in a desultory mood, not quite knowing what to do with ourselves.

The All Blacks over those same last few years had been the converse of the Crusaders, certainly when it came to closing out the big moments. Since 2012, we had lost just twice — once to England and once to South Africa — and never at home. During that time we had come back from the brink on more occasions than I could count. The Ireland miracles in Christchurch in 2012 and in Dublin in 2013, the Ellis Park Epic in the same unbeaten year, the Australian escape in 2014 — all of them illustrated the composure we had cultivated through detail and clarity. We knew instinctively how we wanted to play and by 2015 the structures that had been put in place three seasons earlier were deeply embedded in our game-day DNA.

We had regular leadership meetings for the All Blacks during the Super Rugby season and training camps were instituted to ensure the wider squad was measured and monitored throughout the season. Those camps were critical in methodically building the hype. They were tough, but every player left energised and even more determined to be part of that Rugby World Cup squad. We had also discussed where we were as a team and how we could take our status as world rugby number one and use it to our advantage. Because we had a clear plan on our playing structure and style, the only things that mattered were mindset and execution. If we were the number one team in the world, we thought, let's act like it. Our mindset was based on dominating every team we came up against.

I felt in good shape heading into the international season, certainly in comparison to the year before. I had been able to play 10 games straight through the middle of the tournament and suffered only a minor setback when I took another heavy head knock in a late-round clash with the Waratahs. I sat out two rounds after that and returned for the last game against the Brumbies. With decent mileage on the clock, I was ready to hit the ground running when we got together in Auckland and prepared to depart for a historic first: a test match against Manu Samoa in Apia.

It was crazy to think New Zealand had never played a test match in Samoa, and from the moment we arrived in Apia we realised what all those past players had missed out on. It was an extraordinary welcome at Faleolo Airport, and all through the week thousands came along to watch training, or to wave to us as we paraded in the open-air team bus. Every street was festooned with bunting, front yards filled with shrines to the game. Apia was alive with song and bursting with colour. We were incredibly humbled by the hospitality of the Samoan people and by their appreciation for the team being there. And we were melting from the moment we touched down. The game was slated for a 3 pm kick-off on a Wednesday, which had been declared a national half holiday. It was going to be brutal on the body.

Sure enough, conditions on game day were treacherous. It was overcast and humid and by kick-off afternoon showers had greased up the pitch and made ball handling an absolute nightmare. Looking across at the Manu Samoa side during a thunderous Siva Tau we could all see familiar faces — the likes of Kahn Fotuali'i, Jack Lam, Tusi Pisi and Tim Nanai-Williams — and etched on each of them was a serious determination to do their nation proud. They did more than that on that steamy Samoan afternoon; they gave us a massive wake-up call.

We hadn't exactly rolled out an unfamiliar side for that opening test of the year. Nepo Laulala, George Moala, Brad Weber and Charlie Ngatai were all on debut, but there was more than enough experience around them to ensure things ran smoothly enough. They didn't. The Manu were in our faces all afternoon, forcing mistakes and fatiguing us in the sapping heat. Dan Carter's left boot was the only thing that produced points in the first half, discipline costing our hosts, and it wasn't until the 47th minute that we scored the first try of the match. At 22–9 heading into the final 15 minutes we had a margin but never a sense of security. When Alafoti Fa'osiliva scored for the home side and blew the roof off the Apia Park stand, that margin was cut to six.

We eventually squeaked home. Dan Carter kicked a last penalty to give us a nine-point buffer and the win. The Samoan fans were delighted at the performance of their boys and so they should have been. They were an absolute inspiration that afternoon and taught us a lesson in turning passion into performance. I hope the Samoan people enjoyed the experience as much as we did. Taking the test to America the year before had been special because we could see how it could have a positive impact on the sport there. Taking that game to Samoa was the same, but even more important because it was our responsibility to thank a nation that is so closely tied to many decades of New Zealand rugby success.

Some people may have questioned the validity of the match, but that would be both unwise and unfair. What that week did for us leading into the Rugby World Cup was priceless. It showed us how hard we were going to have to work for everything at the tournament, and it had given Steve Hansen and head trainer Nic Gill an idea: come World Cup time they were going to absolutely flog us on the training field.

The Rugby Championship that year would ultimately be won by Australia. They got the better of us in the first Bledisloe Cup test in Sydney, after we had conquered South Africa in another thrilling encounter at Ellis Park. We had our now customary return to form at Eden Park, blitzing the Wallabies in a second-half onslaught to retain the Bledisloe Cup. It was a special night for us as a team, the last test appearance on home soil for Richie McCaw, Dan Carter, Conrad Smith, Keven Mealamu and Tony Woodcock. Richie also broke the record that night for the most test appearances in world rugby, surpassing the legendary Brian O'Driscoll. We stood in the middle for the post-match presentation. No one had left the stadium, such was their adoration for the skipper. It was a remarkable scene, one that spoke volumes about hard-won respect.

Two weeks later, the squad for the Rugby World Cup was announced at Parliament in Wellington. Yes, I had expected to be on that list of names but to hear it read out was still a relief and a moment to cherish. When we gathered together in Auckland for our final preparations, Gilbert Enoka and sports psychologist Ceri Evans met with the leaders and asked us what our goals were from that point on. Mine was simple: I wanted to win three world cups. One down, two to go.

With the greatest respect to the other teams in our World Cup pool, the Argentinian clash shaped as the one genuinely challenging match in the first four weeks of the tournament, and it was our very first one. We had Namibia, Georgia and Tonga after that opening clash and none of those teams were expected to cause us too many problems. The night before the test against the Pumas we gathered in the team room to watch South Africa play Japan. None of us could quite believe what we saw. In one of the great upsets of all time, Karne Hesketh scored a spectacular injury-time try and the Brave Blossoms beat the Boks 34–32 in Brighton and Hove.

We were thrilled for Japan, in the way that everyone loves an underdog story, but we left the room that night with one prevailing thought: this shit is real, and we could be next. It was a reminder that in world cups all bets are off. Every side saves their very best for the tournament and the following day we were facing a team that was probably the best example of that. Argentina may have struggled in the Rugby Championship, but history showed they knew how to display their talent on the biggest stage.

Stages don't get much bigger than Wembley Stadium and on 20 September we pulled in beneath its famous, towering arch for our first assignment. There was an edge on the team bus, a real focus on what lay ahead for us. None of us had ever played a game at Wembley, and few of us had ever been inside. Twickenham was massive, but Wembley just seemed so much larger. More than 89,000 fans would descend on the home of English football that afternoon, setting a new record for attendance at a World Cup match. It was an atmosphere like nothing we had felt before, and right from the opening whistle we knew we were up against it.

Keep calm. Stay in the blue. There were 23 minutes left in this first game and we were trailing 12–16. We'd already made four substitutions, our front-rowers swapped early in an attempt to take advantage of their tiring big boys, but we still hadn't clicked. We'd had two men in the sin bin — the skipper and Conrad Smith — and we'd created at least two chances to score but fluffed them. I threw a shocker of a pass to Richie to torpedo one of those chances and was filthy on myself for it. We needed to smarten up, and Aaron Smith was the man to take matters into his own hands. Over the next 20 minutes he scored a try and set another up for Sam Cane. The first one broke the Argentinian spirit; we could feel it leave them. The second drove the stake through the heart.

We had already trained harder than ever before the Argentinian game, as Steve Hansen's plan was well and truly in place. After the 26–16 win we were run senseless before the remaining games against Namibia and Georgia, and only started to ease off for the final pool match against Tonga. I could tell from the line of questioning at the media conferences that our form was of some concern to the fans back home and inarguably of much delight to fans from everywhere else. Things weren't coming off in games the way we intended them to, but there was a good reason: we were so knackered from training that we were going into games in a state of fatigue. That was the entire point of loading us up. Steve had absolutely no concerns about our form or any of the external chatter. He just called for trust, and we gave it to him.

In all truth, any frustration we harboured was a by-product of the enormous expectations we put on ourselves. We wanted to be playing perfect rugby right from the opening whistle and that's far from where we felt we were at as we got through a tenacious Namibia and a powerful and aggressive Georgia. The results were never in doubt, but still no one seemed satisfied. Interestingly, though, with every passing week we got closer and closer as a group and the camaraderie we shared was of a level I don't think I had ever experienced before. Absolute faith does that for a team and while we hadn't yet shown what we were capable of in the games, we were training the house down. Every contact session was at test-match intensity as the starting XV went toe to toe with the rest of the squad.

After so many years of touring the UK in November, being there in mid-September was a revelation for us and went a long way to enhancing everyone's mood. On top of that there were days when you would have been hard-pressed to know the Rugby World Cup was on. We gloried in the simple things: getting out and about in our shirt sleeves, enjoying the anonymity London's busy streets afforded us, which was in stark contrast to the World Cup at home where most of the country seemed to be watching our every move; spending a memorable blue-sky day exploring

Wales ahead of the quarter-final against the French in Cardiff, visiting the stunning Pembrokeshire Coast and the famous arc of white-sand beach at Barafundle Bay. In some ways we felt like we were on an old-school All Blacks tour.

It felt good to be out of the spotlight as much as possible, and within the team everyone knew they had a part to play and did their job for the week. Part of my job in the opening two matches was to cover lock, which took me back to my school days. I tried to push Sam Whitelock from tighthead to loosehead lock in the Argentinian game, but he wouldn't have a bar of that. Against Namibia I came off the bench to pack down in the second row with Luke Romano. I thought the scrum went pretty well when I was pushing there too!

Natural order was restored in the games against Georgia and Tonga and my days as an All Blacks lock were over. I could feel my own form improving rapidly throughout those early games, but I could sense that the perception externally was that I was not the player I once had been. That was certainly the tenor of the questions during my media commitments. The accolades I had received in 2013 provided a problematic comparison. I actually thought I was playing better than I had two seasons earlier, but the game had already changed and the plays that had garnered me so much attention then simply weren't possible to execute now. Teams had adjusted their tactics to counter the way we liked to attack.

What many of those critics failed to notice was that we were much more focused on our own defence as a team, and I certainly was personally. Before the World Cup we had all agreed that our biggest improvement was going to come in our defensive structure. Our attack would take care of itself. In fact, it would only get better if we became more accurate in our tackling work.

Wayne Smith had spent hours analysing how we defended and he believed that small tweaks in our alignment — standing wider and marking on the outside shoulder to force players to cut back inside — and aggression would allow us to take our all-round game to unprecedented levels. Those changes made a world of difference to me, and my defensive numbers improved out of sight. If I didn't get chances with the ball, it didn't matter. If people didn't notice my work rate, I didn't care.

After the final pool game against Tonga we drew a line. From the moment the fulltime whistle blew we knew the tournament now came down to three performances. Performances we knew we were capable of. The week that followed was special in every way. For some of our senior players, the demons of 2007 still burned deep within. We were heading back to Cardiff, the scene of one of their most gut-wrenching days. For the rest of us who had not been part of the team when France stunned the world, our motivation was a simple one: it was winner take all from this moment on.

There was an edge to all that we did. We were nervous, undoubtedly, but we found the positive in that and trained with precision and with purpose. The quantity of the last four weeks was replaced with short, sharp quality work. We based ourselves in Swansea, away from the hype of Cardiff, and made the most of our time away from work. By the time we boarded the bus bound for Cardiff after our last Thursday session, we were totally switched on and ready. The events of 2007 were hardly spoken about. This was our team, and our destiny. When we ran out into the deafening noise of a packed Millennium Stadium in which 71,000 fans did their level best to blow the roof open, we felt indestructible.

Right from the kick-off we felt like we were playing three steps ahead of the French. Even copping a good old-fashioned charlie in the thigh in the opening minutes did nothing to lessen my enjoyment of being out there that afternoon. We were men possessed, and when Brodie Retallick scored the first of our four first-half tries we turned the heat up as high as it would go. Dan Carter was in his element in that match, and everything he touched turned to gold. Julian Savea's finishing was a joy to behold. When we broke for halftime at 29–13 there was only one key message: take care of the details and do not let up.

We didn't let up. The second half was a procession of tries as the French fight withered and died. With 15 minutes to go I even managed to get one for myself, which was always a thrill. I remember casting a look at Richie McCaw and Dan Carter after scoring. I could see the joy on their faces and understood what a performance like this one meant to them. I smiled and gave them a nod and jogged back to halfway. By the end of the match we had scored nine tries, which was what everyone would be talking about. We sat in the sheds and thought about how we had defended. France had scored one try in the first half and no points at all in the second. That was what was going to win us a world cup.

We celebrated the victory, and the manner of it, but we knew better than to get ahead of ourselves. We had finally unleashed the performance we knew we were capable of, but we had to reset quickly and think about the semi-final. We would be up against the Springboks and all of us knew that they would be a different proposition. We had been able to bend France before breaking them. The South Africans would not break so easily. They had already come through a tough examination in the quarter-final against Wales and would be match-hardened and ready for us.

No two weeks are ever the same in terms of mental preparation. We had learned to look at this conundrum through the prism of a surfing analogy. Each match week was its own wave and no two waves could be surfed the same way. I had to take things easy at the start of the week as the bruising in my thigh settled down, but by Thursday I was running freely and the body felt good. Our preparation by this stage had become a well-oiled machine, and there was no secret formula to facing South Africa. Front up, be physical was the mantra, always.

We knew that the Springboks were not a team then who could construct tries from deep in their own half. They played the percentages and liked to strike from closer range. The weather on game day was awful, a hard, cold rain falling for most of the afternoon, and that meant we had to be smarter about what we tried to do. We wanted to play fast against them, but given the conditions we weren't able to do that in the traditional way. Starving them of mauling opportunities and penalty points — that needed to be our strategy. Dan Carter put on a masterclass of tactical kicking that day and we resolved to tackle anything that moved.

No two weeks are ever the same. After blitzing the French in Cardiff, South Africa would not be shaken at Twickenham, and we were tearing into them. A converted Jerome Kaino try in the first half was all we had to show for our effort, while Handre Pollard punished us with penalties. We were down by five, in a semi-final of a world cup, but not a single one of us was anything other than perfectly calm at the break. It was a rare feeling at international level. Even though we were behind, we thought we were dominating the match. Defensively we were smashing bodies left, right and centre. When Dan Carter dropped a goal five minutes into the second half, that was the signal to lift our attack. Five minutes later, Beauden Barrett scored and we had our noses in front. That's where they stayed for the rest of the game, with us eventually winning 20–18. It felt like the most comprehensive two-point win we'd ever been part of.

If one play stood out for me, it was a lineout steal from Victor Matfield secured by Sam Whitelock. We were good mates, Sam and I, and had grown up watching Victor earn his reputation as the King of the Air. We had analysed their lineout plays and were prepared for the throw. Winning that ball helped us get down into South Africa's half and close out the game. It was a special moment for Sam and me. We had worked hard on practising those kinds of plays during the week along with Luke Romano who set up all the opposition lineout plays for us to train against. He had a great brain for that kind of analysis, and we were happy it had all come to fruition in that one key moment in the game.

Two down, one to go. We moved into Pennyhill Park in Surrey for the week of the final and could see why the English have their training base there. It was a gorgeous place to stay, surrounded by more than 100 acres of perfectly manicured lawns and garden, a golf course and all the mod cons of a luxury resort. We felt enormously privileged to be there and were thrilled to be out of the bustle of London and once again away from any of the hype building for the final. It would be against Australia, and we couldn't wait.

I roomed with big Luke Romano that week, which was fantastic. Luke just had a great handle on life and loved a chat about anything. He was fastidious in his preparation — his lineout work already mentioned was some of the best analysis I had ever seen — and he had good banter underneath a calmness that was always appreciated around the team. We talked about Australia — their strengths, their weaknesses and what we knew about both. We also discussed the fact that history had no bearing in one-off games. We were going to have to be on our guard.

By the week of the final we were supremely confident in our ability to boss the game, to play like the number one team in the world. That had been the challenge we had set for ourselves — to turn up for games and to dominate. This was our time to show that and to go back to back. Any nervousness was incredibly well-managed through the week. Seven days is a long time to be thinking about that one game, so we took every chance we could to distract ourselves from rugby. On Wednesday I headed into London to see Bridget and the girls, and we took in a show. That it happened to be *Elf The Musical* was something I kept to myself once I got back to the team.

On Thursday Wyatt Crockett was forced to withdraw from the team after sustaining a groin tear. It was tough trying to console my big, clumsy mate that day. After everything he'd been through, he'd finally got a chance to shine in the biggest show of all and now wouldn't be able to take it. We all felt for the Croczilla. Pulling out of the final was a typically selfless act from one of the greatest team men you could ever hope to find. Though he was absolutely gutted, he knew Joe Moody would come in and get the job done.

By Saturday we were fit to bust. Thursday night had been filled with fun as our hotel dinner was transformed into a musical extravaganza by expat Kiwi Geoff Sewell and his troupe of entertainers. Crocky had been instrumental in organising it, and we all sang along and laughed through the evening. There was even a happy birthday moment for me, complete with cake and a Marilyn Monroe imitation from one of the singing waitresses. The next day Luke and I lounged about the room and watched the *Lord of the Rings* trilogy on DVD. I mean, what else would you expect?

We woke to a gorgeous day and the morning was imbued with a childlike sense of excitement and anticipation. I could tell we were all in the zone and the bus ride into Twickenham was amazing. I took the time to look around my teammates, each of them lost for that time in their own world, no doubt picturing the same thing as I was: standing on that podium with the World Cup in our hands. Arriving at the famous gates of that grand stadium we could see the fans streaming into the ground. We thought we had done well during the tournament to make sure we were as respectful and as gracious as possible in every interaction with the British people and walking out onto the ground for warm-up I genuinely felt like this was a home game for us. Having the home sheds was a great feeling — and at least we knew we would have hot water after the match.

Richie, Jerome and I were pumped. We'd talked all week about the need for us to be at our very best. We were going to be the ones who set the tone for the entire team and that meant we had to be on from the very first minute. We sat alongside each other in the shed before the game. We trusted each other wholeheartedly. Nothing further needed to be said. This team knew what it was doing. So many of us had been to the final four years previously. That experience now informed everything we did. We did not have to manufacture some kind of inspiration. If anything, we had to control the excitement of the occasion. Having been there before was enormously helpful for us. We knew what we were getting ourselves into. We were calm and settled. And then we tore off the plaster and ripped into Australia.

The start to the match was ferocious. Right from the opening kick-off we wanted to set the rules of engagement and blood was drawn at the very first breakdown. Jerome was a man possessed, which I always delighted in seeing. I knew that when he was in that frame of mind there were going to be bruised bodies on the other side, and I wanted to join in on the fun. When Israel Folau caught Aaron Smith's first box kick of the afternoon, I was there to melt him. Over the next three phases we knocked them back 20 metres and forced them to scramble into touch. As far as starts go, I couldn't have thought of a better one. They knew then how we were going to be at them all day long.

Only a few minutes had elapsed when we drew our first scrum penalty of the game and kicked for touch. I called a regulation lineout in which I would take the catch and set the drive off me. I had no problems catching the ball, but I landed on someone's boot, my ankle went over, and an intense pain shot through my leg. I passed the ball and hit the deck. I was in a bad way and I knew it. Just five minutes had elapsed in the game. All I could think was, 'This is a world cup final. This cannot be happening now.'

Physiotherapist Pete Gallagher was on the field in a flash. 'Pete, my ankle is stuffed. Just give me a minute,' I said as he arrived on the scene. In the meantime, we had been awarded a penalty from the spot I was now sitting. Pete and I looked at each other. 'Strap it up,' I told him. I got off the ground and tested the ankle. I was in agony, but there was no way I was going off this early into the final. I decided I was just going to deal with the pain and get on with the job. If I could get through to halftime, we could make another assessment. Right now I needed to do my bit for the team, which included the very odd decision at one stage to hoist a midfield bomb — one of the few kicks I had made in my career — which was a challenging enough task without having a bung leg. Fortunately, I was able to chase it and smother Will Genia after the catch.

We had a good first half, but it took 38 minutes before we were able to bag our first try. Nehe Milner-Skudder was the man on the end of the chain, but both Conrad Smith and Richie McCaw were instrumental in the set-up. It was a crucial time to score, and we were able to head back under the stands with the breathing room we felt we had earned. It was hard-earned too. We were in a real scrap out there. I was in a scrap of my own to do something for the pain in my ankle. I sought out Doc Page and we went straight to the medical room, removed my boot, sock and the strapping that was already in place before the game. It was agonising, but there was nothing else for it. Doc grabbed a needle and filled the ankle with local anaesthetic.

By the time I got back to the team most of the talking was done. I knew what would have been said: tempo and defence were our two pillars, and the job wasn't done. By the time the second half began I couldn't feel the pain in my ankle. I couldn't feel my ankle at all, to be honest. One minute into the half, Sonny Bill Williams offloaded a ball to Ma'a Nonu in a three-man tackle. I was on the outside expecting Ma'a to come my way. Instead he saw a gap that wasn't there, and made one for himself, scoring a remarkable try with one boot missing. At 21–3 it felt as if we were on the verge of opening the floodgates, but 10 minutes later Ben Smith was sent to the bin. Things were about to change.

Australia sprang to life and by the 63rd minute had scored two tries and reduced our lead to just four points. No one panicked.

Not on the field at least. The most important tool in our arsenal was our ability to stay in the moment. How many times over the last four years had we proved to ourselves that we could get out of any situation? We stood under the posts as Bernard Foley converted the second try and Richie implored us to keep to our tasks, win the ball and play. Five minutes later, Dan Carter dropped a goal from a lineout win. It was one of the most clutch plays I had ever seen in my life and not one of the forwards knew it was happening. We thought it was coming back to us. So did the Wallabies.

When Beauden Barrett ran on to a Ben Smith kick with just a couple of minutes left, we didn't even bother trying to keep up. We watched him score the winning try from the halfway line.

It was the best view in the world.

15

TAKING THE REINS

It's a Wednesday in Auckland, three days out from the second Bledisloe Cup test of the year. Am I nervous? Yeah, I'm nervous. We have been terrible in the three tests so far. We completely bombed the close-out against the Springboks in Wellington, and I can't even begin to describe how we felt after Perth. Sure, having a bloke sent off with an entire half to go makes everyone's job a bit tougher, but we are better than that. Better than a record defeat.

There's been some heat in the camp, that's for sure. We always knew there would be. I have spent plenty of time in this room already this week, its windows overlooking the harbour and the bridge and the whitecapped waters of the Waitemata. Water under the bridge — a good name for the view, a better phrase for the week. It's my last time here, in this old creaking hotel that we have come to love. No more rides in the service lifts, no more breakfasts in the atrium, no more endless walks down long corridors to while away the hours before kick-off. One last stay. One last test at Eden Park.

We need to simplify things. That's been the message.

Rugby is a simple game, after all. We need to simplify our plan and play with some intent. The words didn't sink in last week. We wanted the intensity to be there, we talked about the way Australia would come out fired up. Did we truly believe it; did it sink in the way it should have? I'm not sure it did. What I am sure about is that this week is going to be better. The clock is ticking, only two more tests before the World Cup and one is against Australia this weekend with the Bledisloe Cup on the line. I am not going to lose that great silver chalice on *my* watch. No way.

As players, we can't just rely on what is given to us. It is massively important this week that we do our homework on what happened in Perth, that we understand the trends, and that we're not caught out again. Assumptions are important, but they are not everything. The subtleties in lineouts are crucial. I've watched the tape, looking for tells from jumpers and from hookers. I've done the same with scrums, looking at whether the halfback is prone to offer the blindside or whether he is trying to shut down the run from the eight. All the little things add up to big improvements.

We've focused on our individual roles and we've let the attack and defence leaders deliver the appropriate messages to the group. I'll take the time to sit down and share intel with the guys who are important to me in every phase of the game. I am a driver in the team and my philosophy is to never leave something unsaid. I'll have conversations with everyone. That has always been my style as a leader: to make sure I am a catalyst for communication. It is far better to talk now so we are all clear when we run out for the game. Develop the clarity, deliver on instinct.

The earlier we can get a read on Australia in this match, the earlier we can find ways to exert pressure. I think back to my days as a cricket captain and realise that kind of leadership has given me a great insight into the feel for a game. Being able to articulate what the challenge or opportunity is and then make a call to get the result. What are they presenting and what is in my playbook to counter it? We have the best playbook in the world, and it's my job to flip to the right page at the right time. It's a job I have always loved . . .

It was just a cheeky aside, really. I told Prince Harry during his royal visit to New Zealand in 2015 that I would see him when he handed over the World Cup later that year. I reminded him of that after he had presented Richie with the Webb Ellis Cup, and we both had a laugh. It was amazing to be out there in the middle of Twickenham, the crowd roaring, the fireworks and lights putting on a show, and the joy writ large on all our faces. We had spent four years working towards this, and we had achieved it. That Dan Carter had iced his career with a wrong-foot conversion was fitting. We weren't just celebrating the win, we were celebrating the international retirement of some of the greatest players to have worn the jersey. We were all stoked to send them off in style.

I spent many a long minute just sitting in my seat in that vast changing room with its bathtubs and years of rich rugby history, taking in the scene as the boys laughed and shared beers and enjoyed celebrating the ultimate triumph. The local anaesthetic had worn off by that stage so I wasn't exactly dancing about the place anyway. A few beers changed that. We joined our partners and families back at Pennyhill; my parents and brother Mark were there and it was an unbelievable night. Relief and pride make a great cocktail to party on. The next day I woke up and couldn't walk. It turned out I had fractured my foot and ruptured the ligaments in my ankle.

I spent the next few weeks in a moonboot after returning to New Zealand. We once again took the Webb Ellis Cup on the road, as humbled as ever by the support from Kiwis all across the country. It was great to finally get back to Christchurch and to move into a new family home. It had been such an intense year that just taking the time to decompress and to be a husband and father again was vital to getting my head right for the following season. I hadn't had any contact with Steve Hansen about the All Blacks captaincy but figured I was in the running for the job. I would have enormous boots to fill but I was ready for the challenge of uniting a new-look side after we had farewelled so many of our veterans at Twickenham.

It was also Todd Blackadder's last year in charge of the Crusaders and still the trophy cabinet was bare. The competition had been expanded to welcome the Sunwolves from Japan and the Jaguares from Argentina, and the conference system put even greater onus on winning derby games against the other Kiwi teams. That had been our Achilles heel in recent seasons and it would prove to be again. Even though we had lost some big names, we still had faith in our squad. One of the youngsters who assumed a massive responsibility that year was a kid called Richie Mo'unga.

My first meeting with Richie was not exactly one of my finest moments. He was still an academy prospect at the time, his partner Sophie the sister of Owen Franks's fiancée Emma. We had been invited to Owen and Emma's wedding at the beginning of 2014, where the story goes the groom made sure he had a protein shake ready so he didn't get hungry during the speeches. Owen is not a beer drinker, but he does enjoy a whiskey. I do not often drink whiskey, and I sure as hell enjoyed one or two that day.

The problem was that Andy Ellis was also in attendance and after he had also sampled a whiskey, he decided it would be a good idea to wrestle me at the reception. Being two competitors, this soon descended into an all-out WWE-style match during which we tried to choke each other out. We soon spilled out of the reception and onto the front lawn where the fracas continued much to the annoyance of our respective wives and the mother of the bride. Richie was duly sent out to split us up (Andy and I would never have conceded) and it was at this point that I turned on him, put him in a headlock, and left him momentarily unconscious.

The next morning, I had no recollection of the previous night's events. Understandably, Bridget was refusing to discuss anything with me, least of all the grass stains that covered my suit. I had to call Andy to find out exactly what had happened. He left out one crucial detail. The following Monday we were back at the Crusaders gym when Richie Mo'unga walked past. I had never met him before so extended my hand and introduced myself. Richie shook my hand, had a brief conversation and wandered off. It was only then that Andy, by this stage on the floor laughing, told me what I had done to the poor kid over the weekend. I don't know how many players started their Crusaders career by being strangled by their captain, but Richie is one of them.

He was also an extraordinary talent. He started every game for us that year as we reached a quarter-final showdown with the Lions in Johannesburg. Again, our lack of consistency had forced us to travel for the playoffs and, inevitably it seemed, Ellis Park was where our season came to an end as the Lions put 42 points on us. We were gutted that we couldn't win a title for Todd Blackadder. He was a man of deep integrity who we all respected. And he had put everything he could into us as a team. That I couldn't deliver a trophy for him over those eight years would stand as one of the few regrets of my career.

It had been midway through that 2016 season that Steve Hansen called to offer me the captaincy of the All Blacks. Even though I had already led the side on nine occasions, I never took it for granted that I would succeed Richie McCaw as a matter of course. When Steve called to make the official offer, I was over the moon. It had been hard at the start of the year to get back into full running and training after a long injury layoff and the break following the World Cup success. To know that I would be taking on this great responsibility spurred me on to work harder than ever.

Unfortunately, fate had another curve ball to throw my way. No sooner had I returned to play than my wrist started to give me all kinds of hell. It was nothing that was keeping me out of games or training, more a non-specific ache that got progressively more irksome as the season progressed. At first I didn't think too much of it, but sooner or later I knew I was going to have to get it seen to. That could wait until the season was over, I thought to myself. When would I ever learn that ignoring my problems did not make them go away?

The thought of captaining the All Blacks can get a man

through a lot of aches and pains, and that's perhaps the real reason I didn't want to kick up a fuss about the wrist. I knew that Wales were coming in June for a three-test series, which would be a big chance for me to stamp my mark on the job for a team that would feature plenty of fresh faces. There was also the added incentive that Wales's coach Warren Gatland would also be coaching the Lions the following year. We were all pretty fired up to show him we would be a tough team to beat.

With the elevation to All Blacks captaincy I began to understand a little more of what made my predecessor tick. Richie and I had enjoyed an incredibly tight relationship in the All Blacks, but it was the ultimate professional relationship, a workplace friendship. I think back to the first time we roomed together, in Sydney with the Crusaders in my first year with the team, and he never once asked me a personal question about my life, family, interests — anything outside the team. It wasn't that he was rude; that information was just superfluous to him. He didn't need it in his head when he had other things to think about.

We had thousands of conversations over the years, but they were always about something that was necessary at the time. In that way you could feel close to him without really getting to know him. It's quite a trick really. We toured with the All Blacks and Crusaders for nine years, played alongside each other in countless matches, drank endless coffees together and played a million hands of cards, but outside of the team our relationship was largely non-existent. I respected that intensely. He was a man who could compartmentalise his life better than anyone else I knew. Now that I was thinking every week about the team and what I could do for the team and what the team could be doing better, I got a greater sense of why he was like that. He wouldn't have been able to do what he did if he didn't have an off switch.

In time I would find mine, but in those first months as skipper, my brain felt overloaded. There was extra scrutiny of every decision I made, there were demands on my time that I had never had to deal with before and, yes, the comparisons between me and Richie were understandable and natural. Was there stress? Absolutely, but I had wanted this job and it was still a lot of fun. What's more, it was a great honour and one I never took for granted.

I was naturally nervous before games, but now I had to be the cool head in a season of great transition for the team. By the end of that year 11 men would win their first cap for the All Blacks, but the train had to roll on, albeit with a different driver. I was not only captain, I was the most capped player in the team. By the beginning of June, I had played 84 tests. Owen Franks (78), Sam Whitelock (73) and Jerome Kaino (67) were the next most experienced players. No one else had reached the 50-test mark.

When combined, the 34 other men named in the first All Blacks squad of the year boasted 551 test caps. To give that some context, the five most experienced players who left at the end of the 2015 season — McCaw, Mealamu, Woodcock, Carter and Nonu — had 707 test caps between them. Losing all of that experience on and off the field would have completely derailed some teams, but not the All Blacks. Between June and October we played 10 tests, winning all of them. Our lowest score was 29 against Australia in Wellington. Our smallest margin of victory was 14 points in the second test against Wales at the same venue. All up, we scored 420 points and conceded just 143.

There is no doubt the first two tests against Wales in June

set us up for the season. The first at Eden Park was a typically rusty opener during which we trailed right up until the start of the third quarter before putting on a three-try blitz to secure the win. In the second we were locked at 10-all until the outside backs got into top gear at the 50-minute mark and added three tries in a 10-minute masterclass. Ardie Savea also chimed in with his first test try, a fine reward for a great spell off the bench in just his second test.

From that point on, there was a change that came over the side. We reset the expectations on the team, pointing out that a lack of experience and a lack of performance were two different things. Everyone in the team was valued, everyone had a job to do, and it was about time we got on with it. The following week in Dunedin, with Elliot Dixon, Liam Squire and Ofa Tu'ungafasi all on debut, we found our groove, winning 46–6 in a display to be proud of. It felt like the train had very much pulled out of the station after that.

Throughout the Rugby Championship the team played sublime rugby. Whether we were at home or on the road the wins, and the points, kept stacking up. A 42–8 victory in the opening Bledisloe Cup test in Sydney was a genuine statement, especially after the struggles we'd had against the Wallabies on their home patch in recent years. We put 50 points on Argentina in Hamilton and 41 points on South Africa in Christchurch. By the time we boarded the plane for Buenos Aires at the start of October, we were confident we could claim a clean sweep.

It was in Argentina at the raucous, post-industrial wonderland of the Estadio José Amalfitani that the wrist finally gave up the ghost. I'm not sure if there was a particular incident or whether it was just the result of a season of neglect, but it was in the match against the Pumas that I suddenly lost my grip, literally. I lost my grip and my ability to flex my wrist. It made it bloody hard to make a tackle and to catch and pass a ball. That was pretty much the two things I did in a game. This was rather problematic.

I spoke to Doc Page about it after the match and once we arrived in Durban the following day I headed straight to the hospital for a scan. The news was not great. I had what was known as a scapholunate advanced collapse, which could best be described as a completely torn ligament between two of the bones in my wrist — the scaphoid and the lunate — coupled with arthritis and cartilage damage. Put another way, my wrist was a bit buggered. I had two options: I could have surgery to attempt to repair the damage or I could play on with the help of a brace. I went with the latter option and that week played the Springboks with the aid of local anaesthetic and approximately 20 lineal metres of strapping tape.

It was still painful, but I figured I could always get it fixed later. How wrong that assessment would turn out to be. For now, though, it didn't matter. On a beautiful day at Kings Park in Durban we cleaned up the Boks 57–15. All up, we managed to score nine tries that day while Morne Steyn kicked five penalty goals. It was a remarkable performance and a record score against South Africa. The Wallabies stood no chance two weeks later at Eden Park. By the end of the Rugby Championship we had scored 38 tries. Between them, Australia, South Africa and Argentina had scored 32.

It had been a dream start to my tenure as All Blacks captain. I believed that the way the new guys all came in and performed showed we had the culture just right. We made them feel welcome and we empowered them to be themselves and to play with their natural instincts. Making mistakes was natural and no one had to feel any shame if they made one on the field. We talked about the trust we had as a group and we connected extremely well over those winter months. We disbanded for a week in high spirits after the last Bledisloe Cup game to regroup and to recharge before leaving for a November tour. It would begin with a test against an improving Ireland side at Soldier Field in Chicago.

I was excited to head away with the team. The energy level inside the camp was outstanding and the new players added another dimension to everything we did. It was great to feel like we could be on the verge of another undefeated season, and those of us who had been to Chicago in 2014 were looking forward to exploring more of that great city. In my state of excitement over how we could make things better, I never stopped to think about anything going wrong. Things were about to go very wrong indeed.

The trouble started the night we landed in Chicago. A few of the boys decided it would be a good idea to explore the city well after they should have been back at the hotel, preferably asleep. We had a team curfew for a number of reasons, the most obvious being that we were a high-performance sports team representing our country. The safety of our team was also paramount. We spent a lot of time on tour in big cities. The curfews were not designed to make anyone feel like they were on a Boy Scouts trip, they were in place to protect us all. The guys who broke curfew that night should have known better, and I took it pesonally.

I didn't want to be spending my Sunday and Monday dealing with the admin of it all. When a player breaches a protocol in our team, we have a process that we have to go through to make sure they know why what they did was wrong, that they accept what they did was wrong, and that they come up with a way to right the wrong. It absolutely grated my gears that these blokes had decided to head off on their own tour. I always believed that we could all enjoy ourselves in the places we travelled within the boundaries set by the team and by the leaders. I guess some people struggled with that notion more than I did. Regardless, I read the riot act, and I got bloody emotional doing it. I wanted them to see how what they did disrespected everything about this jersey and everyone who wore it and cared about it.

I found things like that, as rare as they were in the All Blacks, always sapped me. On Monday night we had planned to go to the Bears NFL game at Soldier Field, but I decided to stay back and rest up instead. I was happy just hanging in the hotel room, glad the drama of the last 24 hours was over, when the phone rang. It was Gilbert Enoka. 'Can you come up to my room mate?' he asked. 'Luke's here with me.' I didn't know what to think as I was heading up the elevator, but when I opened the door and saw Luke Romano sitting with Bert, I knew something terrible had happened. It had. Luke had lost his son.

Hannah Romano had gone to the hospital in Christchurch that day for a routine check-up. She was 37 weeks pregnant and both she and Luke couldn't wait to bring Felix into the world. Hannah was the life of any party and one of the most optimistic and upbeat people I had ever met. She was the perfect foil for a man like Luke who was quiet and considered and loved nothing more than his own company on a hunting trip with his dogs. When the obstetrician started the examination, Felix had no heartbeat. Hannah was induced and their beautiful baby was stillborn.

Luke was absolutely shattered. The sight of that big man

sitting there, haunted and hurt, will likely never leave me. This was my mate; these were my friends. My heart dropped instantly and we both were in tears as we hugged there in the middle of the room. I sat there with Luke most of the night, unable to offer him anything other than my friendship. We all felt helpless, but that was nothing compared to the heartache he felt that night and the trauma of not being beside Hannah. Those two people sharing in the same tragedy, separated by 13,000 kilometres.

Luke departed on the first available flight for New Zealand and I still cannot imagine what the hours on board must have been like for him. We were all shaken to the core and those of us closest to him were in a state of shock for the rest of the week as we tried to get our heads right for the game ahead. At a time like that, rugby seemed the least important thing in the world. Family always came first, and Luke was part of our family. There was also another personal dimension to contend with: Bridget was back home, heavily pregnant with our first son.

When the day of the match arrived, I called Luke to ask if we could wear black armbands for the match to honour Felix. He agreed to the gesture, which added to the emotion of the afternoon. At the same time, the Irish boys were dealing with a tragedy of their own. A month earlier Munster coach and former Ireland test veteran Anthony Foley had died while in Paris ahead of a European club fixture. Many of his Munster lads were in the Ireland team that day in Chicago, but the whole squad was intent upon honouring his memory in the appropriate fashion.

From the moment the Ireland boys lined up in figure eight formation to face the haka, we knew we were in for one heck of a time. The first half was an onslaught in green, and by the end of it we were staring down the barrel of a 17-point deficit. We had not been under this kind of pressure all season and we didn't handle it at all. Five minutes into the second half that 17 points had become 22. It was at the 50-minute mark that we found our attack. TJ Perenara, Ben Smith and Scott Barrett, on debut, all scored tries in the space of 12 minutes and with five minutes left in the match, we believed we were on the verge of another great escape. Robbie Henshaw put paid to that when he crossed for Ireland's fifth try. Joey Carbery slotted the conversion and the game was over.

In the same week the Chicago Cubs had ended their 108-year World Series curse, Ireland ended their 111-year search for a victory against the All Blacks. They were jubilant, as they should have been. On that crisp blue-sky day, they were too good for us. A fortnight later, in Dublin, we managed to square the ledger and we didn't care how it looked while we did it. A new rivalry had emerged at the top of world rugby's pecking order. One for which another chapter would be written a couple of years later. For now, though, the loss tipped us off the cloud we'd been riding during the June series and the Rugby Championship. A second unbeaten year would not be happening, and for New Zealand fans the loss to Ireland was more than just a defeat, it was a tinkering with the natural order of things.

Welcome to the reality of the All Blacks, where 13 wins from 14 games is still not good enough.

The season came to an end with a solid if unspectacular win against the French in Paris, and I was able to take a breath and get my wrist seen to. I was booked in for surgery as soon as I got home, but by that stage the ligament was inoperable. All that could be done was to clean out the joint and remove some stray pieces of whatever they could find. I was going to have to learn how to get a grip.

I had to get a handle on something else as the new year approached. The Crusaders had a new coach and he had a new plan. I was captain of the All Blacks, but I was no longer going to be captain of the Crusaders. I knew this before Razor called me in for a meeting ahead of the start of the 2017 season. The conversation wasn't hard, and at no stage did I feel like my leadership was in question. Razor just knew that leading the All Blacks was an all-consuming job and he needed someone who could be singularly focused on the Crusaders. It just made sense, really. I was going to take time to recover from the wrist operation and the Lions were going to dominate that year's season. I assured him that I would throw my full support behind whoever was handed the job.

I had never played under Razor but having talked to the guys who had, they all told me that he was going to bring something completely fresh to the environment. There was some doubt about whether his methods, honed during his time with provincial and national age-group teams, would translate to Super Rugby, but there was also plenty of excitement about his transformational talents. Razor outlined why he wanted to make the change and create some separation in the roles, and it was a perfectly pragmatic decision. When he told me Sam Whitelock would be handed the job, I couldn't have been happier. It would prove to be an outstanding decision.

Here's the funny thing: I wasn't angry, I wasn't deflated, I didn't feel as if I had failed the team or that I wasn't an effective leader. I knew I still had a massive role to play in supporting Sam with how he captained the side and there was probably a part of me, deep down, that actually did feel a small sense of relief that some of the burden of leadership had been lifted. But, for all that, for all the rationalising of the decision, one thought still stands out and it's one that would make me chuckle many months down the line: I knew then and there that we were going to win the title, and I was a little sad that I wasn't going to be the guy raising that trophy in triumph.

There was something else I couldn't raise in triumph: our first son Reuben was born on 19 January. My wrist was so damaged I couldn't help with him! He was a big lad, too. Bridget once again had to do all the heavy lifting.

16
THUMBSTRUCK

It was exactly the performance we had been looking for and the Bledisloe Cup is sitting where it belongs, in the Eden Park changing room, surrounded by the team that just won it. I've got a beer in my hand and a grin on my face. Sevu Reece and George Bridge are wandering around like lost boys. Hell, those kids were good tonight. We all knew they would be.

Simplify. Be aggressive. Show intent. It's amazing what you can achieve when you stop overthinking things. We had consumed so much information over the first three weeks of the international season, and we had bogged ourselves down. Tonight, we just played. I knew the guys were ready for it; I could feel it on the bus ride to the ground. I looked around the team on the way to Eden Park as I had done so many times before. Then I looked out the window and watched the view pass me by. One last drive along New North Road and its strip of car yards, one last long dip over the Bond Street bridge and past Kingsland's bars. One last slow entrance under the west stand concourse and into the tunnel. One last time through the doors with a left turn before the entrance to the field.

I spoke about doing the small things all night long, going forward and cleaning rucks with pure aggression. We had warmed up with accuracy and purpose, and then the skies had opened. I don't know how the Wallabies felt about the rain, but I told the guys it was perfect for what we wanted to do, and I believed what I said.

We performed 'Kapa O Pango':

Kapa O Pango kia whakawhenua au i ahau / All Blacks, let me become one with the land.

Ko Aotearoa e ngunguru nei! / New Zealand is rumbling here.

We rumbled all right. At quarter time I looked across at the Australians. I could see they were doubting themselves. We all saw it. When Richie Mo'unga swooped on a loose pass to score, we knew we were on our way. At halftime we were 17-nil up, but I wanted more. 'Look me in the eye,' I said to the boys in the shed. 'Keep that killer mindset. There is no letting up tonight and we are going to start with the first 10 minutes of this half.'

We just kept applying the pressure. There was nothing complicated. All it took was focus and determination. When the fulltime whistle blew, we had closed out the game 36-nil. Prime Minister Jacinda Ardern was on stage to hand me the Bledisloe Cup. I could not wipe the smile off my face. One last time, raising that great cup above my head.

In the sheds I call the boys together. I speak to them about the pride they have shown tonight, and about how proud I am of them and of being their captain. I remind them of how hard they have worked over the last month to get that one crucial performance. There is only one last thing to add: I tell them that we are only getting started. There is one goal left this year, and I know all about the power of a goal . . .

I may not have been playing when the Super Rugby season kicked off, but I loved what I was seeing. Scott 'Razor' Robertson had imbued the entire Crusaders organisation with some kind of Peter Pan magic. The team was absolutely sparking and Rugby Park had come to life. Muhammad Ali was our thematic touchstone for the season; we were on a quest for greatness. There were only two pillars to Razor's organisational philosophy: come to work happy to be there, and whinge up. If any of us had a problem, it had to be sent up the chain, not left to fester lower down the ranks. It was a fresh voice, and a fresh and technicolour philosophy. Everything was upbeat, an awakening of the senses.

The promotion of Sam Whitelock proved as inspired as I thought it would be. Through the early rounds his captaincy was smart, ballsy, uncompromising and inspired. Twice in the opening three rounds, against the Highlanders and the Reds, Sam had led the lads out of hopeless situations and they had found a way to win. I couldn't wait to get back out there, but I knew I needed to bide my time and let my wrist strengthen as much as possible.

I still couldn't really grip with my hand so had been following a regime of finger exercises to try to compensate for the lack of movement. I started looking at ways to change my tackling style too. I finally returned for the round seven match against the Sunwolves and backed up the next week against the Stormers.

Both matches were in Christchurch and both resulted in 50-point wins. It was great fun playing a rejuvenated style of rugby based on constant movement and all-out attack.

Given my lack of grip, I had been working with a wrestling coach on different ways to hold during the tackling process. I hadn't really tried to implement too much of what I had learned over the first couple of games back, but I decided to try out some of the techniques against the Cheetahs in Bloemfontein. Unfortunately, I discovered that my thumb was no match for a giant Afrikaner's knee. I can't even remember who, or what, it was I was trying to tackle. It may as well have been the side of a barn. What I do recall is that the Cheetahs scored off that play, and my thumb was toast.

I hauled my ass off the turf and got myself back to the team assembled behind the posts while we waited for the conversion. I can assure you that hearing and feeling your bones crunching is never a pleasant experience, but when Doc pressed my thumb there was something else that added to my growing discomfort: this was only my third game of the season for the Crusaders and it was now just eight weeks until the first test against the British and Irish Lions. It wasn't just my thumb that broke that day. My spirit did too. I sat in the changing room in a daze, stared into space through the halftime talk and barely registered the rest of the team filing back out for the second spell. I stayed in my seat and there, alone, started to cry.

I couldn't stop the tears. I sat there hunched over in that changing room and let the sobs come. I suddenly felt a long way from home, rudderless and adrift on an ocean of despair. What had I done to deserve this? Self-pity had me in its crusty old clutches and I was torn from them only when Doc came back into the sheds at some point in the second half to ask if I wanted to go straight to the hospital with the local liaison officer. I figured it was as good an option as any; it wasn't as if I was playing much of a role for the team sitting under the grandstand feeling sorry for myself. I performed a one-handed packing job and left the ground, bound for the local hospital and a night to remember.

The first room I walked past at Rosepark Hospital appeared to have been recently decorated with a substantial volume of blood which, while mildly terrifying, at least allowed me to put my own problems into perspective. On balance, it was obvious that someone was having a far worse day than I was. Whether the doctors noticed my reaction to that scene or not, I don't know, but from that point on, I could tell they were doing their best to keep me separated from the harsh realities of their daily existence and I was grateful for that. I was X-rayed quickly and the liaison was charged with quickly ferrying back my imaging to the ground so Doc could take a look. The short story was I needed surgery, and I needed it then and there. If I left it until I got home, I would be forced to wait for the swelling to subside and that could take up to a week. The clock was ticking for me, and everyone knew it.

There was no debate to be had. Before I knew it, an orthopaedic surgeon had been summoned to the hospital to operate on the All Blacks captain's hand. You have to give it to the South Africans, there was no fluffing about, no waiting around for red tape to be cut through or for forms to be filled out. For all I know the surgeon may well have been about to fire up the barbecue and settle down with some beers on his day off, but sure enough, within minutes he was standing beside me in the consultation room and — this comes as no surprise — we were chatting about rugby more than the surgery.

'I'm telling you, Kieran,' he boomed in his deep Afrikaans accent. 'I can guarantee I will have you ready for those Lions in the first test, and then you can go out there and destroy them.'

I had to laugh at that. I don't know what it is about the Afrikaans accent, but it can make the most reassuring sentence sound like a death threat. From that point on, I was at the mercy of the surgeon and the hospital staff and, barely six hours after I had left the stadium in Bloemfontein, I was coming to from the general anaesthetic and posing for a thumbs-up photo in the recovery room. It was then that the Crusaders doc came to take my wallet and my phone and to give me a few last comforting words before leaving me for the night. It was a restless sleep, and a lonely one. Despite the very best efforts of the nurses and medical staff at the hospital, I wanted to be anywhere but there. I wanted to be in an alternate reality, one in which I wasn't facing another uncertain recovery, one in which I was not eight weeks out from the biggest moment of my captaincy career with a busted hand and a mind furiously scribbling pictures of worst-case scenarios.

Being bitter and twisted rarely helps with anything, but that's just how I felt after I was released from Rosepark and reunited with the Crusaders. I had a couple of extra days in South Africa with the team, counting down the hours until I was cleared to fly back to New Zealand to begin recovery. I put on a brave face around the boys because I knew they still had a job to do the following weekend against the Bulls, but my brain was in full self-sabotage mode and I needed to distract myself as much as possible. It turned out that I would be sharing a plane home with my old mate Sam Whitelock who had been cited after the Cheetahs game for throwing an elbow into the face of prop Charles Marais and subsequently handed a two-match suspension. I know this sounds ridiculous, but it was nice to share a long-haul trip with someone in a fouler mood than I was.

My old mate the surgeon had been bullish about my chances of being fit and ready to face the Lions but, naturally, I harboured my own doubts. It was pleasing then to see a specialist as soon as I was back in Christchurch who had nothing but praise for the surgeon's skill and who shared the optimistic prognosis. From that point on, I resolved to stop agonising and to start prioritising. I couldn't do a damn thing about what had happened and I couldn't change the fact I was unable to play. What I could do was seize control of the rehabilitation and do everything required to get my thumb right. That was going to involve a lot of bike work and a lot of sweating through Nic Gill's running programme. In my kitchen hung a wall calendar. I found a permanent marker in the drawer and circled the date of the first test, 24 June 2017. I was going to make it, no matter what.

The only stipulation around recovery was to avoid any kind of contact, which is not exactly an ideal way to prepare to face one of the biggest and most aggressive forward packs in world rugby. It was what it was, though, and so I would head to Rugby Park each day and get through everything on my programme. I was happy to be in the company of the Crusaders, to feel like I was still a part of the season, even though I was largely confined to the back fields while the guys got through their team training. If I wasn't outside running, I was in the gymnasium submitting to the particularly sadistic torture of the watt bike, pedalling out 50-minute sessions twice a week and sweating through my teeth. The one bonus of sitting on a bike for that period of time was I was able to use visualisation techniques to think about how running out onto

Eden Park was going to feel, and how I was going to make an impact for the team in that first test.

I had something else to take my mind off the pain of these sessions: the America's Cup. Like so many other Kiwis, I was captivated by Team New Zealand's epic performance in Bermuda and I was inspired by the sheer grit of the 'cyclors' as they powered that boat to yachting's ultimate prize. It was not hard to feel like a kid again, pretending I was one of them and that the harder I pedalled the faster that boat would go. They were motivating days for me, and a catalyst for my own imagination to run — or ride — wild. I have always had a great capacity for visualisation, whether it was picturing how I was going to implement a new move on the field, or planning my running lines to fit within a team structure. I would write it down in my book just once and then roll it over again and again in my mind until it was so deeply ingrained that it became instinctive. I used that same method now to get me through each session, no matter how tough it was.

Through continual visualisation I have come to understand the shifts in a game and to see the patterns unfold before me on the field, whether it be the opportunities for attacking space or the wisdom to think a few moves in advance so as to get myself into the perfect position on defence. Maybe I always had a touch of that ability, or perhaps it was honed on the cricket field when as a captain I had to read a batsman's next shot and adjust my field constantly to set the ideal trap. Time and experience have only enhanced that skill, but it is one any successful rugby player should always be working on. The game may last 80 minutes, but the result is decided by a thousand split-second decisions. Of all the things I try to bring to my game, I believe that vision is the greatest asset I possess.

I have found that on tour I can devour my downtime with this kind of thinking. Sure, I can switch off when I need to with a game of cards or a coffee and a laugh with the boys, but in those many hours of time alone I often drift into my own dreamscape, directing my own silent movies as I slide into sleep. To be honest, sometimes they are not so silent, and many a roommate would attest to being kept awake by me yelling out lineout calls in my slumber. I never thought of sleep talking as a secret weapon, but it obviously has worked for me, if not for the poor bastard stuck listening to it instead of getting his own shut-eye. Bridget would also tell you there has been many a time when she has been woken by me sitting bolt upright in bed calling plays. Fortunately, I haven't taken to regular somnambulism, although Wyatt Crockett once had to guide me back to my bed on tour after I went wandering in the night. I was probably trying to subconsciously escape his snoring.

As the weeks unfolded, I stayed in regular contact with the All Blacks staff who had remained eternally positive about me getting ready for the opening test. It was unbelievably encouraging to have their unwavering support, and in the few phone calls I had with Steve Hansen, the message was always the same: 'It doesn't matter about now, when the time comes you will be here and you will be playing.' I had made my peace with the fact I was not going to get a game before that opening test at Eden Park and I just had to trust in the fact that I had been there and done that in terms of getting the kilometres on the clock in the test-match environment. My mood improved with each new week, aided in no small part by the fact the Crusaders had reached the end of May without dropping a game. A week later, against the Highlanders in Christchurch, Mitch Hunt pulled off one of the great game savers when he drop-kicked a winning goal from 45 metres, sending the team and its fans into raptures and entering New Zealand sporting folklore.

That same night, 3 June, the British and Irish Lions opened their New Zealand tour against the Provincial Barbarians in Whangarei. I was glued to the television for that first match, as enthralled as the rest of the country with what was shaping up as the biggest sporting event for Kiwis since the 2011 Rugby World Cup. The Barbarians were a throw-together side written off by many as having absolutely no chance of competing with a team of international superstars, and yet they led 7–3 at halftime and were in many ways unlucky to finish the game on the wrong side of a 13–7 scoreline. The media and the public were quick to deride the Lions performance, and that criticism was only compounded four days later when they suffered a 22–16 loss to the Blues.

I saw things very differently. What I saw was a Lions team patiently bedding in their plans to win test matches. Everything about their structure and style was designed for the grind. If you looked through the results and the understandable lack of combinations, you could see how Warren Gatland was piecing together the puzzle, utilising his key playmakers in very specific areas of the field to control tempo and set the game rhythm. The public and the media saw the rust, but I could see the sharpened steel beneath.

This was a team that cared not a bit about scorelines and pretty pictures, and that's not to say it wasn't one stacked with players who had sensational skillsets. The British and Irish Lions had simply come to New Zealand with an obvious and ingenious plan: shut the space down, win the collision, kick accurately and often, and make every single inch of territory harder than the last for the opposition to win. Two weeks before the first test they came to Christchurch and kept a Crusaders side tryless — a side that had so far that season scored 74 tries. The final score was 12–3. No matter what happened from that point, the All Blacks had been put on notice and not least because the Crusaders side that day was stacked with them. It was a high-stakes game for both sides and the Lions showed just how effective their approach could be in those situations.

Everything that the tourists would bring to the test arena was on show that night at AMI Stadium. Their defensive line was an absolute wall, their kick-chase, especially from the box, was incredibly effective, their forwards were unwavering in their commitment to the breakdown. Their style was anathema to the typical New Zealand player, but that was also their strength — they challenged you to take risks and punished you if the bets didn't pay off. I was gutted for the guys in the Crusaders who would never again get the opportunity to play against a team that only came calling every 12 years, but I could only tip my hat to the Lions. If that's the way they wanted to play, all power to them. They were going to be hard to beat.

I knew that as All Blacks we were going to have to play smart. Discipline was going to be paramount lest their kickers be given a chance at points or to pin us in our own danger zone and drive from attacking lineouts. I knew we were going to have to win the aerial game to ensure we had a constant source of possession, and once we did have the ball we were going to have to be patient, to build phases and break down their rush defence. Teams that generate line speed will never concede the gainline on every play, but they can be broken down with long periods of sustained attack. Just as a woodpecker eventually makes its nest, a patient attack strategy will always find the gap in a rush defence.

Of course, there was never going to be a sudden desire within the team to change the way we wanted to play the game. We enjoyed the freedom of expression that came with the territory and sought to perform with speed and with width. It had not been our style to continually come around the corner and run off the halfback or to rely heavily on kick and chase. At some point in any game we may have to utilise those tactics, but an All Blacks side is not designed to play that way from the outset; we back our skills and our catch-pass and believe inherently in the accurate execution of an expansive system that delivers points. That was certainly our mindset when the team assembled in Auckland a week out from a pre-series test against Samoa at Eden Park. Though I wouldn't be playing in the match, I assembled with them. I was back where I wanted to be.

A week is a long time in rugby and, as it turns out, it's also a long time in any injury recovery. We had in-depth discussions with the specialists about whether I should suit up to face Samoa as I desperately wanted to get some game time ahead of the Lions series, but ultimately the risk of rebreaking the thumb was deemed too great. With another contact-free week, the risk would drop to much more acceptable levels. There were no guarantees, of course, but ultimately I had to trust in their expert opinion. My fitness, I told myself, would be fine, and my instincts would flood back to me once I finally took the field. That lonely night in a Bloemfontein hospital felt like a distant memory. I was back, surrounded by some of my best mates, and inside a team I would do anything for. All that mattered now was preparing the side for Samoa and the Lions.

We knew this was going to be as big as a world cup in terms of the pressure to perform and we wanted to embrace the pressure and the expectation in the same way we had been able to do in 2011 and 2015. Because of that, many of the initial conversations as a team centred on how we were going to get ourselves mentally ready for what was coming — the extra media scrutiny, the travelling fans, the need to stay completely on task over the three tests knowing that the Lions would undoubtedly improve over the course of the series. In the leaders' meetings we focused not so much on tactics but on personal improvement. We had earlier in the year undertaken an internal skills survey, and that had given us a foundation upon which to grow our own leadership capabilities.

The feedback I received as part of this process was genuinely encouraging. Essentially, the team just wanted me to back myself more, to get more demanding when it was clear that I needed to be. I was, in effect, being given licence to get shitty. I knew I had a habit of holding back rather than letting the rockets fly, but my instincts also told me that if my default setting was frustration then my efficacy as a leader was going to be greatly reduced. What I needed to do was find a better balance — to be comfortable knowing it was part of my job to fire a shot from time to time, as long as I was sure that it would hit the intended target.

It was timely advice for me because I'd already had an entire season as captain, and I knew that I had probably stepped back a little in terms of being prescriptive. I put a lot of faith in the other leaders around me, wanting to be as collaborative as possible, and I was happy to delegate responsibility to others. The guys enjoyed that approach and they believed the openness with which I led had helped foster a good learning environment for the younger guys in the team. For all that, though, they still wanted me to take a bit more control of the team's destiny, to be more forthright with my opinions and my expectations. They wanted me to be a captain. If something needed to be said and done, it was up to me to say it and to do it.

Once everyone had arrived in Auckland, Steve and I outlined exactly where we were at and what the expectations were going to be over the next few weeks. The biggest issue was always going to be the lack of time we could spend together before the Lions series began. June series have long posed a problem for preparation, one that can't be completely assuaged by mini-camps and short training days, but we had to acknowledge it and move on. Everything about those opening sessions is designed to energise the team, to have them walking out of the room knowing they belong there and thinking they would do anything to be part of the next chapter of All Blacks history. Unfortunately, over the next few days, things got somewhat over-egged.

Effective theming requires simplicity and as All Blacks we had a deeply ingrained set of principles which encapsulated performance, professionalism, humility, hard work and humanity. As it transpired, the management team were looking for ways to add some extra threads to what was already a well-woven fabric. Derek Lardelli, the man who had composed 'Kapa O Pango' for the All Blacks and who was rightly lauded for his work in Maori arts, presented to us the story of Pouakai, the great eagle of Maori legend. It was a sensational piece of symbolism for what we wanted to be and all we wanted to achieve, but I could sense that Derek — and this was hardly his fault — was speaking to us without having been briefed on what we already had in place, and therefore the impact of his message was somewhat muted.

Compounding the issue was that nothing had been shared with the leaders prior to Derek's presentation or before several others that were put on for us by the management team. As such, we hadn't had a chance to think about how we were going to stitch together the extra detail, to make it relevant to how we wanted to act and how we wanted to think. Again, in isolation, each of the talks was incredibly powerful, but the overall result was an added complexity around our messaging when simplicity was a much better approach. As leaders we can't preach what we don't understand and while we understood the urge to look at the challenge ahead of us with fresh eyes, perhaps we built up that challenge too much, and allowed it to muddy the usually crystal-clear waters of the All Blacks world.

I enjoy standing in front of the team on the first day of any new season and delivering that message of expectation. I love looking around the room and seeing that focus on the faces of my teammates — it tells me just how badly they want to be there and how much they are prepared to do to stay there. It doesn't have to be complicated at the level we are performing at, and by and large it never is. Perhaps that's why all the extra thematic effort put in ahead of the Lions tour stands out for me. It was rightly intentioned but, in my mind at least, never driven by the current that already flowed within the environment. There were simply too many tributaries and none reached the river that ran through us.

Our team room — wherever we may be in the world — is our whare, and it is there that we remind ourselves of our identity as a team. In that whare stands the outline of our All Blacks way; the standards that we live by are illustrated there for all to see, represented through the ancestry of the team. Through my experience I had learned that if we focused on those things — things that have stood the test of time for more than a century of All Blacks rugby — then our processes never needed to be questioned. It was nothing new to the team, but it had gained a new prominence in our thinking ahead of the 2015 Rugby World Cup. I feared that rather than adding another dimension, the new material was subtracting from the power of an existing set of messages that worked well. I guess there was only one way to find out.

17

A ROAR DEAL

The break has been good after the Bledisloe test. It's been important to get away and draw a line under what has been this year, and what is still to come. I love being at home with Bridget and the kids, just feeling normal again after the intensity of the Rugby Championship and the attention that goes with it.

Tomorrow the coaches will name their squad for the Rugby World Cup. Only 31 names will be on that list and I know that the next 24 hours will be filled with anxiety for so many players. We all want a shot at it. We've all worked hard to be in the selection frame. We have one match left, against Tonga in Hamilton, before we depart for Japan. I'm excited by what lies ahead and filled with a healthy anxiety. We have been here before, gone back to back. All the ingredients are there to give this a good shot, and the expectation will be massive. It always is . . .

The pressure to perform is always there when you are in the All Blacks, but without question it had gone up a level as the red tide of Lions supporters flowed into Auckland and the tour continued to saturate every newspaper page and sport programme. It would have been impossible to float free of the sense of anticipation that flooded the country, even if I wanted to. As it was, I felt invigorated by everything that was going on around us. The city was alive with visiting fans which provided a festive edge to the camp, and the 12-try victory over Samoa in the first Friday outing was more valuable to us than the 78-nil score would suggest. It signalled the start of what we all hoped would be an unforgettable three weeks.

In my downtime, when I was alone in my room with just my thoughts for company, I would shut out the distractions and think through all that needed to be done. They were intensely reflective times for me as I trawled through the list of unknowns, and the various scenarios that would be presented at Eden Park. I thought about the team's needs and I thought about my own position. Would I get through the game without mishap? Would I have the requisite fitness to play the full 80 minutes? It may sound counterintuitive, but there is value to be found in uncertainty. I thrived on that nervous energy, and when I looked around the team at trainings or in meetings, I could see that everyone was completely dialled in to the week.

Apprehension is a natural by-product of the will to win and everyone deals with it in different ways. As All Blacks we have learned to acknowledge the misgivings while not allowing them to dominate our thinking. Clarity of purpose requires calmness, and as the week progressed and I took a more active role in training, the tension began to subside. I had a specially made brace to protect my hand which afforded me some much-needed peace of mind, and we rapidly increased the intensity, session by session. It was an amazing feeling to lead the team that week, and not just because of the long road I had taken to get back into a position to contribute. There was a genuine sense of occasion, a boys' own adventure bonhomie that infused all that we did, while a healthy element of anxiety offset any risk of overconfidence.

We are so accustomed, when we play at home, to running out in front of crowds which are almost exclusively on our side. Conversely, we know that when we are overseas — at Ellis Park or Twickenham, Murrayfield or Stade de France — there will be very few fans cheering for us. It is part and parcel of our place in the world and we have always enjoyed the stark contrast of home and away occasions. What took me be surprise — threw me a little to be honest — was the sheer number of Lions fans packed into Eden Park as we walked out onto the turf before warming up for the first test. Eden Park was supposed to be our fortress, our dark, foreboding castle, the black hole into which was sucked any last hope the opposition had. Someone had left the gates open and in had washed a sea of red.

I had never experienced anything like it at home and was probably a little angry with myself for not pausing during the week to consider, and to address with the team, how different the atmosphere at Eden Park might be. I remember hearing the chants for the Lions during the warm-ups and thinking, 'What is going on here?' I know I wasn't alone in feeling slightly unbalanced by the scene around us, but it had a galvanising effect on the team and, dare I say it, on our own fans who were probably taught a lesson in how to be vocal that night and throughout the series. I made a mental note to find the person who sold all those tickets to the tourists, parked it, and got down to work. I couldn't do much about the number of away fans in the crowd, but I could certainly help find a way to keep them quiet.

There was nothing quiet about those moments leading the team out ahead of kick-off. Very few — if any — of us had experienced a crowd like it, and Eden Park was alive with the anticipation of what was to come. The scene was set for an absolute thriller and right from the opening exchanges I knew this was going to be a royal rumble. The first quarter was one of the most brutal I had ever been involved in, their pack as tough and as tricky as any I had ever measured up against. We threw ourselves at two-man tackles, fought off frustrating holds at the bottom of rucks, and tried to keep our cool at lineout time when they continually took up space and yelled incessantly over our calls. They had every trick in the book, learned through years of psychological grind in the European club game and in the fierce heat of the Six Nations.

Fortunately, our faith in the catch and pass game paid dividends through the opening exchanges. Beauden Barrett kicked the first three points after 13 minutes and Codie Taylor finished off a special play a few minutes later to score the first try and to give us some confidence in our game plan. We held a 10-point advantage until close to halftime, at which point I chased too hard on a deep kick to Liam Williams, and left the door open behind me for an 80-metre counterattack, sealed by Sean O'Brien in the corner. It was at that point I had to face facts: these guys were nowhere near as one-dimensional as people had assumed. That try, complete with an expert block on Sonny Bill Williams who led the chase line behind me on the play, was all the evidence we needed to show us that the tiniest mistake could prove incredibly costly against a team as smart as this.

With a five-point buffer at the break, there was no panic under the stand. We had already lost Ben Smith with a head knock and Ryan Crotty with a dud leg, but we had the utmost trust in Aaron Cruden, who had a wealth of experience, and in Anton Lienert-Brown, who had made a massive impact a year earlier. We knew that we had a quality bench, stacked with players who were adept at injecting an extra element of pace in the later stages of the game. We also knew we had enough potency out wide to inflict more damage on the Lions if we could continue to stress their defensive line. Over the next 40 minutes, we managed to work the ball with accuracy and with speed, and Rieko Ioane showed the world his class with a second-half double. The game was essentially decided with 10 minutes to spare, having worked our way to a 30–8 scoreline, but we were still chastened by Rhys Webb's try in referee's time that allowed for a scoreline which better reflected the closeness of the contest.

Of course, it also gave the Lions a massive shot of confidence. That was something we would live to regret.

The late concession of points notwithstanding, we were rapt with the performance at Eden Park. In terms of setting out our store for the series, we could hardly have done more. On a personal level, I had got through all but three minutes of the match and, although there had been moments when I felt like I was sucking on fumes, I had been able to impose myself physically and lead the team with the clarity and certainty they had been demanding. I had been substituted late in the match and had run to the sideline to a standing ovation from the Eden Park crowd. I didn't want to dwell on that or to get ahead of myself, but it was a most generous and humbling gesture from the fans and one that I privately acknowledged later that night when I allowed myself a satisfied smile before falling into a restful sleep.

The squad was in great spirits the next morning as we

packed the team bus and headed for the airport and the flight to Wellington. It is one of the great joys of the job to travel around the country between matches with our fellow Kiwis and fans. I can't imagine what it must be like for superstar teams in other sports who operate in a cloistered world of private travel. I think it is one of rugby's greatest assets, that easy, comforting connection with fans and with the wider public. Walking through the airport and boarding the plane there was a buzz about the tour and about the result from the night before. How could anyone not feel energised by that? We certainly were. It reminded us all of what a privilege it was to be playing for the All Blacks during this special tour.

We had a relaxed day on the Sunday, briefly meeting up as a leadership team to discuss any concerns we had about the game just played and what we needed to be mindful of as we prepared for the second test. The general consensus was that we could not afford to be complacent. The scoreline may have suggested the victory was a comfortable one, but it never felt that way while we were playing, and it was imperative that we found the right balance in our messaging for the week. If we built up the challenge too much, we risked restricting the natural instinct for expression. If we allowed the team to think things were going to come easily, we were in danger of underestimating the Lions' ability to bounce back.

There was plenty of chat that week about what the Lions were trying to achieve and how we would counteract that. Again, we couldn't afford to be too focused on them, to the detriment of our own game plan, but players such as Conor Murray were singled out for attention. He was by far and away their best kick threat and because of his accuracy from the box the Lions seemed to always have a chance to regather or, at worst, force a hold or tackle near the sideline, cutting down our options to counter through their outstanding line speed. What we knew — or thought we knew — above all else was that we needed to reset our expectations ahead of the second test. There was no way we were going to simply turn up to Westpac Stadium and think we had the game in the bag.

I didn't think about it until a long while after the fact, but on reflection there was something missing in the week that followed: that electricity that had coursed through the team ahead of the first test simply wasn't there. It is natural after a tough game like the one at Eden Park that some of the energy is diverted into recovery but, even so, snap and crackle still needs a pop. It wasn't that the training lacked intensity or that the guys weren't enjoying themselves in the environment and among the public during our promotional commitments. I think that we simply hadn't given ourselves enough credit for the way we performed at Eden Park. In essence, we hadn't found the balance I spoke about.

As it was, I was massively keen to get stuck in again and I am sure the rest of the guys were. Much to our disappointment it rained a murder ahead of the game, which dampened the spirits of the fans and certainly made us think hard about how we were going to adjust to the conditions. We were still confident in our ability to play in the wet, but there is no denying we would have much preferred a dry surface. When you seek to play with width you always want ideal conditions for quick passing, knowing that every transfer takes that little bit of extra caution when the ball is slippery. Although we are talking fractions of a second, that is the difference between finding the space and being smothered by the tackle. We had to be smarter, plain and simple.

Adding to our own misgivings about the weather was the fact Warren Gatland had made some timely, crucial changes to his starting line-up. Owen Farrell had shifted to second-five for the second test, allowing Johnny Sexton to slot in at first-five, and having two great decision makers so close to the ruck posed a massive threat. On top of that, the athletic Maro Itoje had returned to the starting line-up at lock and their talismanic captain Sam Warburton — an intensely skilled and seemingly fearless player who we all had enormous respect for — was leading them out. Right from the opening whistle it felt as if they had found a better mix of personnel for their purpose and the first quarter was a torrid affair during which neither side was willing to give an inch.

Then things got complicated. With only 23 minutes on the clock, Sonny Bill Williams came in to assist Waisake Naholo in a tackle on Lions wing Anthony Watson. It was a regulation play, or should have been, but Sonny got himself tangled up and caught Watson with a shoulder to the head. Referee Jerome Garces wasted no time in reaching for the pocket and Sonny became just the third All Black to be red carded in a match. We came together as a team as Owen Farrell lined up the penalty and my sole thought was how I was going to keep everyone calm. I had a chat to Beauden Barrett about making some adjustments in how we used the ball. Getting around the rush in the wet had already proved tough, and it had just got much harder. We needed to work for territory through our kicking game and communicate well on the chase.

I was surprised when the coaches put up Jerome Kaino's number as soon as the kick had been taken, but it was a great call to ensure we had our full complement of backs on the field. We had designed a pod attack structure that could still function if we were a forward down but would have been rendered ineffective if we didn't have the numbers in the backline. Simply put, we wouldn't have been able to use the full width of the field. It was a big moment for Ngani Laumape, who entered the game for his test debut, while Anton Lienert-Brown got the rare privilege of packing down on the side of the scrum when we needed an extra man. Patched up, and a man down, we managed to make it through to halftime with the scores locked at 9-all. We felt like we were very much capable of pulling off a remarkable win, and then we bottled it.

Adversity is a compounding equation. When you start to think about the things that haven't quite fallen into place, nothing seems to work the way you want it to. We came out for the second half and did exactly the opposite of what we knew: we second guessed every pass, played for safety rather than for structure, kept things close to the ruck where we could be picked off in two-man tackles, and kicked as a last resort rather than to a clear and concise plan. We were suddenly thinking about outcomes instead of trusting our plan, and I was as guilty as anyone else in the team. At times when it normally would have been my instinct to throw the pass, I tucked the ball and took on the line, fooling myself into thinking that was the safe option, and that the safe option was the best option. For all that, however, we kept winning penalties and Beauden kept kicking them, taking us out to an 18–9 lead at the end of a third quarter that we should really have dominated more than we did.

We were asking a lot of a forward pack that was a man down and, having not been able to properly capitalise on our territory and possession advantage, the Lions struck. A simple midfield wrap play between Sexton and Farrell created space down the right-wing side and the Lions were able to recycle quickly before shifting back to the left and sending my opposite Taulupe Faletau over in the corner. What pissed us off most about the play was that the Lions were also down a man at the time — Mako Vunipola had been sinbinned for a clumsy challenge.

We still had our noses in front, but there was no doubt the last 15 minutes were going to test us to the limit. When Beauden kicked a seventh penalty — a record against a Lions side — we restored a seven-point margin but, tellingly, it was seven-pointers that we were unable to find. The Lions, on the other hand, were invigorated by the chase and after their big hooker Jamie George burst through a disconnected line to set up a Conor Murray try, Owen Farrell added the extras to tie the scores at 21 apiece. Maybe we just didn't see the opportunities for space in behind as well as we could, or maybe we should have trusted our skills more than we did, or maybe we spent too long looking at the scoreboard rather than at the on-field picture — whatever the reason, we were left to regret our conservatism and execution when Charlie Faumuina was penalised for tackling opposing prop Kyle Sinckler in the air and Owen Farrell kicked a penalty to seal the game and level the series.

Left to lick their wounds and count the 'what ifs', the boys sat devastated in the changing room after the match, strapping tape and boots strewn across the floor, engaged in dozens of reflective half-hearted conversations about what had just unfolded on the pitch. It was a tough scene to walk into after I had finished the post-match media obligations, and inside I was feeling the same way the rest of the team was. I couldn't show that emotion, though, couldn't be seen to have let the result get me down. I walked around the room and shook hands with the guys, doing my best to lift their spirits. Sonny was probably the most disappointed man in that room and he wandered over to me to apologise for being sent from the field. I could see how much he was hurting, but the loss was not on him and I needed him to know that. I had known Sonny for a long time and had enormous respect for him. As big as those shoulders of his were, this was not a burden he needed to carry.

Once everyone had cleaned up and changed, we came together in the room one last time to talk through the night and to get ourselves ready for the week ahead. My message was a simple one: we still had the chance to win a series at home next weekend, and our preparation was going to be perfect. Any thought of wallowing in defeat was to be dispelled then and there, left to linger with the shower steam that swirled above our circle. Through the haze of that loss we would resolve to put things right at Eden Park. I briefly imagined the scene inside the Lions shed, not 50 metres away down the dim concrete-block corridor. I had no doubt that my counterpart was in a much better mood but no less determined to win the third and final test.

I wanted to enjoy the next week as much as I could, knowing full well that I would never again have the chance to play in a series like this. Auckland teemed with Lions fans, all of them proudly clad in jerseys and jackets, drinking their way through a week in the City of Sails. It felt as if you couldn't leave the hotel without seeing a bunch of travelling supporters wandering through downtown Auckland or occupying a street-side table at a waterside bar or restaurant. It felt too as if the media contingent had doubled, the British and Irish journalists as partisan as the fans. I enjoyed their company and the interest they brought to the series and, while I didn't read or watch a lot of the coverage, it was fun to front up for media conferences and to take stock of just how much interest there was for the match in New Zealand and abroad.

Fatigue is a major factor in a three-test series and the match in Wellington had taken plenty out of us. We redoubled our recovery efforts earlier in the week to ensure our bodies would be in the best possible shape for the decider, but for all the physical considerations, I was much more concerned about our mental state. We needed to snap out of the cycle of overanalysis and get back to trusting our instincts. Unfortunately, anxiety had taken up residence inside the camp, and I could feel it in everything we did. For the first time, I felt sure that the management team were searching for problems that didn't exist. It manifested in myriad ways, from extended meetings to spreading the emphasis of the week across too many areas, to the way in which messages were delivered. When you have a team as tight and as together as the All Blacks, everyone picks up on that kind of vibe. We were pretending to be cool and collected, but none of us truly believed in that act. It was as if we were carrying on the performance while the set fell down around us.

Even though we knew deep down that we were letting things get to us when we shouldn't have, we still trained well and maintained our faith in the group of players we had and what we could do on the field. While I was able to keep my distance from the ongoing reportage of the series, I know there were others in the team who weren't as capable of shutting out the noise. It's almost impossible when you spend time on social networks not to dive head-first into a festering pit of opinion and criticism, and there were plenty of young guys in the team who probably didn't need that in their lives while also dealing with a type of test-match pressure they had never experienced before. It was pointless to think we could somehow isolate ourselves from the outside world completely, but I did want us to head into that third test inspired by what we had within us. That was where the magic lived. We just had to believe in it.

I did have something else to consider that week: the deciding test was also my 100th for the All Blacks and I was set to join a very select group of players, all of whom I had taken the field with during my international career: Richie McCaw, Mils Muliaina, Dan Carter, Keven Mealamu, Tony Woodcock and Ma'a Nonu. I understood the significance of the milestone and allowed myself a few moments during the week to think back to those Saturday mornings at Drury, running around on the cold, wet grass with my mates and loving every second of it. Would four-year-old me really have dreamed he would play 100 times for his country? He probably did, and now that dream was coming true. Still, what would the moment mean unless we got the result we wanted? That had to be my focus, leading the team. That and now finding a whole bunch of tickets for everyone in my family.

I had known for a long time that the third test was going to be my 100th, but anticipation alone could not prepare me for the intense emotional rush of running out onto the field in a packed Eden Park, by myself. My mind whirred and spun, filling up with images of all the moments leading to this point, and all the people who had helped me get this far. I felt as if I floated out there, carried by an incredible electrical energy that I hoped would stay with me forever. I savoured those few seconds, that lifetime, and then turned to watch the rest of the team run out to join me. I don't think I have ever been more ready to rip into a game than I was right then.

I can't really tell you much about the game. I can't really tell you how Beauden knew his little brother Jordie was expecting the cross-kick, nor can I tell you how a kid like that, on debut, had the wherewithal to knock that kick into the hands of Ngani Laumape to score. I can't tell you how we created space for Jordie to score his own try on the other side of the field, nor whether we ever felt like we had control of the match. I can tell you how tough it was to stay patient and to try to break through their forwards and how hard we worked to stay disciplined on defence. I can you tell you what it was like to watch Owen Farrell kick a 77th-minute penalty goal to lock the scores up at 15-all.

I can tell you this too: all I said to Beauden under the posts was, 'Kick it to me.' So if that passes for a plan then I guess it was. We had to get the ball back; it was as simple as that. We had often used the set-up we now assembled into for restarts so it was familiar to all of us and I just ran as hard as I could to chase the kick. I had barely enough energy left to get there but in desperation I leapt for it, putting just enough pressure on fullback Liam Williams for him to misjudge the catch and knock the ball forward . . . into the arms of his retreating hooker Ken Owens. Referee Romain Poite blew for a penalty to us. This was the moment! And then, it wasn't. Suddenly, there was just absolute confusion as the Lions boys implored Poite to take another look at the decision. He blew time and signalled for the Television Match Official. I had absolutely no idea what was happening. What was there to check? We stood there for those agonising few moments, watching the footage on the big screen certain that once time was called back on Beauden would kick us to victory. We couldn't hear what was being communicated to him through the TMO and then wondered why Poite was also conferring with his assistant referee. All I heard was the word 'accidental', which was all I needed to hear. 'Ref,' I said, 'that is a penalty every day of the week.'

When he called time back on and awarded us a scrum instead of the original penalty I was in disbelief. I would later ponder in the post-match interview why an infringement that had for a long time been penalised was suddenly adjudged to be accidental and worthy only of a scrum. I did my best to stay calm on the field, but I did not want to let it go. You can say what you like about opportunities to score we may have missed during the game, or penalties we had given away — including a very dumb one from me that resulted in Elliot Daly kicking three points from his side of halfway — but when it comes to crucial refereeing decisions, all you want is for the officials to get it right. I think they just completely screwed up that call, and there was no justifiable reason they should have. The law was very clear, and we all knew it. I know the Lions boys knew it too, but I can't blame them for doing their best to convince the referee to review his decision. We would have done exactly the same thing.

In all honesty, we still had a chance to win that match from the scrum and we gave it one last shot, albeit with much of the wind already gone from the sails. In our anger we rushed the final play and failed to keep our composure. We made the crucial break to get within dropped goal range but then were caught in that indecision zone between setting up for the snap and going for the try. When we were finally bundled into touch and Poite blew for fulltime I was just deflated. The series deserved better than the finish it got. The fans and players did too. I stood there stunned for a few seconds and in my frustration again questioned the referee for the call he had made. It may have been more a statement than a question, actually. I think my words were, 'Mate, that was just a ridiculous call.'

It was the fast-rising realisation that we had missed our chance that hurt most, and then hot on the heels of that came the sickening feeling that I had let everyone down. There wasn't a lot of time to process those complexities before a television camera was shoved in my face and I was asked for my thoughts on the match. I can't even remember the questions to be honest, or even who was asking them. I was still grappling with what had just happened, trying to come to terms with the fact the series was over, and it had ended in a draw. I had to address the non-penalty, cautious not to betray my real thoughts on the matter, and I was mindful that the Lions deserved an enormous amount of credit for how they had played, especially in the last two tests. It was only later, on the stage alongside Sam Warburton as we raised the cup together and had a laugh, that I properly considered that he too would never get another shot at winning a series like this.

For all the disappointment, to have my silver 100th cap presented to me on the stage by fellow centurion Keven Mealamu was a special moment. I would later say in the press conference that 'I'm proud to make 100 tests but would probably swap all of them for a win', but I don't think that was entirely true. To stand there with my daughters Elle and Eden and my baby boy Reuben — who would steal the show during my speech by doing what all good babies do and bursting into tears — gave me a chance to put the series and the match in perspective. Bridget was also there to share that ceremony with me, having to save the day as usual by grabbing Reuben from my arms. I loved them all so much, and I was so honoured to be up there representing their sacrifices. I watched Eden running across the stage, trying to catch raindrops on her tongue, and realised that even if some people wished to define me by series won, lost or drawn or by the number of caps next to my name, I wouldn't let myself be defined by that.

As the presentations concluded and both teams gathered for a group photo on the stage, the rain continued to fall and the remaining fans drained away from the saturated ground and out into what remained of the wet Auckland evening. I indulged myself one last time, picturing the alternate reality I had imagined for many months in those minutes before sleep — the one in which I raised the cup as the captain of an All Blacks side that won a series against the Lions. It wasn't hard to put on a brave face out on the field, but everything caught up with me once I was back in the changing room.

We had all put so much into winning and now tears came to fill the empty places we had saved for celebrations. Emotions were heightened further when the boys performed a haka for me, and for Aaron Cruden and Charlie Faumuina, who were leaving New Zealand after the Super Rugby season. There was no point in sugar coating this one, we were disappointed because we cared, and because we cared we let that disappointment sink in. By the time both teams arrived at the post-match function in the city it was close to midnight and, still, I don't think either team really knew how to feel.

We finished the night in the team room, which was once the old Farmer's Department Store Grand Tea Room and was now the function space for the Heritage Hotel, its floor-to-ceiling windows affording commanding views across the waterfront and the harbour, its vaulted ceilings and distinctive chandeliers a throwback to its art deco sophistication. We shared more than a few beers and then played cricket, like a bunch of kids in the backyard, and by the time we were done we had at least filled the room with a few laughs, and reminded ourselves that even when the stakes are high, it's only a game.

18

BACK AGAINST THE WALL

There's a time lapse I keep in my head. A little kid standing in a car park next to a muddy field beside a motorway. He's crying because all he wants to do is join his brother in the team playing rugby that winter morning. He doesn't care that they are bigger and older than him. If they can do it, he can too. His parents finally relent, and he runs as fast as he can out onto the field.

He's older now, and a big kid is running straight at him. It's another field in another winter. He will tackle him because that's what he loves to do. There's no better feeling than marking up on the biggest kid on the field and driving him back, knocking the fighting spirit right out of him.

He's at school, dressed in his number ones on a Friday afternoon. His mates are scattered around the courtyard, games are being played, lunches are being eaten and jokes are being told. There's a girl there, older. She's looking at him. He's looking back at her. Tomorrow is the biggest game of the season and the whole school is excited. None are more excited than he is.

He's in his beat-up old Corolla, driving the Desert Road with that girl who looked at him at lunchtimes. They are on an adventure together, neither knowing exactly how the story ends but happy to be writing this part of it together. Everything will work out for them; they are sure of it.

He's surrounded by stars, the biggest names in the game. He is shy and out of his depth. He goes with the current, bides his time, learns from the best. He'll find his voice soon enough. Work hard, listen, keep your head down, mate.

He's on the big stage, exactly where he dreamed he would always be. There are no tears now, just the adrenaline rush from the crowd, a national anthem to the tune of 50,000 voices. A challenge steeped in history. He wants to be here, where for that one brief moment he is that little kid again, fearless and indestructible . . .

In medical terms, this was the situation: I had a severely herniated disc between the L5 and S1 vertebrae or, more plainly speaking, between the lowest vertebra of the lumbar spine and the top vertebra of the sacrum — the lower part of the spine above the tailbone or coccyx. The disc is the rubbery cushion that sits between the vertebrae and mine had begun to push out through its protective shell and was rubbing against the spinal cord, sending sharp, shooting pains down my left leg.

It came on late in the 2017 season, after the Crusaders had beaten the Lions on Ellis Park to win the Super Rugby title and Sam Whitelock had raised the trophy above his head and the drought had been broken and Wyatt Crockett and I had stood there in the middle of that great stadium and held that trophy between us, the last two Crusaders from the last successful crusade.

It came on after we had retained the Bledisloe Cup and ran South Africa off the park in Albany to the tune of 57-nil. What a night that was to be a part of. We all wanted to bottle the lightning after that. There was only 40 kilograms on the bar, but as I lifted it for a commercial shoot the following week, I felt a pain in my backside. I didn't think much of it at the time but dutifully told physio Pete Gallagher and muscle therapist George Duncan and asked them to just massage my ass, quite literally. We were flying out to Argentina that day, and all week the pain stuck around. I played the game that weekend as if nothing was really wrong and then jumped on a plane bound for South Africa.

At this point, things took a turn for the worse. The pain now spread down my hamstring. As soon as I bent forward it felt like I had been shot in the back of the leg. I couldn't tie my shoelaces during the week but, hey, it was probably just a pinched nerve. It will go away in time. Forget the fact I couldn't tie my shoelaces without feeling like my leg was about to explode. It's just a nerve.

I just kept going, accepting that my training and game play was going to be accompanied by pain. I played in South Africa and I played in Brisbane against Australia in the wet. We were beaten 23–18 that night, which really pissed us off. The pain was not an issue while I was playing, but once I was at rest it was just a constant battle. We arrived back home after the Australian loss and I just carried on with my normal training. I then exacerbated the problem by giving myself a low-grade hamstring tear while running. I don't know whether it was related to what was happening with my back, but it certainly didn't help.

I didn't make a fuss. By the time we departed for the end-of-year tour the hamstring was better, but I was on painkillers constantly, just to provide some relief and to allow me to get to sleep. Even then it wasn't enough to take care of the constant ache. I didn't play in the tour opener against the Barbarians, as much as I would have liked to lock horns with my old mate Andy Ellis who captained the famous club that day. I suited up for France on 11 November, Armistice Day. By this stage I had been living with the nerve issue for two months. I twinged a hip flexor in the test and was forced from the field. When it rains, it pours.

I didn't train much the next week in Scotland. I ran on Thursday and my calf was so fatigued I could barely get through the session. I somehow pulled myself through the week and was ready to play at Murrayfield when my left leg decided to stop working. It was absolutely terrifying. It felt like I had done a thousand calf raises and there was just nothing left to give. I don't know what I was thinking playing an entire test in that state, but it just meant so much for me to be out there that I didn't want to tell anyone I wasn't okay. I was gone at halftime and I knew I had to tell the boss. I said to Steve, 'Mate, I can keep going but I can only give you what you have already seen from me and no more. Hopefully no less, either.' He just looked at me and said, 'Well, I think we need you so do what you can.'

It was a tough test. All I could think was that I needed to go out there and somehow influence the game, if not by being at my absolute best, then just by my presence. It seems a touch conceited, but I was the captain and it was my responsibility to take control and guide the team home. Maybe if things hadn't been so damn close, they would have decided to do without me. I don't know. When I get injured in a game, my first thought is always, 'I'm an 80-minute player. How do I get to the end of this?' It's a survival instinct honed over years of playing the game. I knew I had the resolve to make it to fulltime, that I could get into position and cover the key elements of my job. But there was no explosiveness in me that day, no chance that I was going to pull something miraculous from the bag of tricks.

It was frustrating and frightening, especially as the game was an epic. We had not been able to score a single point for the first 37 minutes of the match and Scotland were playing with a flair we simply had not seen coming. Our discipline was average, but fortunately it had not cost us more than a solitary penalty, and we were able to equalise just before the break. There was no question that I wanted to be out there for the second half, and as it turned out we were able to string a few phases together, putting Codie Taylor in the corner for the first try five minutes into the second spell and working our way upfield five minutes later for Damian McKenzie to chase through a midfield grubber and score under the posts.

This was when we were supposed to pull away and break the Scottish resistance, but not this day. A Richie Gray try brought Scotland back to within five points, with a quarter to go. In the 66th minute Beauden Barrett finished what many would probably consider one of the tries of the tour, working off a midfield merry-go-round of Sonny Bill Williams and Damian McKenzie. His conversion gave us a 12-point buffer. Still they kept coming back. Huw Jones finished off a fantastic right-side move and scored 10 in from touch. Finn Russell converted, of course, and with five to go Scotland were within reach of a historic victory. We were out on our feet. Already our tackle count was almost twice that of Scotland. Wyatt Crockett had followed Sam Cane to the sinbin, I was operating on one leg, and we were clinging on, just.

Scotland poured into us with everything they could muster

and with seconds remaining set a ruck 15 metres from the right touchline, just on our side of halfway. They cleared quickly and I watched as Russell started to run, straight at me defending three wide. I had no choice but to come in for the tackle, doing my best to track outside-in to disrupt the pass and prevent him finding the space wide. He played it perfectly, passing just as I moved to make the tackle. I didn't commit fully, enabling me to bounce back out and chase the receiver, but as I swivelled, my leg just did not work. I had to bounce onto my right to get moving and Stuart Hogg saw the space that my moment's hesitation opened. He ran straight onto an inside ball and blitzed between Anton Leinert-Brown and me. He was away for all money.

I watched on helplessly as he burned past Damian McKenzie and evaded the diving tackle of TJ Perenara. He was just 10 metres shy of the corner flag — 10 metres shy of a try that would have levelled the scores. And then, out of nowhere, Beauden Barrett smother-tackled the poor bastard into touch, forcing him to throw a forward pass in the process. Before we even had time to pack a scrum, the referee blew the end. I think it took the crowd about five minutes before they realised the game was over. I couldn't even begin to describe the level of adrenaline coursing through me. It was one of the grittiest and, dare I say, luckiest wins of my career, and I was, above all else, glad it was over.

My closest mates in the team knew I was struggling, but we needed to keep our cards close to our chests. After that Scotland game, though, if you had been in the stands, you would have seen the captain of the All Blacks unable to walk back to the changing shed. I shuffled from the field like an emperor penguin and did my best to grimace through the post-match. The next day, I couldn't walk at all. That was about the time I called Doc and said, with characteristic rugby understatement, 'I think I may be done for this tour.'

Things loosened up a little over the course of the morning, but I knew there was something far more serious going on than any of us had originally thought. I spoke to Steve about it and told him that there was no way I was going to be able to play. He just told me, 'We'll see how you go.' That was on a Sunday. On Monday in Cardiff I was sent for a scan which revealed a frighteningly large bulge in my lumbar spine. It was massive. It should have been given its own name. With trademark candour, Doc jabbed me with a cortisone injection to ease the pain, but I knew it was never going to work and I told him there was no way I was going to be able to play. He just told me, 'We'll see how you go.'

The next morning, I was named to start against Wales.

Luke Whitelock was training with the team so the contingency was there. I was listed to lead the side that weekend, even though I had told Steve not to name me. Figuring it was all smoke and mirrors, I played along with the charade and made a promise not to give anything away when, the following night, he and I attended a testimonial dinner for the great Welsh lock Alun Wyn Jones. I was absolutely thrilled to be there for Alun Wyn and even more delighted when I was presented with my Rugby Centurions jacket by the man himself.

The Rugby Centurions club is the brainchild of former Springboks captain John Smit and was launched in 2017. I became the 53rd member, joining such luminaries as Philippe Sella, Jason Leonard, George Gregan, Bryan Habana, Brian O'Driscoll and Gareth Thomas, not to mention a few of my old All Blacks mates. The club prides itself on having 'the toughest membership in the world' and it points out that only 3 per cent of international players will ever reach 100 test caps. John wanted a vehicle for those who have been fortunate enough to reach that rare milestone to give something back to the rugby world. I was very honoured to have got a foot in that door.

I spent most of the evening pretending I wasn't in agony and that I could actually walk. Despite the great spirit of the occasion, I was more than a little relieved when it was time to head back to the team hotel. The next morning, things took another unexpected turn, this time while I was — and there's no delicate way of putting this — in the middle of my morning ablutions. At some point while doing the business, the pain escalated from barely manageable to unbelievably excruciating. I somehow managed to clean myself up, fall face-first off the toilet seat and crawl to the bed. There was to be no relief once I got there.

Obviously, the bulge in my back had now found an entirely new part of the nerve to put pressure on because the pain was unrelenting. It was akin to having a thousand needles jammed into my left leg from the foot all the way to the thigh, and there was no escaping it. It didn't matter what position I squirmed into, it did nothing to alleviate the agony. I eventually plucked up the will to phone Doc, and though I can't remember my exact words to him, I believe the gist of it was, 'I need you rather soon.' To his credit he was at my door within a few minutes with a cornucopia of approved pain medication (only the best for you, sir) and he proceeded to dispense as much as his professional licence would allow. None of it worked. And there were some fairly hefty drugs on offer. I am no pharmacologist, and I am certainly no dispensing chemist, but when you are suffering the kind of nerve pain that tramadol won't budge, you know you have a serious problem.

While I was going through the eleventh layer of Hades in

my own room, Doc headed downstairs, presumably to tell the coaches that their captain was in a heap upstairs and may be a 50:50 proposition at best for the weekend. When he returned, he gave me something to help me sleep and I slowly drifted off. I had all of two hours' sleep and woke up in the same amount of pain I had been in to begin with. It's fair to say at this point I must have been slipping to a 40:60 at best, even in Doc's optimistic eyes. My old mates Sam Whitelock and Aaron Smith dropped by not long after I woke up to see how I was getting on and they could both tell that things were pretty grim. They left for the afternoon training with instructions to send Doc back to top up my medication. I dozed when I could and tried not to cry in between visits from various teammates. Luke Romano made sure every time I woke up there was something to eat next to the bed. I was aware that I was still technically named in the team. I would have laughed about that had I not been quietly sobbing.

There is an emotional limbo you exist in as a player when you are sitting by a teammate who is badly hurt. Part of you doesn't want to be reminded that on any given day it could be you sitting or lying in their place. Part of you is working overtime to convince yourself that these sorts of things couldn't happen to you, that they are freak occurrences rather than near certainties. Still another part of you doesn't want to be there at all because you fear it will prey on your mind the next time you are on the field. I could see all those emotions at play on the faces of the boys as they popped in to visit. I appreciated their company and their concern, but they were now just two days out from a big test and I wanted them to be fully focused on that.

For my part I slipped in and out of fitful sleep, trying to find my focus through the fog of drugs. There were harsh realities to

269

face but nothing but the constant pain to cling to as I fell deeper into my despair. Was this going to be the way my career ended? Dosed to the eyeballs on a cocktail of hefty medications, alone in a nondescript hotel room? There was no off switch for the mind or the body. One way or another I was just going to have to ride this one out. At least I'd been scratched from the team list.

The following day there was the slightest relief. I did my best to get through another day in bed, wrestling with my demons, and then hauled my carcass downstairs later in the evening for a stretching session with the team. It was a Friday ritual for a small group of us and I had not missed one since it had been implemented several years before. I wasn't going to start now. I got through the session and the next day sat uncomfortably in the stands at Millennium Stadium as the season came to a close with a 33–18 win over Wales. Sam Whitelock captained the side and played out of his skin, notwithstanding a 10-minute spell in the bin. Sam Cane was also massive that day as the team's defensive pressure provided plenty of transition opportunity for points.

It was the end of a troublesome tour for me, but not the end of my tour of troubles. Bridget and I had planned a break in New York following the conclusion of the season and I was not going to let her down by cancelling a trip we had both been looking forward to. I hadn't told her just how bad the back had been over the last week in Wales but as soon as she saw me, she knew it was more than simply another niggle, another side effect of a career in a collision sport, and she saw right through the bravado, as she always did. We managed to take in the sights, walking around that great city and allowing ourselves to be consumed by its relentless hustle and intoxicated by its grand scale. I figured if I could overload the rest of my senses, the nerves might just concede defeat and let me rest. I figured wrong.

All the advice I had received on tour was that I would just have to give the disc time to settle and that surgery would be something I should best avoid. I respected that opinion but knew it couldn't hurt to seek a surgeon's point of view, which is exactly what I did when I arrived back in Christchurch. Within a week, Rowan Schouten had me on his operating table, and in little more than an hour the procedure to scrape away the offending disc was complete. When I emerged from the anaesthetic daze, the pain was gone. It may go down as one of the best feelings I have ever had in my life, but it came with a caveat: Rowan had warned me that it would be at least 12 months before I was feeling back to full fitness, but I could be back playing in half that time if I worked for it.

Two days after surgery I began to wean myself off painkillers which, considering the dosage I had been taking, was a process that needed to be managed with care. My early optimism took a hit when the symptoms began to return, but I much preferred that to the thought of continuing on a regime of opioids that only served to mask the real recovery process. I knew that I had to deal with this with my feet firmly on the ground rather than with my head in a constant cloud, which is exactly how I had felt for weeks. Every athlete at the professional level is prepared to suffer a certain amount in order to keep competing. It is a physiological penance for the sin of self-obsession and blind faith in one's own ability. I was simply paying the toll.

Perspective comes from all angles. Being out of action for six months was hardly ideal for the Crusaders, and it was less than perfect for the All Blacks, who still had a June series against France to prepare for and would now almost certainly be without their captain. Then again, I had already set my sights on being in Japan in 2019 and so to have this chance to prepare the body and the mind for what was going to be a gruelling year was one that I had to view, personally, as a positive. I didn't just want to be in Japan, of course. I wanted to win the Rugby World Cup.

I have never been much of a man for writing down goals or typing out detailed plans. Mostly, I have been content to form an idea of where I want to be and of what I want to achieve and then hone it into a guiding principle or, more accurately, a destination on my mental map; 'I think therefore I am', or something like that at least. Far be it from me to overreach on my philosophical expertise. I found Gilbert Enoka particularly helpful as I began to formulate a plan for me to return to play. I knew I was going to have to prioritise certain things, which is never easy when you just want to be able to give your all to every team you are part of. The surgery and attendant recovery had to be viewed as an obstacle and nothing more, something to be navigated around rather than derailed by.

It seems counterintuitive, but the easiest way to take on any challenge is to first admit your vulnerability. Were doubts stalking me about my chances of making it to a third Rugby World Cup? Absolutely. They snuck into my sleep at night and perched on my pillow. Did I need some reassurance that I was still entrusted with leading the All Blacks on that campaign? Of course I did. I also needed to be aware of the impact the injury had had on me, and on those around me.

I was reminded by Bert Enoka of something I had said to him three years earlier. When he had asked me in the lead-up to the 2015 Rugby World Cup what it was I wanted to achieve, I had told him I wanted to win three world cups. That was still my goal. My desire was undiminished.

I want to stress that there was no arrogance at play when I said that. I just saw it as a natural progression. We were heading into a tournament then to win it, and what better way to motivate me through the 2015 edition than to set a future goal pursuant on success in the present. Having articulated my goal, I had enjoyed listening to the other senior players in the team and hearing — genuinely hearing — what they were saying. Desire is the fruit of ambition. It is not the words that matter so much as the emotion that is being expressed. Learning to differentiate between those two very separate things was important to me as a leader.

I was at Rugby Park every day as I recuperated from surgery. I wasn't necessarily in the meetings, at least not early on because that would have absolutely done my head in — not because I would have been bored by the detail, more because I would have been amped up and beside myself at not being able to be part of the quest. Instead I just tried my best to be around, if not completely within, the team and everything that was going on. The boys had a massive start followed by a couple of losses but soon got back to winning ways and went undefeated through April and May. I had a plan for my rehabilitation and resolved to do everything I needed to do to get back into action. I couldn't do hard work, but I could still work hard.

It was good to be in that space without being fully immersed in everything that was happening with the Crusaders. I could drop the kids off at school and pick them up at the end of the day, and in between I could focus on me and my recovery. There was a fantastic spirit at headquarters and it was easy to turn up to the gym and get through the session knowing everyone else was giving it their all. The playing roster, the coaches, the support staff and the executive had all been rejuvenated by the 2017 title win, and Razor's energy was tantamount to a communicable disease:

all who came into contact with him caught some of it. He was the very definition of infectious.

In some ways the reality of a long recovery made things easier. I knew, and my coaches knew, that I wasn't going to be playing for a long time and as such there was no pressure to rush my return. I could stay connected to the Crusaders without weighing myself down with any added concern that my absence was being monitored on a daily basis. Sometimes the less serious injuries are worse in the sense that you feel compelled to get over them quickly and get back into the starting line-up.

Relieved of the grind of game week, the analysis loads of daily meetings and training runs and the interminable travel schedule that goes with the territory, I was free to think outside the game for the first time in what felt like forever. Although I had been relieved of the captaincy duties at the Crusaders, I was still a leader in the team, and still the All Blacks skipper. Those roles, while absolutely cherished, do extract enormous amounts of mental energy and I was probably slow in realising just how much. Having been forced to the sidelines, I could recalibrate my head space for the challenges still to come. On 6 July, against the Highlanders, I returned to play.

It was so important to me to get myself back for the last few weeks of the campaign, and to return as part of Wyatt Crockett's 200th Super Rugby match was extra special. Who would have thought my old mate would have a stadium named after him? Wyatt was subsequently left out of the team for the semifinal, and I thought he deserved to be there on merit. I know most of the guys felt the same way. After the team was named I sat down with Razor and had it out with him. Wyatt didn't want to make a fuss but I had to get it off my chest. It didn't change anything —

he was again left out for the final — but it was important to me to go in to bat for such a good man.

As it was, everyone came to terms with the call, and the Crusaders won a second consecutive title. To do it at home was a memory to cherish forever. We celebrated long into the night, but already my mind was turning to the All Blacks season. There was something else preying on my mind that night. My back wasn't good. It was all too obvious that I had returned to play sooner than I should have.

As the Rugby Championship began, I did my best to put the ongoing issue to the back of my mind. I was short of a gallop in terms of my match fitness for the year, but I had a full All Blacks programme to get me right and that environment always filled me with confidence in my ability. We started the Rugby Championship with two big wins against Australia, and a good showing against the Pumas on a brilliant and historic night in Nelson. The city put on a carnival atmosphere all week and it was great to play a test in one of the smaller cities. We headed to Wellington to face the Springboks the next week and after getting the jump early we let them back into the match.

In the end we lost by two points and my decision to eschew a shot at goal in favour of going for a try was roundly criticised by the public and the media. We spoke about it after the game as a team. South Africa were tired, they had a man in the bin, and we had the ability to pull that play off. We got tight and knocked on metres from the line. Would I have made the same decision again? Absolutely.

We got our revenge in a thriller at Loftus Versfeld to claim the title, and before the end-of-year tour I sat down with Gilbert and Steve Hansen. I had to be honest with them: my back was killing me. They listened to me and then asked where I wanted to go and what I wanted to be. They told me to acknowledge the back and the injury but equally acknowledge the fact that I could play through it, that it was not enough to prevent me from giving it my all. It was such an honest and healthy chat to have because I had started to believe that I was being limited mainly by my subconscious fears and not by my physical woes. Bert was a master at getting me to reframe my mindset. I thought, 'Shit, yes there is a fear in my life, something that is preventing me, at some level, from breaking the shackles of my own self-doubt.'

It seems weird to think that I needed this to be explained to me, but when you allow your niggles and your aches and your pains to start controlling your thoughts, you are destined to end your career well before your time. I guess the biggest issue was thinking too far ahead; if I went out and damaged my back further what would that mean for the Rugby World Cup? I was so close to realising the dream of leading the team on the biggest stage of the game and I was now playing it safe because that desire was eating me up. Some people might have thought 'I have nothing to lose'. All I was thinking was how much I had to lose.

It was to be a tour defined by a loss. It could easily have been defined by two. On 10 November we faced England at Twickenham in a highly anticipated match pitched largely as a battle between Eddie Jones and Steve Hansen. It was an awful afternoon, and the rain started to fall as soon as we ran out onto the field. The partisan crowd were in full voice and the English forwards were full noise. We bashed, we probed, we jabbed — nothing worked. England, on the other hand, raced out to a 15-nil lead, a lead we clawed back late in the half to turn just five points in arrears.

The second half proved as tough as the first and we sneaked in front only courtesy of Beauden Barrett's boot. For the entire last quarter, we felt like we were just holding on. When Courtney

Lawes charged down a TJ Perenara box kick late in the game and Sam Underhill ran around Beauden to score, our hearts were in our mouths. Marius Jonker eventually called the play back for offside, and we clung on to win 16–15. The English fans were incensed. Our fans were unimpressed. Worse was to come.

I genuinely believed I was getting back to some good form on the tour. During the games I was feeling really good, as if for those 80 minutes I was entirely unencumbered by the issues that had plagued me through the year and still plagued me off the field. I had built well through the Rugby Championship, and my metrics in terms of the way I was covering the field and making my tackles were, on balance, where they needed to be. Of course, I made one mistake that would come back to haunt me, and that was to drop a ball against Ireland, in an intense test we would go on to lose.

Funny, isn't it? Just getting myself into a position to make that pick-up was the real skill, and nine times out of ten I would have caught that ball and we would have scored. People see outcomes, but they never see the construction. The outcome of the game was Ireland won, 16–9, and Aviva Stadium went berserk. As a team we hate to lose and we sat inside those sheds after the game in a sombre mood. Did we think we had played poorly? Not really. Certainly, there were things that we could have done better — chances that we could have taken — but ultimately Ireland were tactically superior and that was something we knew we were going to have to live with, and change. In the review of the match we saw every opportunity we left out there and part of the problem was that we had been conned into playing the confrontational game.

Did it sting? Absolutely. But ultimately those are galvanising moments for a team that seeks to be the best. For some it was the first time they had been in that kind of situation, with the eyes of the rugby world on them in a match of such magnitude. For the rest of us it was a timely reminder that rugby is a game that rewards intelligence as well as brute force. It was up to us now to find that balance and perfect it.

The following week we headed to Italy for one last match. For the first time in my career I led the haka. It was an enormous honour, one that was widely depicted as an act of defiance on my part. That couldn't be further from the truth. I had a team that was hurting, one that needed to make one final push for the year. I wasn't trying to prove anything to the public. I was standing in front of my men and leading them. We posted a big score at Stadio Olimpico and afterwards we sat in the sheds and shared a beer and reflected on the season. I'm not sure whether the public gets enough of a chance to see the camaraderie we have as a group — maybe that is just for us to savour — but I looked around the team after the final test and reminded myself of what a privilege it was to lead this bunch of lads. This old dad with his bad back and a whole lot of kilometres on the clock still loved every minute.

That December, Bridget and I headed away for a friend's wedding celebration. It was a beautiful Northland affair, the scorching sun drying off the long grass in the hay paddocks, the pohutukawa in full crimson bloom above sand as white as bleached bones, the whirr and click of cicadas providing the seasonal soundtrack. We spent a wonderful weekend on the coast, lounging about on the beach. And then I threw my back out, chucking a damn frisbee. I couldn't sit down properly for a week. In fact, I couldn't do much for a week, other than to think that there must be a special kind of cruel humour in the universe when a man can return from back surgery to play half a year of tough footy only to be undone by a kid's toy.

19

ONE LAST MISSION

It was as if I was hearing the wheels on a lock spindle click into place. The combination: 31 players' names. The All Blacks team for the Rugby World Cup was announced on 28 August, in the home dressing room at Eden Park, the same room in which we had celebrated our 2011 triumph, and in which none of us had ever experienced the aftermath of defeat. The moment was a thrilling one for me, the culmination of months of anticipation. Now that I knew exactly who was sharing in this last mission, I felt a rush of energy and excitement. The venue for the announcement was symbolic of course, but several days later an even more symbolic moment would be shared between us, on the side of Hikurangi mountain, as we greeted the rising sun before anyone else in the world.

The Thursday after the team announcement had been a whirlwind of logistics as we headed in groups to all corners of the country that we were now representing on the biggest stage in the game. I headed to Queenstown to see the kids at Wakatipu High and loved the time I got to spend there. Being around youngsters always recharges me and makes me ever more aware of the privileged position I find myself in as captain of this team. It was important for us to get out to as many places as possible, to take stock of who we played for and why. We returned to Auckland that night and the following morning embarked on a most special trip.

Our leadership team and core management had been planning something like this for months. We had one opportunity to do something unique that was all about our values and culture as an All Blacks side, away from the gaze of the public and the interest of the media. We wanted a chance to connect with each other and with our place, our origins, and our shared and respected ancestry as New Zealanders. With the help of artist, composer and performer Derek Lardelli we had settled on a trip to the East Coast. Derek had put much thought into the destination: Hikurangi is sacred to Ngati Porou and is regarded as the first part of Maui's great catch to emerge from the ocean. The way Derek explained it, the mountain also connected us with the new light and connected Aotearoa with Japan, our two nations linked by the Pacific's ring of fire. It was perfect.

We flew into Gisborne as a team on Friday morning and jumped aboard a bus bound for Ruatoria and beyond. No one outside the senior leadership team knew anything about the trip, which made everything about it even more exciting for us. We stopped off at Tolaga Bay and took a dip in the cold water and bombed off the famous wharf. It was as if we were on a school trip again, just a bunch of excited kids enjoying a mysterious adventure. It was as Kiwi as it comes, but there was another great surprise just up the road in Tokomaru Bay where a group of gorgeous ladies had gathered waiting for us, ready with their voices and guitar. We pulled over and got off the bus as the ladies struck up a rendition of the old folk song 'On The Ball', written in 1887 to boost morale for — ironically — a hapless rugby team that was dubbed 'The unscorables'! It was wonderful, standing there in the afternoon sunshine seeing how passionate they were for us and for the moment. Derek then led us in a waiata as a response, and we did our level best to sing 'Te Aroha' for our new friends. That one moment touched our hearts in the most profound way.

From there we headed north to Hiruharama for a wonderful afternoon and a delicious feast, and we were honoured with the most incredible haka, which left us tingling for hours afterwards. We arrived at the base of Hikurangi, where our home for the evening was an old woolshed and a hastily pitched tent for our communal dining. We split into our mini teams to prepare dinner and clean up and lit a bonfire for the evening, around which we shared a few beers and more food. Derek then led us in a conversation about where we had come from to be here. He talked about 'Kapa O Pango', the haka he had composed for the All Blacks in 2005. After his lesson we lit the scene with car lights and ripped into our own haka practice. Our guides, all Ngati Porou, challenged us back with a haka of their own. It was incredible. We practised harder than we ever had before, learning from our hosts and from each other. None of us had ever experienced anything like it.

We had very little sleep that night and were woken in darkness to pile into 4WD vehicles and ATVs for the drive up the mountain. It was a 45-minute trek to the place where Maui's waka had been stranded, and as we arrived, the sun slowly rose above the horizon. We performed our haka for the new day, and I made a commitment to the team: we will bring the Webb Ellis Cup back here. This is where it needs to be returned from the land of the rising sun, to the first mountain to see the sun — from creation to completion.

*   *   *

Our time together at Hikurangi connected us like never before, and while we had one final test to get through — against Tonga in Hamilton — we were focused only on preparing as best as we could and getting one final performance under our belt. We knew by doing everything well that week, we could set a tone for the World Cup. None of us were under any illusions: in world cups you cannot afford to miss one beat in preparation because any team can trip you up. We were not going to stumble in the last test on home soil, and our performance that day — a 92–7 victory — showed where our heads were at. It was great to have Eden with me at the game too, especially on her birthday. The next day we assembled in Auckland one last time before flying to Tokyo. The time was upon us. It was suddenly all very real.

We arrived in Tokyo and bussed straight to Kashiwa to the north-east. Kashiwa is a relatively new city in Chiba Prefecture and the city officials had arranged with New Zealand Rugby to host us for the few days before the tournament began. The welcome was unbelievable and everywhere we went it seemed as if thousands of people were there to greet us. It was incredibly hot, with temperatures in the mid-thirties and humidity off the charts. We trained as hard as was humanly possible, knowing that everything was leading to the biggest game of our lives: South Africa in the opening match of the Rugby World Cup. That game was all I could think about. That game would define our tournament. Every single one of us knew what was at stake.

The few days spent in Kashiwa reminded us all that we were at a Rugby World Cup and the official team welcome simply reinforced that notion. Receiving our tournament caps was the ignition point for the fire we would need to bring to the first pool match against South Africa. Everything from that point became a calculation in preparation, a fanning of the flames. I had been forced to sit out the final two days of training in Kashiwa with an abdominal strain, which had only served to strengthen my resolve. I had been through so much just to make it to Japan. I was not about to let it slow me down for too long. By the time we arrived in Tokyo for game week, I had made up my mind that the strain was just another inconvenience and nothing more.

The South African game could not come soon enough. We trained with a collective energy that gave me an enormous amount of confidence and we spoke as one about the need to make a statement in our first match — not just as an All Blacks team, but as an All Blacks team at the Rugby World Cup. We had long acknowledged our desire to use the expectation of victory as a force for good. Now, we came at that equation from a slightly different angle: it is not enough to accept the standard expectation; it is time to rewrite it forever. We wanted to be the ones to draw the line under a decade of dominance. There was something else, too: I wanted to show the team how much captaining them meant to me and, going back to the lessons we had learned in Ngati Porou country, I asked TJ how he would feel operating with me as a second kaea, or leader, during the haka. He was incredibly receptive and told me the boys would go nuts if we made that happen.

I was grateful to TJ for making that plan a reality for me, and as the 70,000 fans at Yokohama Stadium settled in the heavy and humid evening air of Saturday, 21 September, we stood before the Springboks and laid down our marker. 'Taringa whakarongo . . . Kia rite! Kia rite! Kia mau!' In the moments I felt those powerful words escape my mouth, an enormous energy flooded through me. Right then, with my team in formation behind me, and our greatest rivals standing before us, I felt indestructible. A minute later we set up for the kick-off with George Bridge ready to chase a kick down the middle. At that point Jerome Garces, the referee, told us we still had 90 seconds to wait. By that time, South Africa had read the play, and we immediately had to reset our plan. I couldn't help but think, 'Here we go again.'

As it was, South Africa would score the first points — Handre Pollard kicking an early penalty to remind us that our discipline had to be spot on. The first 20 minutes were typical of the games between us: big contacts and tentative advances, a period of testing defensive lines, and settling on schemes to bust the game open. We had come into the tournament with an attack plan that was still taking shape, but we had all bought into what we wanted to achieve: take the game wide, come back to the middle, split the line, and hit either side to get every one of our playmakers involved. We wanted to cause chaos and to keep teams guessing. When Handre missed his second penalty attempt of the match at the end of the first quarter, it was time to flick the switch.

In the next seven minutes, the boys went ballistic. First George Bridge tapped back a box kick for Richie Mo'unga to hit Sevu Reece with a screamer of a cross-field kick, setting up a break down the right-hand touch. Ardie Savea took the inside ball and set the ruck 15 out from the Boks' line from where Ryan Crotty found Beauden Barrett who pierced the defence and offloaded for George to finish the try. A few minutes later Anton Lienert-Brown went straight through three tiring defenders and fed Scott Barrett with an inside ball for a try under the bar. In those two plays we had effectively taken the game from South Africa, and we would go on to win the match 23–13, all but guaranteeing us top spot in the pool. We had never looked further than that opener; now we had a night to enjoy the victory, and 10 days to prepare for Canada.

September became October. The early autumn heat showed no signs of abating as we travelled to the resort town of Beppu, famed for its hot springs and sands. It was an epic week of training as Nic Gill upped the ante on our running and fitness work. It was so similar to 2015 in the approach: get a big first pool game out of the way and then work as hard as possible on the training field. By the time of the Canada match, we were all feeling the effects of a heavy schedule, and with the roof closed at Oita Stadium, it was like we were playing a game in a sauna. I don't think any of us had ever perspired as much in a game before, and accurate handling was nigh on impossible. As it was, we managed to get through a spirited contest with a 63-nil victory. The Canadians were a great bunch of lads and the people of Oita and Beppu were enormously welcoming. We really did feel it was a home away from home.

I was rested for the Namibian game four days later in Tokyo, and despite a slow first half and the need for a halftime tune-up from Steve Hansen, the boys prevailed 71–9 with a second-40 slaughter job. I watched on from the stands that match, happy for the rest ahead of the following match against Italy in Toyota. As it transpired, that game would not take place on account of Typhoon Hagibis, which left over 80 dead and threw the final week of the group stage into chaos. It was a tragedy for our hosts, and we felt their pain. All we could do was take stock of how precious life is, and turn our sights on the quarter-final which, thanks to three weeks of Japanese heroics, would be against Ireland. Nothing motivates an All Blacks side like revenge. We had Dublin on our minds for the best part of a fortnight.

We were so keyed up for the match at Tokyo Stadium we

could have played it twice. Our rivalry with the Irish had grown exponentially since their breakthrough victory in Chicago in 2016, and their follow-up win in Dublin two years later. We wanted to crush them so badly. After the Italian cancellation we trained as well as I can remember, and we hit game day with a level of focus that was awe-inspiring for me as a captain. The night was perfect for our game plan, but to illustrate just how fired up I was, I lined up to lead the haka with TJ and all but blacked out. 'Taringa whakarongo . . .' was all that would come out. At that exact moment, I lost all thought and physical response. There was no 'Kia rite! Kia rite! Kia mau!' I remember seeing TJ looking at me as I regathered myself. It felt like an age had passed by the time I snapped back to reality. 'Kia whakawhenua au i ahau!' It was the strangest experience of my career.

Fortunately, the incident passed and when the ball was kicked off we were into our work. Everything we did seemed to pan out the way we expected it to. By the end of the first quarter Aaron Smith had scored two tries and we had taken the wind from their sails. Beauden Barrett added another after the break, and then I popped up a pass for Codie Taylor to score a fourth. It would be 67 minutes before Ireland scored a point in the match, and we added three more tries to secure a 46–14 win. It was one of the sweetest victories of my career. The team was humming. And next up was England in a Rugby World Cup semi-final. Of course, nothing's ever straightforward; I had torn my calf muscle . . .

The 'what ifs' come in waves. What if I had been able to train with the team that week instead of watching from the sideline? What if I had been out there just to offer a little more direction, or reassurance, or assistance? What if we hadn't started the game so poorly? What if we hadn't let in that Manu Tuilagi try in the first two minutes of the match? What if we had held onto the ball more, and not kicked for touch or, worse, took the ball across it as often as we did? What if we hadn't got tight on defence? What if we had done more in the game to keep our emotions in check? What if?

On Saturday, 26 October, our quest for a third straight world title fell apart. It was torn apart actually, our plan hijacked by an English side that was simply too good for us. From the opening whistle they took the game to us and never allowed us to find our rhythm. That's the objective point of view, naturally. The emotional one is different. We lost a world cup semi-final 19–7, and when the final whistle blew, I could not look my team in the eye. I felt so much responsibility for them. I had made promises to them, promises now that meant nothing. I stood there on the field in Yokohama as the English fans went delirious, and I stared at the ground, empty.

I had run more in the game than in almost any other test match I had played. My eye was bleeding. My knee was already starting to swell. My calf, ironically, had been fine in the match. The rest of me was broken. I broke down in the sheds, regathered myself for the press conference and went to have my eye stitched up. When I returned to the changing room, I showered alone. Tears were washed away, but the pain could not be scrubbed clean. It was my 34th birthday.

What if.

We took the bus ride back to the hotel in stunned silence, every one of us in his own universe of regret. Most inhabitants of the vast city we drove across would have had no idea that 31 rugby players on a bus were either in tears or on the verge of them. We got back to the hotel to greet our families, my wife. Alone with her, I broke down again. Sitting in my room were three cards from my children. The following day they arrived with three more.

Elle's said she didn't love me any less.

Eden's said I should have got her to play because she is sneaky and would have scored tries.

Reuben just had a question: 'Are you happy, Daddy?'

Right then, in that moment, I was.

Two days after the semi-final I sit in the vast lobby of the Conrad Hotel. I have stitches in my eye, a knee that I can't bend, a calf strain as well as a strained abdomen. The what ifs still come in waves. The questions linger. The pain has not been erased and it may never be. But I have three great kids and one heck of a wife. I have a family to treasure. I have been able to play for my country 126 times and go the distance in 105 of those games. I have been to the top of the mountain and I will climb out of this valley. I may not reach the summit this time around, but I refuse to live down here. I have one last chance to lead my country, to finish a career that has taken me from a paddock beside the motorway to the biggest stage in the sport. And I have done that alongside some of the best friends I could wish for. My story has more to be written, there is more to be done. Maybe that next chapter will have a happier ending for the fans. Maybe there really are no guarantees.

But yes, Reuben, Daddy is happy. And he's enormously proud to have been an All Black.